F. D. Reeve, well-known for his translations of nineteenth and twentieth century Russian literature, is the author of *The Russian Novel, Aleksandr Blok,* and *Robert Frost in Russia,* as well as of a novel, *The Red Machines,* and two volumes of poetry.

Mr. Reeve has taught at Columbia University and at Wesleyan University, where he served as Chairman of the Russian Language and Literature Department.

contemporary russian drama

SELECTED AND TRANSLATED BY FRANKLIN D. REEVE

WITH A PREFACE BY VICTOR ROZOV

PEGASUS / NEW YORK

for Ernest and Winifred Simmons

ACKNOWLEDGMENTS   The translations were made from the following sources:

V. Rozov, *Alive Forever,* from *Večno živye* (drama v trëx dejstvijax), *Literaturnaja Moskva,* I (Moscow, 1956), pp. 626–680.

N. Pogodin, *A Petrarchan Sonnet,* from *Sonet Petrarki* (drama v trëx dejstvijax), *Literaturnaja Moskva,* II (Moscow, 1956), pp. 300–351.

E. Shvarts, *The Naked King,* from *Golyj korol',* in his posthumous volume *P'esy* (Leningrad, 1960), pp. 90–164.

V. Panova, *It's Been Ages!,* from *Skol'ko let, skol'ko zim!* (p'esa), *Novyj mir,* 7 (July, 1966), pp. 3–38.

L. Zorin, *A Warsaw Melody,* from *Varšavskaja melodija* (liričeskaja drama v dvux častjax) (Moscow, 1967), 51 pp.

Mr. V. S. Rozov's important, generous contribution to this volume is deeply appreciated.

CONTENTS

PREFACE

Several times in various countries I have been asked, "How does the growth of television affect the theater in your country, in the Soviet Union?" And I have happily answered, "You know, not at all." I had in mind the fact that millions of "theaters in the living room" have not killed people's desire to spend money for tickets, to dress up a little in the evening and head for a show, even if the theater itself is located very far from their house.

In the Soviet Union there are about five hundred permanent, professional theaters. We have theaters for drama, light opera, opera, and children's theaters. Clearly, historical development was such that the role of the theater in our country was special: it has never been simply an amusement palace. In Russia, people have gone and still go to the theater chiefly for spiritual nourishment. And the audience seeks to leave the theater not merely relaxed and amused but, above all, enriched emotionally, intellectually, and esthetically. Outstanding Russian theater people have called the theater a Temple. Those who go to the theater feel the same way. It is incredibly difficult to get a ticket to such Moscow or Leningrad theaters as The Contemporary, The Vakhtangov, The Theater on Taganka, The Gorky Great Dramatic Theater. People may have to stand in line a whole freezing winter night to get a ticket to the better productions of any theater.

Several days ago, as I was coming out of the metro at Mayakovsky Square, I saw, still underground, by the escalators, many people waiting, many young people especially, continually asking passersby, "You don't happen to have an extra ticket?" They did not say what theater they wanted to go to. On Mayakovsky Square there are The Theater of Satire, The Moscow Council Theater, The Contemporary, Obraztsov's Puppet Theater, and the Chaikovsky Concert Hall. People did not care which one they got into. And the closer you get to any of these theaters, the more people there are seeking that cherished "extra ticket." It is like that almost every evening during the theater season.

In 1966, theaters throughout the country performed 350 different plays. That included only plays of which there were more than one hundred performances. The authors of the plays were as widely different as you can imagine—from Euripides to Albee. Most of the plays, however, belonged to Soviet dramatists. Sometimes, a very popular play, put on in several theaters, will have more than two thousand performances in the course of a year.

I have allowed myself this brief introduction only to emphasize that the five plays included in this anthology are a drop in our theatrical ocean. Although a drop may present definite, concrete facts, it never can take the place of the overall picture.

All five of these plays have a strong stage history. Shvarts's *The Naked King* opened at The Contemporary in 1962 and is still being performed regularly. Vera Panova's *It's Been Ages!* opened in 1966 in Leningrad, where the author lives, at The Gorky Great Dramatic Theater under the direction of Georgy Tovstonogov, one of the best contemporary directors. I have seen this subtle, poetic play, and the magnificent performance of its actors. *A Warsaw Melody* opened very recently, staged by the oldest director in the country, Ruben Simonov, at the Vakhtangov Theater, of which he is the director. The famous actors Yulia Borisova and Mikhail Ulyanov have parts in this play. At any one of these three plays the theater is overflowing, and at the entrance stand those same long-suffering men and women hoping, before the curtain goes up, to get an odd "extra ticket." My play *Alive Forever* has been fortunate, too: it has been in the repertory of The Contemporary for more than ten years. *A Petrarchan Sonnet,* a play by the late and very important Soviet dramatist, Nikolai Pogodin, had enormous stage success in its day and provoked heated debate in the press. Although the play is now being presented in smaller towns, I hope it will again appear on the stage in the capital.

I am happy to see this new anthology of Soviet plays published in the United States. A good deed! May it be one more slim plank laid across the gulf to build the bridge.

VICTOR ROZOV

Moscow
October 1967

INTRODUCTION

The theater is a cultural barometer, especially in England and Europe where repertory companies modify tradition by introducing new plays and new techniques into an established body of work. Often, as in the Soviet Union now, new repertory companies arise to present the new plays, and the traditional theaters, a little dusty but solid and revered, continue the old plays in the old style.

In the 1920's, the theater in Russia was bright, dynamic, experimental. In the 1930's, the cultural atmosphere changed. The theater became routinized. Through long years of high physical but low intellectual pressure it hung steady on "socialist realism" and "conflictlessness." The era was full of personal tragedies and national calamities, but none of this could be picked up by the theater. Everyone now agrees that, from the viewpoint of importance for the theater, the period from the mid-Thirties to the mid-Fifties was a waste.

In the period when plays recording problems of collectivization, production norms, and social duty were the only new material introduced into the classical repertoire, audiences were aware that new motivations, such as fulfilling the plan or serving the Party, did not adequately describe the psychology or the life of the farmer, the worker, the white-collar man. The vogue of the "positive hero" introduced no new historical or philosophical issues, nor even a new aspect of human behavior. For all his big words, the positive hero was false, everyone knew, a manipulator of slogans and forms, not a mirror of actual life. The plays were shoddily written. The propaganda offended: it was intolerably unrealistic.

In the middle 1950's, change began. Conflictlessness was thrown out as a category. Socialist realism was (and still is) repeated as a phrase, but the many varieties of interpretation reduced its usefulness. Wise heads now avoid it altogether. Dramas, comedies, and light satires by Arbuzov, Rozov, Shtein, Sofronov, and others changed the theater. Social criticism first appeared as modification of standard, tame forms—romanticized complaints leading to resolutely happy endings. Quickly, however, playwrights turned away from the artificial solutions of the modern, "well-made," socialist-realism dramas to plays of fresh construction characterizing daily life. There were problems: successful presentation of new material required altering accepted forms, yet without stage innovation and experimentation new material could not be introduced. Either way, audiences could not be interested.

The caliber of Soviet Russian theatrical presentation has always been high. "Classical," conservative, superbly disciplined, and exceptionally devoted, the actors and directors were world-envied experts in their line of work. It proved easier, and to everyone, especially to audiences, more appealing and more urgent to change the intellectual content of the theater. As Mark Shchëglov said in an article "The Realism of Contemporary Drama" published a decade ago, "the drama, the theater, actually and truthfully represent life, emotions, and events but not in life's form, as some used to think, but in the form of art." Over the past decade, without significantly dethroning the prevailing convention of naturalism, Soviet theater people have altered the form of art. That is, they have made it possible to put on plays in which the argument, elaborated according to established conventions, reflects the conditions of life.

The strikingly common characteristic of the five plays gathered in this anthology is romantic disillusion: life is not "positive," nor necessarily productive, nor always good. Life is, simply, what people live, remembering old promises. Most interesting in life is the pattern of human motives. Most interesting of human motives and relationships, most intimate, and most individualistic is the love affair. Each of the five plays collected here turns around a romance.

Four of the plays are dramas; one is a satiric comedy. In the dramas, a kind of disillusion prevails: the love affairs are frustrated, although the desires which caused them are ennobled. In the comedy, the lovers live happily ever after at the expense of the official machinery which tried to frustrate them. In this simple sense, all five plays say that only the content of life itself is fit material for the theater. Theatrical conventions exist to reflect what happens in daily life and to transform life into meaning, not despite but by means of artistic distortion. Staged unhappiness, say these plays (like the superb 1957 Soviet film *Don Quixote*), is true-to-life. "True" artistic manipulation of what real people fail in leads to meaning and understanding. In sum, these playwrights have brought to the theater what Mark Shchëglov hoped for a decade ago:

The intellectual side, the political tendencies of a work of art *cannot* have effect *despite* its artistic primitiveness but only *as a result of* its high artistic merit. Only in that way nowadays can art contribute to education in the spirit of communism—in which case, "art and propaganda are synonymous" (Saltykov-Shchedrin).

Art, apparently, has certain eternal, invincible laws corresponding to the potentialities of our esthetic response. Apparently, there are things which you cannot get away from, things which, in the art of the theater, give specific delight and enchantment and bring forth a special *dramatic force.* This force—the force of transformation—united in itself two decisive "poles": *naturalness* and *conventionality.*

The basic failures of contemporary dramas, which keep them from being genuine "plays of life," as seen from this corner, follow from the fact that we have forgotten about this decisive, double nature of dramatic art, about the specific "dramatic force," about precisely those qualities which make it art. . . .

So far we still make use of only the first and elementary aspect of dramatic art as "imitation" of life, seeking to embody as "literally" as possible in some "average" canonical dramatic form some given contemporary theme, some crucial conflict of our times. The attempt to create life-like literalism without taking into account the specific nature of drama, the failure to understand the profundity of "reincarnation" in drama and in the theater, conceals as if under a shroud many fruitful, artistically universalizing potentialities of this genuine, popular art.

By and large, the contemporary Russian theater has not made the technical experiments or advances which please audiences in Poland and France, in Stratford, Ontario, and Minneapolis, Minnesota, in the small, "off-Broadway" theaters of the Western world. Soviet Russian theatrical work, in the hands of such actors as Angelina Stepanova, Yulia Borisova, Oleg Efremov, carries on the traditions of Kachalov, Tarkhanov, Ilyinsky, and others. The professional level is high; the ensemble is exquisitely trained; the timing is perfect; the interpretation is clear; but, Mikhail Zharov recently complained, in the many symposia on the new Russian theater the actor is ignored by the director and by the playwright. His complaint confirms that the Russian theater, like the technically skilled society which it measures and projects, is now chiefly concerned with redefinition of goals and reassertion of a proper function.

The new plays, often put on in new theaters or in theater clubs, indicate a longing to expand the "intellectual side" of the theater and to make "political tendencies" represent actual experience. Victor

Rozov's *The Reunion* (about the lives of members of a high school class), Alexander Shtein's *Applause* (about a father-son conflict in attitudes toward the theater and society), and Alexander Volodin's *The Appointment* (about a good man involved in bureaucratic conflict who accepts promotion to keep the wrong man out) treat themes publicly unutterable when the new period began. They help break down drab theatrical literalism by reintroducing such techniques as the voice of *conscience* over the microphone, the open stage, multilevel sets, and the use of fantasy and irony leaning toward the grotesque. Volchek's *Court Chronicle* and Radzinsky's *A Hundred and Four Pages on Love* have provoked lively discussion, much of it in the press.

None of these plays suggests the "Theater of the Absurd" nor even the (Albee/Pinter) drama of empty, domestic bitterness now in vogue in other European and American theaters. None suggests the fierce, sardonic political and social satire which has come from West Germany. Perhaps the Russians' continued respect for individual dignity, their prevailing faith in the goodness of life (no matter how unlucky any one man's life), and their conviction that drama, like any art, must be socially responsive and/or socially definitive combine to keep in center stage characters who, despite their losses and griefs, do not opt out. Perhaps a kind of general prudishness is partly responsible for the absence of plays treating homosexuality, drug addiction, alcoholism, racial oppression, and spiritual boredom, but, more importantly, such themes are minor and aberrant (and, most Russians would say, not significant) aspects of the life of a society which has firm and cohesive goals and which expects its artists to see, to judge, and to show how. The increasing number of productions of Western European and American plays opens a window on life abroad (although, by and large, Russians are more understanding of us than we are of them) and encourages greater inventiveness in using domestic material, but it is hard to think of a satirist more inventive than Shvarts or of skilled playwrights whose ears are closer to the ground than Rozov, Panova, or Zorin.

The plays in this anthology cannot represent the variety of Soviet dramatic offerings today—from puppet theater and folk dance to opera and classical tragedy—but they may show how, in the past decade, details of individual life have become meaningful for all society. They are love stories. One ends happily: that is, the lovers are united; social hypocrisy and cruelty are exposed. The play is a satire. Four end sadly: that is, the lovers, parted by forces beyond their control, readjust to (perhaps, vanish in) social life. All of them are made without regard to "isms" and with respect for those "things which . . . bring forth a special *dramatic force*." As we read or watch them, we see that the dramatically structured love story, one of the oldest and most conventional of plots, has reacquired significance through its opposition to established social norms and to declared (as opposed to "felt") obligations.

A new romanticism has burst forth in Russia. The past decade has been a period of the personal anecdote, the faithful memoir, the touching story, and the lyric love poem, all celebrating the integrity of the individual and of his ideals against formidable opposition. Nagibin, Solzhenitsyn, Kazakov, Voznesensky—these names are well-known abroad as those of writers who have found vitality, dignity, and nobility in the average man's search for "self." The authors of the plays in this volume also assert imagination and sentiment and the rights of the individual against the indifference of "the system" and the classical strictures of the now-defunct "socialist realism." In detailing quests for spiritual and emotional adventure and for modern chivalric love, in emphasizing transcendental aspects of daily life (music, song, poetry, wine, heroism), these plays are characteristic of their time. Literate and sophisticated, they show concern for language, for character development, for construction. They tell the world that a new sense of style has come into Russian life. In their firm, often humorous, always sympathetic new humanism, they excellently propose still greater changes in the decades ahead.

F. D. REEVE

contemporary russian drama

alive forever

A DRAMA IN THREE ACTS

BY VICTOR ROZOV

CHARACTERS

Fyodor Ivanovich Borozdin, *a doctor, 57*
Varvara Kapitonovna, *his mother*
Boris, *his son, 25*
Irina, *his daughter, 27*
Mark, *his nephew, 27*
Veronica Bogdanova, *18*
Anna Mikhailovna Kovalyova, *a history teacher, 52*
Vladimir (Volodya), *her son, 21*
Stepan, *Boris's comrade, 24*
Anatoly Alexandrovich Kuzmin, *Boris's co-worker, 29*
Dasha, *17* }
Lyuba, *18* } *Boris's co-workers*
Antonina Nikolayevna Monastyrskaya, *33*
Varya, *a worker in a soap factory, 20*
Nyura, *a bread cutter*
Misha, *a student*
Tanechka (Tanya), *a student*
Nikolai Nikolayevich Chernov, *business manager of the Philharmonic Society, 48*

ACT I

SCENE 1   *Veronica's room. Veronica is sitting on a sofa, her legs under her. Boris, standing on the windowsill, is tacking up a blanket, darkening the room.*

VERONICA   Lower, make it lower!

BORIS   I can't, it won't reach.

VERONICA   There's a crack at the bottom! [*Runs over to the window, yanks the blanket down.*] Let go, let go! . . . [*The whole thing gives way.*] Oh, hold it, hold it! . . . What a man! . . .

BORIS   For the third time. You can't do it like that, Veronica! I've told you: I'll tack it on top and then do the bottom. You can't do it like that! [*Hops down from the windowsill.*]

VERONICA   You've already said that! *You* can't do it! I'll do it myself, I'll do it myself! . . . [*Climbs onto the windowsill but can't reach the top.*] Give me the chair.

BORIS   The chair won't fit on the windowsill.

VERONICA   You refuse—all right! [*Gets down, takes the chair; it doesn't fit on the windowsill. Then* VERONICA *takes some things off the desk and moves the desk over toward the window.* BORIS *tries to help her.*] Get away, I'll do it myself! [BORIS *keeps helping.*] Boris, you're in my way. Get away, do you hear!

[BORIS *steps back.* VERONICA *moves the desk over, puts the chair on it, climbs up, reaches the top, measures it with her eye, gets down, picks up the blanket, a hammer and nails, and again climbs up. Tacks the blanket on, drops a nail.* BORIS *doesn't move.* VERONICA *gets down, puts several nails in her mouth, holding them in her teeth, and climbs on to the chair once more.*]

BORIS   Don't swallow a nail.

[VERONICA *works without saying a word. At a slant, crookedly, still she somehow manages to fasten the blanket up. She gets down, looks it over—the crack at the bottom is even bigger.*]

VERONICA   Now, that's different.

BORIS   Yes, much better.

VERONICA   Better than it was. [*Covers the crack with books.*]

BORIS   And the flowers can go on the bookshelf.

VERONICA   One more word and I'll throw you out. Don't worry, the Germans won't come.

BORIS   I don't know about the Germans, but the police certainly will.

VERONICA   Let them.

BORIS   They'll fine you.

VERONICA   Oh, stop it!

BORIS   Yes, they will. And if you don't pay you'll be sent off to hard labor or put in prison for violating blackout regulations.

VERONICA   You can make all the fun of me you want. I'll leave the window the way it is, and as for the police or prison or your witticisms—phooey! there! [*Turns around and knocks a little statue off the desk.*]

BORIS   To make it more convincing knock over the lamp and the vase, too.

[VERONICA *suddenly laughs, runs to the sofa, sits down with her feet under her.*]

VERONICA   Only, don't you come near me! I hate you! Borka, don't come near me, you hear! [BORIS *sits beside* VERONICA. VERONICA *nestles up to him.*] Tell me, am I very silly? Very?

BORIS   No, not very.

VERONICA   But you're clever, you read everything, you study and work. Tell me, Borka, are you a genius? [BORIS *laughs.*] A genius, a genius! You've read everything, know everything. . . . Tell me, how many people live . . . [*thinks*] in India?

BORIS   About three hundred fifty million.

VERONICA   But how do you know that, how do you?

BORIS   I read it.

VERONICA   Where?

BORIS   But everybody knows it.

VERONICA   Everybody! You mean, I'm the only one who doesn't. Then I *am* a special ignoramus; yet still you say you want to marry me. All right, tell me, why do you love me?

BORIS   I don't.

VERONICA   Nonsense. . . . But I like that. Such a clever man, yet loves a silly girl. So, where's justice? There isn't any. Isn't and shouldn't be! Listen, Borka, please make me clever, because when

Papa's friends come to the house, his oh-so-scholarly friends, I sit
and shake: maybe someone will suddenly ask me something.

BORIS   You'll go to the institute. . . .

VERONICA   Sure. . . . Very likely. What'll I take as a present to the
admissions committee?

BORIS   Maybe that! [*Points to the statues on the desk.*]

VERONICA   Oh, that's nothing. Mavrik, our cat. [*Picks up a statue.*]
He was on the windowsill, sprawled out in the sun, three hours there,
and so I did a clay from life. Yesterday . . . Only, don't you say
a word about this. . . . [*Goes up to the closet, takes a statuette
out.*] I did this. It's called "Mama's Up." Look: one of her eyes
is still asleep, stuck shut, her hair's in a mess, bathrobe and slippers, yawning. . . . Mama saw it, said not to show it to anybody.
Hide that foul thing as far away as you can, she said. Don't you
dare say you saw it!

BORIS   So, take it to the admissions committee.

VERONICA   For shame! I'll take this and . . . [*Picks up the hammer
and aims it at the statue.*]

BORIS   Don't!

VERONICA [*hiding the statue away*]   During the summer I'll do something special. . . . I'm a silly fool, a fool, but I have some ideas
of my own, too, yes, I do, don't laugh. And you know: I'm not
afraid of the war. When you're with me, I'm not afraid of anything. Not of anything in the world! Though, actually, that's not
true. Tell me, could you do something right now that's a very,
very unpleasant thing for you to do?

BORIS   What?

VERONICA   No, tell me: could you?

BORIS   I could.

VERONICA   Borenka, pet, put the blanket up over that damned little window. I'm afraid of the police.

BORIS   You won't pester me?

VERONICA   No, no. I'll sit here like a mouse. If you want, I won't
even look. I'll shut my eyes and won't open them until you tell
me to.

BORIS   Sit there and shut your eyes.

[VERONICA *sits with her eyes squeezed shut.* BORIS *goes to the window.*]

VERONICA [*after a pause*]   Can I talk?

BORIS   You can.

VERONICA   I'll recite you a poem, all right?

BORIS   All right, go ahead.

VERONICA   Listen.

> The long-billed cranes
> Are flying overhead,
> Gray ones, white ones,
> Ships in the skies.
> Chug-a-rum, the frogs
> Stroll along the shore,
> Hopping here and there,
> Catching flies.

You like it?

BORIS   Full of significant content!

VERONICA   I think that's the first poem I learned when I was little.

BORIS   And the last.

VERONICA   Just you wait! . . .

BORIS   I didn't say a word.

VERONICA   Tell me, can the army take you?

BORIS   Of course. I even wanted them to. . . .

VERONICA   You'd volunteer?

BORIS   Why not? If I decide to, I will.

VERONICA   You're so smart. You know, Borka, that's not good. You know very well you'll get deferred, and so you're showing off.

BORIS   What makes you think so?

VERONICA   All intelligent people will get deferred, I know it.

BORIS   So, according to you, only idiots will fight?

VERONICA   I won't talk to you anymore.

BORIS   If there is a deferment, it'll be for only one of us, either me or Kuzmin.

VERONICA   But who are you comparing yourself to?

BORIS   He knows the practical side a hundred times better than I do.

VERONICA   Stop, stop! . . . So what if your Kuzmin knows everything in the world. . . . Who got the prize on May first? You or Kuzmin? Who received an expression of commendation and gratitude not so long ago—you or Kuzmin? You yourself told me about it proudly. You work in a plant that's nationally important, and that's that! . . .

BORIS   Veronica, this is a serious conversation. I've been wanting to talk to you about . . .

VERONICA   But I don't want to. And don't you dare call me "Veronica," you hear! Who am I? [BORIS *is silent.*] If you don't say

right away who I am, you know what I'll do? First I'll open one
eye, then the other, then I'll jump up and run over to you
and . . . [*Does all this as she speaks, stands beside* BORIS *on the
windowsill and grabs the blanket, threatening to pull it down.*]
Who am I?

BORIS Squirrel . . . Squirrel . . . Just don't pester me.

VERONICA That's right. [*Goes around the room with the air of a
conqueror.*] Can I ask you another little question, can I?

BORIS You can.

VERONICA What are you going to give me tomorrow?

BORIS That's a secret.

VERONICA You won't say?

BORIS Not for anything.

VERONICA Well, you don't have to. Only, if it's something tasty,
I'll eat it right up and forget it. Give me something I'll remember a long, long time, until I'm an old woman. We'll be grandpa
and grandma together and we'll look at it and say: that's the present
Squirrel got when she was eighteen. I'll live to a hundred, and
I'll have a hundred of your presents. [BORIS *has finished the blind,
climbed down from the windowsill, and now puts the tools away.*]
I like its being dark: from the windows across the way you can
always see what's going on in here, but now . . . Kiss me. [BORIS
kisses her.] Good . . . and nobody can see. [*A knock on the door.*]
Come in, come in.

[STEPAN *enters.*]

STEPAN This the Bogdanovs?

BORIS Stepan!

VERONICA I'm Veronica Bogdanova.

STEPAN Oh! . . . [*To* BORIS.] That the one?

BORIS Yes.

STEPAN [*greeting* VERONICA] I'm Stepan. [*To* BORIS. *Speaks in fits
and starts, breathing heavily.*] Got the notice . . . just now. . . .
Ran over to you . . . it's there, too. Your family's upset . . . said
you were here . . . I ran over. . . .

BORIS For what day?

STEPAN The crackpots, you understand—for today, with all your
things. Run down to the office, get your release . . . settle things
there. . . . I told the bookkeeper's office . . . they'll wait. . . . And
leave a power of attorney. . . .

BORIS Today?

STEPAN   At ten tonight. I'll just have a swallow—got to hurry. [*Goes to the decanter, drinks.*]

VERONICA   What is all this?

BORIS   Well, you see, Veronica, I thought I'd be here for a few more days still, but now . . . The notice has come . . . the army.

VERONICA   For you?

STEPAN   Me, too. We both volunteered. . . .

VERONICA   [*to* BORIS]   You're going? . . . By yourself? But me? What about me?

STEPAN   I can see you have something to talk over—I'm off. [*To* VERONICA.] Don't cry, girl, your Borka is a great fellow! Ah, my family's waiting at home, too! . . . What can you do with them! . . . Don't be sad. So long! [*Runs out.*]

[VERONICA *and* BORIS *are alone.* VERONICA *looks at him uncomprehendingly.*]

BORIS   It had to be this way. . . . Couldn't be any other.

VERONICA   No, no. He said you did it yourself, volunteered. That means I'll be alone. Why did you? You know I love you.

BORIS   Right now everything's fine, quiet, understand, but war's coming, already has, Squirrel. I sent in the application myself, that's true. . . . I didn't want to tell you for the time being . . . tomorrow's your birthday. . . . And now—I have to go. How could I do anything else? You know, things are going to be hard for everybody now. It'll be hard to work, to study, to live, and hardest of all to fight. If I'm honest, I've got to be where it's hardest of all, you understand?

VERONICA   Of course, of course . . .

BORIS   Nothing's going to happen, I know that. And afterwards we'll live together a long, long time, until we're a hundred. Let's go over to my family's, I'll explain everything to you and you'll understand, wise and clever.

VERONICA   What's there to explain? I understand everything. I'm not a fool.

BORIS   You angry?

VERONICA   Go on, they're worrying about you at home.

BORIS   And you?

VERONICA   I'll come. Soon. Very soon. I want to be alone . . . a little . . . a few minutes. Go on, go on.

BORIS   Only don't be late, Squirrel.

VERONICA   No, no, I won't. [*Suddenly throws herself on* BORIS's *neck.*] Borya! My Borenka!

BORIS   Come, what are you doing, why? Don't.
VERONICA [*letting go of* BORIS]   I won't, I won't.
BORIS   Let's go together.
VERONICA   No, no . . . You go on.
BORIS   Don't start crying.
VERONICA   No, no . . . I won't. [BORIS *goes up to* VERONICA, *starts to embrace her.* VERONICA *moves away.*] I'll come.
BORIS   I can't leave like this.
VERONICA   Oh . . . [*Kisses* BORIS.] Now go. [BORIS *leaves the room.* VERONICA *goes over to the door, stands there, listens. Silence. She notices his books on the little table by the coat hanger. She picks them up.*] Forgot his books.

SCENE 2   *A room in the Borozdins' apartment. The dining room and part of the front hall can be seen. Varvara Kapitonovna is packing things into a duffle bag. Mark persistently practices a passage on the piano.*

VARVARA [*shouting*]   Irina! . . . Mark, stop a minute, please. [MARK *stops playing.*] Irina, bring the iron!
IRINA'S VOICE   All right!
VARVARA   Time's flying, flying. . . . And nobody's here. Does he know?
MARK   Stepan ran over. He'll tell him.
VARVARA   But is he at Veronica's?
MARK   He wasn't at work, so he's there.
VARVARA   Not telling anybody anything. That's not like Borya.
MARK   It's just like him. To let everybody know afterwards.
VARVARA   Deciding by himself, without talking it over with anyone.
MARK   Yes, rather odd.
VARVARA   Get his cuff links out of his drawer, would you? The ones in the pen-case.
MARK   Don't forget to add a pair of starched collars.
VARVARA   No objections from you. They won't take up much room, and it'll be nice for him. Veronica gave them to him.
MARK [*gets the cuff links*]   I doubt he'll have much time there to wax lyrical.

[VARVARA KAPITONOVNA *wraps the cuff-links in paper, puts them in the bag.* IRINA *enters, the iron in her hand.*]

VARVARA [*taking the iron*]   Well, your father coming finally?

IRINA I called him. He's in the operating room. And still no Boris.

MARK Vanished!

VARVARA [*ironing a shirt*] Can't he stay over until tomorrow?

MARK The notice specifies ten tonight.

VARVARA Just a piece of paper and yet it whisks a man away, just like that.

MARK Yes . . . And there's nothing you can do about it.

VARVARA [*drawing* IRINA's *attention to the shirt*] You gave this to him, remember?

IRINA Did I?

VARVARA [*to* MARK] Call Fedya up once more—maybe he's free now.

MARK [*dialing*] I don't know how to tell him.

VARVARA Don't do it all at once; it would be like a bolt from the blue.

MARK [*into the mouthpiece*] The hospital? Is Doctor Borozdin free now? Find out, please. [*To* IRINA, *pointing at the piano.*] Close the lid or the dust will get in. [*Into the mouthpiece.*] Uncle Fedya? Uncle Fedya, could you come home immediately? Oh no, nothing special. Boris has pulled another trick, that's all. . . . [*To* VARVARA.] He's swearing mad; I don't know how to handle it.

VARVARA Let me have it. [*Takes the receiver.*] Fedya, it's me. No, no, no, Mark didn't mean that. Nothing has happened. When are you going to be finished today? No, please, don't get upset. Let me say it again: absolutely nothing has happened. We're home here, quiet and peaceful. . . . Here's Irina now. . . .

IRINA [*taking the receiver*] Papa, Boris is leaving for the army in an hour. An emergency? Seems he himself applied as far back as the twenty-third. No, he isn't here. But come home; you can curse as well at home. [*Hangs up the receiver.*]

VARVARA Brought everybody up short, the whole house.

MARK It's all strange. He was in line for deferment, we know that for certain. And Stepan said . . . He's up to some kind of foolishness, something foolish.

IRINA It was foolish that he didn't say a word, but everything else, maybe, is very right and sensible.

MARK We're just waiting for you to go and become an army nurse.

IRINA If the time comes, I will.

MARK But I think that if the upper echelons find it necessary to leave a man here, in the rear, it means that he's most needed right here. Anybody can hold a rifle.

VARVARA Time's flying, flying.

MARK If I get a notice, I'll go, I won't cry over it.

IRINA   It's nasty of him if he's still over at Veronica's.

MARK   What did you think? That he'd stay over there until the last minute and just run in here for his things? Though in this kind of thing you don't understand very much, anyway.

[BORIS *enters.*]

VARVARA   Borenka! Borya!

IRINA   What's happened to you, out of your mind?

BORIS   You want to know why I didn't tell you anything? Here's why: just so there wouldn't be any of these *oohs* and *aahs* and long discussions. Nothing else. [*Looks at the things which his grandmother is getting together, at the table* IRINA *has set, and becomes confused.*]

VARVARA   It wasn't right, Borenka.

MARK   We were waiting and waiting for you.

IRINA   What's the matter with you?

MARK   Did you and Veronica have an argument?

IRINA   You think we're criticizing you? Why I . . . I envy you.

MARK   What did I tell you!

IRINA   Blockhead of a conservatory graduate. [*Goes out.*]

MARK   She's stern.

VARVARA   You should have told us, Borya, at least told your father.

BORIS   [*pointing to the knapsack*] Grandma, what's all that for? I need just what's necessary.

VARVARA   But everything seems necessary.

BORIS   The main thing is to make it as light as you can. Did you call Papa?

VARVARA   He'll be here in a minute.

MARK   He swore like a trooper over the phone.

BORIS   [*giving* MARK *notebooks and a drawing*] Take these to the plant tomorrow. There you'll find Kuzmin, Anatoly Alexandrovich; give them to him. Or call him up.

MARK   What for? Sure, I'll take them. We need to buy some wine; I'll go get it.

BORIS   Not necessary.

MARK   Oh, this is an occasion.

BORIS   The traditional toast on saying good-bye, drowning our sorrow?

MARK   I'll get a little red wine, for your success. [*Goes out.*]

VARVARA   Maybe it is tradition, but all the same I'm certainly going to have a glass. . . . Why did you come without Veronica?

BORIS   She'll be here in a minute.

VARVARA   What's wrong with her?

BORIS   She'll be here. . . . [*Rummages in the drawer from which* MARK *took the cuff-links.*]

VARVARA   I put them in, Borya. Will you go straight . . . to the front?

BORIS   Probably. [*Sits down at the table, writes.*]

VARVARA   And so it's reached us. Both the Anosov sons had to go. Every family is upset, has its farewells and tears. The Sorokins are leaving Moscow, say it's dangerous. What do you think, Borya, will they bomb Moscow? [BORIS *keeps writing.*] Probably will. But maybe not . . . What comes will come! . . . They're moving so fast. . . . I won't go. It's better to die here than traipse around from a corner in one stranger's house to another. It's a time of trouble. . . .

[BORIS *has finished writing. Takes the bundle which he came in with and opens it up. It's a big plush squirrel with fluffy tail and ears. Tied to it by a ribbon is a wicker basket with gold nuts.* BORIS *unties the ribbon, empties out the nuts, puts a note on the bottom, pours the nuts back in, ties the ribbon and again wraps the bundle up.*]

BORIS   Grandma, I want to ask you a favor.

VARVARA   What, Borenka?

BORIS   Tomorrow morning, as early as you can, take it over to her.

VARVARA   What is this? No, no, I'm not asking anything. So you mean, give it to her and . . . ?

BORIS   Tomorrow is her birthday. And also: if it's hard for her— you know, the war and all—help her.

VARVARA   And if I die?

BORIS   You've no right to die, especially now when you have so many secrets.

VARVARA   Then I might just up and do it! . . .

[FYODOR IVANOVICH *enters.*]

FYODOR   A-ah! Twenty-five years old and still, forgive me, such a fool! What are we—children? Is this a game? Hide-and-seek? Are you trying to be romantic? Will-power! Where's Irina? Where's Mark?

VARVARA   Irina's in the kitchen making coffee, and Mark went out to buy some red wine.

FYODOR   Coffee? Red wine? No sense of style, people have no sense of style. [*Shouts.*] Irina!

[IRINA *enters.*]

IRINA   Finally!

FYODOR   In my wardrobe, up on the special shelf—bring it. [IRINA *goes out.*] And where's Veronica?

BORIS   She'll be here in a minute.

FYODOR   Where is she?

BORIS   Home, busy.

FYODOR   Busy with what? That's not good. Ought to be here—her fiancé's leaving.

BORIS   Not her fiancé.

FYODOR   Then who?

BORIS   Oh, just leaving.

FYODOR   What does that mean, "just leaving"? "Just leaving"— that's suspicious.

BORIS   I don't mean it that way.

FYODOR   How *do* you mean it?

BORIS   Stop picking.

FYODOR   What happened, did you have an argument with her?

BORIS   No.

FYODOR   Be careful! In moments like this, Boris, there must be only joy, only plain-dealing. [*To* IRINA, *who has come in carrying a vial.*] Dilute it according to the rule. [*To* BORIS.] Then there'll be something to remember when you're there, a place to come back to, a desire to keep on living, living despite all the bombs and machine-guns. Living in order to come back here to the people closest to you in the world, to come back as a hero, your head high in the air!

[MARK *enters.*]

MARK   I got it.

FYODOR   Red wine?

MARK   Yes.

FYODOR   Well, you can guzzle it yourself. We'll find something more substantial. Everybody here? Sit down. [*They all sit down around the table.*]

IRINA   Mark, don't sit there, that's my place.

MARK   Did you buy it?

FYODOR   Nobody did, but you know I don't like people coming and going at the table. We've sat like this for twenty years and we'll sit this way for another fifty. [*To* BORIS.] You used to sit in that place when you were no bigger than this, you could hardly reach the table. And it'll be yours until you have a family of your own. And when Irina gets married, I'll toss her chair up into the attic.

IRINA   As soon as I finish struggling with my dissertation, I will.

FYODOR   You ought to look over my notes, I spent thirty years collecting them: quotes, facts, observations. Thought of writing a book, getting a professorship. I worked, worked, and kept thinking, I'll do it later, but now I see it's too late.

IRINA   I'm almost finished looking through them.

FYODOR   Well?

IRINA   My conclusions later.

FYODOR   Oho! I'm afraid you're going to give them an F?

IRINA   We'll see.

[*Preparations at table are over.* FYODOR IVANOVICH *raises his glass.*]

FYODOR   May you live long and happily, Boris!

[*Everyone drinks. A knock on the door.*]

MARK   Veronica! [*Runs to the door.*]

[DASHA *and* LYUBA *come in.*]

DASHA   Hello!

LYUBA   Hello! Boris Fyodorovich, we're here from the plant. . . .

DASHA   We were appointed to give you these presents and on behalf of the plant committee to say . . .

LYUBA   And the Young Communist cell . . .

FYODOR   Be strong and brave, Comrade Borozdin, to the last drop of your blood, beat the cursed fascists, and our factory here, in the rear lines, will fill and overfulfill the norms. . . . All of us know that—don't worry, we won't let you down. Instead, why don't you sit down and join us in toasting my son Borka on the long road ahead of him?

DASHA   But what about the presents?

FYODOR   But we'll accept the presents. What's there? [*Opens the package.*] A safety razor, a soap-box, stationery, envelopes . . . just what there should be. [*Opens the second package.*] Pastries. All Napoleons.

LYUBA   We bought that ourselves on the way. We always used to see Boris Fyodorovich get these pastries in the snack bar.

FYODOR   Have some, Boris, more—you'll fight like Napoleon. That's a present that means something! We've all had one round, so now let's have the second. [*Pours.*] Life on this terrestrial globe still isn't set up so well and orderly as we'd like—here you are leaving. To you, Boris! [*Drinks.*]

DASHA   I saw my brother off yesterday—Mama cried so.

FYODOR   And you?

DASHA   I did, too.

FYODOR   On behalf of the local committee or just simply as a member of the family?

DASHA [*laughing*]   As one of the family.

LYUBA   But we have nobody to see off—three of us sisters and Mama . . . It doesn't seem right—everybody has people going.

FYODOR   Yes, when ours come back, you'll envy us.

MARK   That's just what's so terrible: not everyone will.

FYODOR   Whoever doesn't will stand like a monument reaching the sky. And his name will be pure gold! To you, Boris. [*Drinks.*] [*A knock on the door.*] Must be someone on behalf of the management.

VARVARA   Come in.

[KUZMIN *enters.*]

KUZMIN   Hello. Excuse me, please, this is the wrong time: you're saying good-bye to your son, I understand. . . . Excuse me, I didn't even introduce myself. Kuzmin—Boris Fyodorovich's comrade at the plant. Boris Fyodorovich, naturally you didn't behave completely honestly. . . . Excuse me, I mean not completely correctly. You tried to get ahead of fate. But it goes without saying that it would be ridiculous to criticize you for that, especially for me to. You refused a deferment though, probably, it would have been you who would have gotten it. I'm staying behind. [*To everybody.*] Of course, maybe, that's wrong, but war, the front . . . you know, somehow they don't attract me. You know, it even makes me feel sick when boys shoot keys: they take a regular, old-type key and stuff the stem full of match heads, plug it with a nail, and then throw it with a smash against a wall. Extremely unpleasant. Of course, if I'm needed, too . . . why, as they say, I'll take the bayonet in my hands. . . . Boris Fyodorovich, I'm sorry, last week we were talking about the connecting tube for the journal. . . .

BORIS   Yes, yes, I did the calculations. I just asked my cousin to take them over to you. Here. [*Hands the notebooks and drawing to* KUZMIN.] It works out in theory, but I can't swear that it will in practice. Check it.

FYODOR   Comrade Kuzmin, join us at table.

KUZMIN   I thank you, thank you—couldn't possibly on any account. Have to rush. [*To* BORIS.] I promise you to work tirelessly, to do the work of two, of ten. By the way, Lyuba, though you are a young laboratory assistant, you have to know how to do things right: you went out and left the apparatus on the table. Dust could get at it. It cost two thousand in hard money. So maybe you and I won't manage to work together. [*To everyone.*] Once more, please, excuse me. Well, Boris Fyodorovich, till we meet again! [*Shakes* BORIS's *hand.*] Let me embrace you. [*Embraces and kisses* BORIS.] Only please don't let anything happen to you . . . or I'll feel extremely awkward. [*Smiles.*]

BORIS   Good-bye, Anatoly Alexandrovich. Nothing will happen, we'll have a chance to work together again.

KUZMIN   [*to everyone*]   Best of luck. Curse this war. How it gets in the way of everything! [*Goes out.*]

FYODOR   Well, he'd never make a Chapayev.°

MARK   I'm glad Boris is going instead of him. A coward. You're probably going because of him, Borka, aren't you?

BORIS   He's not a coward.

LYUBA   Just a civilian through and through.

BORIS   An experienced, knowledgeable man. But I have to be there. You understand, there . . . I don't want to talk about it.

FYODOR   Then don't. An intelligent man will understand anyway, and there's no point wasting your breath on fools.

IRINA   Borka, you're my own brother, but I feel as if I were seeing you for the first time.

FYODOR   Outpourings of family sentiment later. Why isn't Veronica here?

BORIS   Well, she said she might not make it. She and I already said good-bye.

FYODOR   I heard what you call her—Squirrel. You were here in the room whispering away and courting, and there I was with my ear to the door, eavesdropping. That's fine she's a squirrel! Let her come here more often, hop around, for Irina's serious beyond her years, and to Mark music is the whole world, and Grandma has finished her hopping.

VARVARA   Yesterday in the management office they were telling us

---

°Chapayev, V. I. (1887–1919), a workman who, in command of a division in the Urals during the Civil War, became a Red Army hero. Furmanov's novel *Chapayev* (1923) and a famous film (1939) made him a popular figure.

how to put out incendiary bombs, so maybe I'll still have to do some hopping—on the roof.

BORIS ˙ It's time for me to go, Papa.

VARVARA Already?

FYODOR Well, if it's time, it's time.

IRINA [*giving* BORIS *a little book*] If you have a free moment, take a look. Lermontov. [*Embraces and kisses her brother.*]

MARK If you'd told us earlier, I'd have gotten something ready.

BORIS Give me your fountain-pen, if you'd like to.

MARK You found the right moment to worm it out of me! Take it and be sure to write often. [*Kisses* BORIS.]

VARVARA Before, I'd have hung a little cross on you, but now I don't know what to give you—maybe a button off my dress. . . .

FYODOR Splendid, cut off one of her buttons, the biggest, there, the one on her belt.

[BORIS *takes a knife and cuts the button off.* GRANDMA *gives it to him and blesses him with the sign of the cross.*]

VARVARA Still, that's better.

FYODOR Well, there's nothing for me to give you, but you won't forget anyway, all the times I scolded you. I won't go see you off—I'm too tired. Give me your eyes. [*Kisses* BORIS'S *eyes.*] Here, the girls will see you off.

DASHA Sure.

LYUBA We will.

BORIS [*quietly, to* MARK] Don't you come.

MARK Why not?

BORIS Stay with Father.

MARK All right. Just to the street-car.

VARVARA [*taking* BORIS *aside*] Borya, what's the address where you're going now?

BORIS It's all right, Grandma. It's even better this way. Tell her I'll write on the way. If she comes now, give that to her [*nods at the package*], there's a note in it.

MARK We're off!

VARVARA Let me have a last look at you.

FYODOR Grandma! . . . [*All go out except* FYODOR IVANOVICH *and* VARVARA KAPITONOVNA.] Have just another little swallow.

VARVARA Do, Fedya. [FYODOR IVANOVICH *is about to drink but pushes the glass away.*] Can't drink alone?

FYODOR I can't. [*Gets ready to go out.*]

VARVARA Where are you going?

FYODOR   To duty in the hospital.

VARVARA   You were on duty on Friday.

FYODOR   I'm relieving Fyodorov—the old man is very tired, and, after all, I can't sleep anyway.

[FYODOR IVANOVICH *goes out.* VARVARA KAPITONOVNA *tidies up in the hall. The doors into the room are shut.* VERONICA *enters carrying a bundle.*]

VARVARA   Veronica, here you are!

VERONICA Hello, Varvara Kapitonovna!

VARVARA   Hello, hello! Borenka kept watching the door the whole time.

VERONICA I wanted to get him something to take with him. I went into a store, but when I came out I couldn't get across the street—all the soldiers who had been called up were marching through . . . whole columns of them . . . The street-cars had stopped, the automobiles, too . . . everything had stopped dead . . . only *they* were marching, marching. . . . An awful lot of them . . . Grandma, please ask Borya to come here a minute. . . . I don't want to go in.

VARVARA   He's already gone, Veronica.

VERONICA Gone? Where?

VARVARA   But don't you know? . . . To the assembly point. Let's go in.

[VERONICA *mechanically follows* VARVARA KAPITONOVNA.]

VERONICA Quickly as . . . I wanted to get . . . and then—they all were marching, marching . . . Where did he go?

VARVARA   He didn't say. Probably someplace in Krasnaya Presnya. Irusha and the girls went to see him off.

VERONICA What girls?

VARVARA   Came by from the factory. On behalf of the Komsomol and the local committee, I think. Nice girls, very nice. And Fedya behaved very well. Thank god, everything went off without any tears.

VERONICA Without any tears . . .

VARVARA   Borya left a note for you, and here it is. [*Gives the package to* VERONICA.]

VERONICA What's this?

VARVARA   For tomorrow—you have a birthday. There's a note in there.

VERONICA [*undoing the package*]   But where's the note?
VARVARA   In here. No?
VERONICA   Nowhere. Maybe he put it on the table?
VARVARA [*searching on the table*]   Can't find it. He must have forgotten it in his hurry, he probably took it away with him.
VERONICA   Forgot?
VARVARA   He'll write you soon.
VERONICA   Good-bye.

[VERONICA *goes toward the door. At that moment,* MARK *enters.*]

MARK   Hello, Veronica. How come you were late? . . . Oh, what sad little eyes you have. . . . Don't go, wait here a while. Sit down. You're like one of us. We all love you, honestly— Uncle Fedya was just talking about it. There's some kind of bright light in you, a little star. . . . Don't be sad, follow Boris's example. What a fellow—smiling, witty . . . if only he stays alive. [*Opens his music.*] Sweet Veronica, mankind fights without respite—if not in one place, then in another. Once our turn comes, we'll fight, too, we won't let our face get pushed in the dirt. [*Sits down at the piano.*] But as I see it, the chief thing even in wartime is to keep the rhythm of normal human life. Not to give up your joys, your cherished wishes even to war. So, there's a war on; but I'll keep practicing and training my fingers. Like this. [*Plays a passage.*] Like this! . . . [*Plays.*] Like this! . . . [*Plays.*] [VERONICA *gets up to go.*] Stay, Veronica; here with us it's as if you were beside him. And you know, music is a special help in moments of sadness. Listen. Grandma, don't rattle the dishes.

[MARK *plays the piano. The sound of marching feet breaks through the music—outside the window columns of soldiers are marching past.* VERONICA *listens to the marching feet, slowly goes over to the window, opens the blinds.* GRANDMA *puts out the light and also goes to the window. Then* MARK, *too, comes up. All three look out the window.*]

VARVARA   The Moscow men are going.
MARK   There's something triumphant in it . . . and terrifying.
VARVARA [*softly, out the window*]   Come back alive!

ACT II

SCENE 1 *A completely different, strange room in which the Borozdins settled after being evacuated from Moscow. However, we recognize several things from the previous scene. Veronica and Anna Mikhailovna are in the room. Anna Mikhailovna is drinking coffee at a little table and reading a letter. Veronica is in her favorite position, on the sofa with her feet tucked under her.*

ANNA [*putting the letter down*] You want some coffee, Veronica?
VERONICA No thanks. [*A pause.*] [*Speaks without thinking.*] The long-billed cranes are flying overhead. . . .
ANNA The last box. It'd be good to get some more somewhere.
VERONICA How about the marketplace? The black-marketeers always have some.
ANNA Too expensive. I rarely drank it in Leningrad, on account of my heart. But my husband liked it, especially in the evening, before working. He worked a lot in the evening.
VERONICA Anna Mikhailovna, did you love your husband very much?
ANNA Kirill and I were together for twenty-nine years, and to say I loved him wouldn't be saying the half of it. He was a part of me. He, Vladimir, and I made up one whole, indivisible. But, as you see, in this world anything can be divided.
VERONICA You're a strong woman, Anna Mikhailovna.
ANNA Just seems so.

[*A pause.*]

VERONICA   The long-billed cranes
                     Are flying overhead,
                     Gray ones, white ones . . .

Pooh, some silly lines have stuck in my head! . . . We've been living here in these rooms a whole eternity but I still can't get used to them, it's as if I were exiled.

ANNA [*again taking the letter up*]   Volodya will soon be out of the hospital, but if only he'd say approximately when. Just as irresponsible as ever. And he's twenty-one today.

VERONICA   Today? Congratulations.

ANNA   Thank you. He's a wonderful boy. I don't even have a picture of him—absolutely nothing was left.

VERONICA   But we brought a lot of things, all thanks to Mark's efforts.

ANNA   Yes, your husband is a very practical man.

VERONICA   But I don't need a thing. I wish I were like you—alone.

ANNA   Fyodor Ivanovich loves you—no less, I think, than if you were his own daughter.

VERONICA   But I can't love him.

ANNA   He understands everything, Veronica.

VERONICA   I know, I know. . . . What time could it be now?

ANNA   Probably a little after five.

VERONICA   The endless days.

ANNA   I don't know Boris Fyodorovich, but they. say he was an intelligent and reliable young man in the best and highest sense.

VERONICA   Was? He's missing in action—not necessarily dead!

ANNA   Of course, of course. I just didn't express myself right.

[VERONICA *crosses the room, goes up to the window.*]

VERONICA   March, but what a snowstorm.

ANNA   In Leningrad we always have a snowy March. [*A pause.*] May I ask you a question? If you don't want to answer, don't; I won't mind.

VERONICA   Yes?

ANNA   Why did you marry Mark Alexandrovich?

[*A pause.*]

VERONICA   You don't take any sugar?

ANNA   I'm economizing. When Volodya comes I'll bake something.

VERONICA   I used to have so many, many tasty things. And I still do. [*Goes to the wardrobe, takes the squirrel out.*] See. A whole basket of golden nuts. [*Lost in thought.*] When I got out of the subway, I ran to the house. . . . But there . . . everything ruined . . . smoking . . . I wandered along the streets . . . and came to the Borozdins. . . . Late at night . . . Only Mark was there. . . . He talked to me a long time. . . . Talked well, I thought. . . . Nothing from Borya . . . Fyodor Ivanovich wouldn't be home for

days at a time. . . . But Mark . . . In short, I thought I was saving myself. . . . I did something I can't repeat . . . terrible. . . .
You understand me?

ANNA   Yes.

VERONICA   Thank you. [*After a silence.*] You like the toy?

ANNA   Very much. Probably made to order. I never ran across anything like it in the stores.

VERONICA   Some time I'll wrap it up and go away, without anybody knowing, alone.

ANNA   Where?

VERONICA   I don't know. To the very end of the world. [*Very softly.*]
I'm dying, Anna Mikhailovna.

ANNA   What do you mean, Veronica!

VERONICA   I am, Anna Mikhailovna. . . . I signed up here to study,
I couldn't, I quit. I worked in a factory for just two weeks—left
that, too. Everything's falling apart.

ANNA   It's the war, Veronica.

VERONICA   Yes . . . it's hard to study, work, live. . . . No, no. You,
Irina, Fyodor Ivanovich, Mark—you all are anxious about things,
you work, you live. But me . . . I've lost everything.

ANNA   You still have your life, Veronica. It's all still ahead of you,
a long life you can't see the end of.

VERONICA   But why live? What for? Here, you teach history, you're
intelligent, tell me—what's the meaning of life?

ANNA   [*after a pause*]   Maybe it's in what remains after us. This
house was built, I'd guess, in the middle of the last century. The
men who put up these brick walls have disappeared, but here, in
these terrible days, you and I have found refuge. Or this cup—I
don't know whose hands made it—but now I'm drinking coffee
out of it; it's useful, lovely. Didn't your teachers leave a mark
deep inside you? From generation to generation men pass on to
others the work of their hands, their ideas, their flights of spirit.
Go work, Veronica. Don't look inside yourself for answers to
your questions; you won't find them there. And you'll never find
justification for yourself—you're too honest for that.

[MARK *enters.*]

MARK   Hasn't Nikolai Nikolayevich come?

VERONICA   Is he supposed to?

MARK   He hasn't come?

VERONICA   No. [ANNA MIKHAILOVNA *starts to leave.*] Stay a little
longer, Anna Mikhailovna.

ANNA   I'm going to my own room—Mark Alexandrovich is probably tired.

MARK [*insincerely*]   You're not in the way, Anna Mikhailovna, stay.

ANNA   I have to go teach soon. [*Goes out.*]

MARK   If Chernov comes, be more polite to him, please.

VERONICA   He's repulsive.

MARK   He may be a hundred times more repulsive to me than to you, but it can't be helped—he's my boss.

VERONICA   And keeps borrowing money from you he'll never pay back.

MARK   But what an administrator he is! He arranges the most profitable concerts.

VERONICA   It's disgusting to see how you fawn on him.

MARK [*sternly*]   I never fall on him. . . . I mean, frawn on him . . . I mean . . . Oh, what an idiotic word!

VERONICA   You've stopped studying completely, Mark.

MARK   Yes, sometimes I get desperate. Oh, this war, this war! . . . Well, never mind, it'll end. The chief thing now is to get through it. You understand, the chief thing is to get through it! [*A knock on the door.*] Come in.

[CHERNOV *enters. He is a reliable, dignified, well-dressed man.*]

CHERNOV   Good evening, Veronica Alexeyevna.

VERONICA   Hello.

CHERNOV   Mark Alexandrovich, forgive my intrusion. . . .

MARK   On the contrary, Nikolai Nikolayevich, we're delighted. Please, take off your things.

CHERNOV [*taking off his fur coat*]   The Germans have gotten through in the Caucasus somehow, did you see that? Doesn't matter, we'll show them who we are. May I put my hat on this little table?

MARK   Please do, please.

CHERNOV [*moving into the middle of the room*]   Nice here, comfortable, warm . . . My wife and children are in Tashkent. . . . I live like a waif.

VERONICA   I'm going to the store, Mark.

MARK   All right, go ahead. Maybe they've got some cigarettes now; get some.

VERONICA   All right. [*Goes out.*]

CHERNOV   I'm simply enchanted by your bride, how forthright she is, how pure.

MARK   Don't be offended by her, Nikolai Nikolayevich.

CHERNOV   I was speaking completely sincerely. That childlike lack

of self-control makes her simply enchanting. I was looking for
you today at the Philharmonic. . . .

MARK   Yes, yes, I heard.

CHERNOV   I hate to bother you, but rescue me, Mark Alexandrovich.
My wife writes that she hasn't a kopek.

MARK   How much do you want, Nikolai Nikolayevich?

CHERNOV   Literally as much as you can spare. Say, five hundred
rubles.

MARK   [getting the money]   Certainly, Nikolai Nikolayevich.

CHERNOV   I keep a record of everything, and don't you worry. . . .

MARK   Heavens, Nikolai Nikolayevich, heavens!

CHERNOV   And one other little request: you couldn't ask Fyodor
Ivanovich to get some medicines, could you?

MARK   [frightened]   Which?

CHERNOV   Some sulfa, opium, camphor.

MARK   No, no, what do you mean! Uncle Fedya is morbidly scrupu-
lous. Out of the question to ask him for that.

CHERNOV   Well, then, don't, don't.

MARK   Maybe there's some in his medicine cabinet in the house—
I'll have a look.

CHERNOV   No, if it's really awkward, don't.

MARK   That's all right. . . . [Goes out and comes back with the
medicines in his hand.] Here's all there is.

CHERNOV   Many, many thanks. You tell Fyodor Ivanovich it was
for me. I hope he won't mind, it's really nothing. [Hides the
medicines in his briefcase.] Are you going to Antonina Nikolayevna's today?

MARK   I may.

CHERNOV   Tell her I'm sorry I can't come, I'm too busy. By the
way, let me offer you this box of candy. [Takes a box out of his
big briefcase.] Make it a name-day present. Antonina Nikolayevna
will be delighted. It's not very sumptuous, but you add something, tie something on top. Oh, maybe even this little toy [points
to the squirrel which VERONICA left on the sofa]. It would be
rather nice, I'm sure. What with the war, we have to show how
imaginative we are in all we do.

MARK   What do I owe you?

CHERNOV   Nothing, nothing. We'll settle later. It's nothing. I'll
leave it, all right?

MARK   Fine, Nikolai Nikolayevich. Thanks.

CHERNOV   [putting his coat on]   They wanted you to appear in the
hospital tomorrow—a benefit, naturally, but I shifted you to an-

other brigade; I think you'll do pretty nicely. You can use it, I expect?

MARK Thanks, Nikolai Nikolayevich.

CHERNOV [*saying good-bye to* MARK] Say good-bye to your wife for me.

MARK Good-bye, Nikolai Nikolayevich.

[CHERNOV *goes out.* MARK *goes over to the closet, takes a suit out, goes into the next room to change.* IRINA *enters quickly.*]

IRINA Who's home?

MARK [*shouting from the next room*] Don't come in—I'm dressing.

IRINA Anna Mikhailovna, Anna Mikhailovna! [ANNA MIKHAILOVNA *comes in.*] Congratulate me! I'm still out of breath! . . . I did the most complicated abdominal operation today—it came off absolutely successfully. Father watched it, complimented me. The fellow was all set to turn in his ticket, as they say, you know, to give up the ghost, but I took the chance, with Father's permission, of course. Isn't there any tea? I'll wait for Father for dinner.

ANNA I can bring you some coffee.

IRINA Please do, I'm dying for something to drink. [ANNA MIKHAILOVNA *goes out.*] Mark! I performed a miracle today! A resurrection from the dead. [ANNA MIKHAILOVNA *comes back in.*] You understand—he was dying. But now he'll live! He will, he will! [*Runs to the phone.*] The hospital? Who's this? How's Sazonov in Ward Forty-five? This is Borozdina speaking. Complains of the pain? That's all right, he'll have to for a while. Wanted something to eat? He did! [*Hangs up.*] Wanted something to eat—that's an important sign. I've worked up something of an appetite myself. [*Hungrily eats a sandwich.* MARK *enters, ties his tie in front of the mirror.*] Really, to understand it all you have to be either a doctor or dying. This is the thirty-second one I've brought back to life.

MARK You ought to cut a notch the way soldiers do on their rifles: they kill a fascist and cut a notch. You should, too, even in the operating table.

IRINA You're changing, Mark, and not for the better.

MARK And I don't see how a person can root around in somebody else's guts, do amputations, resections, and then dance for joy.

ANNA Success in any job brings a feeling of satisfaction and joy.

MARK You mean that if an undertaker has made a fine coffin he'll rub his hands together in satisfaction?

ANNA Maybe it's paradoxical, but he probably would.

MARK   Ahh!

IRINA   You sensitive soul, what are you all dolled up for?

MARK   A concert.

IRINA   Tell me another—you have Wednesdays off.

MARK   I'm telling you I have a concert, a chef's concert.

IRINA   Where?

MARK   In the food-workers' club.

IRINA   [*getting up from the table*]   Thanks, Anna Mikhailovna. I want to go put some things down in my notebook.

ANNA   Don't overwork yourself, Irina Fyodorovna. I've been noticing that every night you keep writing and writing. . . .

MARK   Really, what are you doing there, compiling a chronicle?

IRINA   Sure. "These tales of by-gone years . . ." [*Goes out.*]

ANNA   I think she's getting her doctoral dissertation ready.

MARK   Aha, traveling post-haste! She'll spend her whole life as an old maid, mark my word.

ANNA   What makes you think that?

MARK   When a young woman works so furiously it means she's burying something down inside her. [*Fastens the squirrel onto the box of candy.*]

ANNA   Are you going to take that little squirrel with you?

MARK   Yes . . . A little boy has his name-day today, and I'll drop it off on the way.

ANNA   I think your wife attaches special importance to it.

MARK   That doesn't matter, I'll get her something else.

ANNA   You ought.to talk to your wife, Mark Alexandrovich, she's very depressed.

MARK   Yes, I know. And I don't understand what she wants. She has plenty to eat, she's warm, she doesn't need a thing, as far as I can tell. You talk to her, Anna Mikhailovna. I just can't stand it; sometimes I don't even feel like coming home. [*Puts his coat on.*] Tell Veronica I won't be late. [*Goes out.*]

[IRINA *enters.*]

ANNA   No matter, it isn't right.

IRINA   What isn't?

ANNA   Your cousin's wife left a lovely little plush squirrel on the sofa, it must have been a present from somebody.

IRINA   From Borya.

ANNA   That's what I thought. But just now Mark Alexandrovich tied it on to a box of candy and took it away to some little boy.

IRINA God knows what's happening! A concert! . . . I felt it! . . . Little boy! That little boy is called Antonina.

ANNA What do you mean, Irina Fyodorovna?

IRINA Yes, yes. You have to be as stupid as Veronica not to see anything.

ANNA Maybe you're wrong?

IRINA Wrong! Our operating-room nurse lives in the same house as that person I've mentioned. . . . I don't talk about it so Father won't know.

ANNA The poor girl, I feel so sorry for her.

IRINA Well, can you imagine, I don't in the least. She's like a doll. Sits there on her little sofa all hunched up as if she had been drowning and someone had just pulled her out of the water.

ANNA That's true enough, Irina Fyodorovna, but she has a kind heart.

IRINA You're the one with the kind heart, Anna Mikhailovna. You ought to have known her before: she laughed so that she made you envious. She did some sculpting, planned on going to art school. She had talent! . . . But now? The most that will come of her is to be a housewife. And probably a bad one at that.

ANNA You're making the judgment of an energetic woman. The girl has lost her parents. . . .

IRINA I know. At first even I couldn't look at her without tears coming to my eyes. But the days go by . . . In this hellish war you have to stand firm and not turn into sour milk. Or else what would happen? Nobody's happy now; nobody *can* be.

ANNA You still feel resentment for the loss of your brother, Irina Fyodorovna.

IRINA Yes, for him, too.

ANNA [*sharply*] And that's a mistake! War cripples people not just physically; it destroys a man's inner world—and maybe that's one of the most terrible things it does. You understand how the wounded feel when they cry and groan and carry on so that they even interfere with your curing them. There, you're patient, sympathetic; but here . . .

[FYODOR IVANOVICH *enters.*]

IRINA What kept you?

FYODOR The boys were being sent off: some home, some to the rest and rehabilitation battalion. Are we going to eat?

ANNA I'll have it ready in a minute.

IRINA   No, no, I'll do it myself.

ANNA   It's no trouble for me, on the contrary—and it makes me feel one of the family.

[IRINA goes out.]

FYODOR   Where's Veronica? Where's Mark?

ANNA   Mark Alexandrovich said he had a concert, and Veronica probably went out for a walk.

FYODOR   I don't like the house being empty. Can we soon sit down to table all together, the way we did in Moscow? [IRINA comes in.] What about you, Anna Mikhailovna?

ANNA   I just had some coffee. [Goes out.]

FYODOR   Well, if there's just the two of us, there's just the two of us. Give me the decanter. We have to celebrate your successes. You're superb, Irina.

IRINA [handing her father the decanter]   You ought not to.

FYODOR   I'm tired. [Pours.] Have a little swallow, would you like to?

IRINA   What next! It's awful stuff!

FYODOR [emptying his vodka glass]   No mail?

IRINA   No.

FYODOR   I understand. It was a silly question. . . . No matter, let's be patient. Have you sent the money to Grandma?

IRINA   Yes, this morning. Think of her sitting there in Moscow, like a watchman!

FYODOR   Stubborn, stubborn. Doctor Bobrov has his eye on you, did you notice?

IRINA   As if I had nothing else to do!

FYODOR   What's this, barley is it?

IRINA   How should I know—eat and don't ask.

FYODOR   It would be nice to have buckwheat. [VERONICA enters.] Just in time, sit down. Did you make the gruel?

VERONICA   I did.

FYODOR   Marvelous! Sit down.

VERONICA   I've already eaten. [Goes past the table, sits down on the sofa.]

FYODOR   Three days now and the snow keeps coming and coming.

VERONICA   Yes. [IRINA starts clearing the table. VERONICA goes up to her.] Let me do that.

IRINA   That's all right, stay seated. [VERONICA moves back. IRINA carries the dishes out.]

FYODOR [going up to VERONICA]   Well, how are things?

VERONICA   What?

FYODOR   Had a walk?

VERONICA   Yes.

FYODOR   [*not knowing what else to say*]   That's fine. . . . You know, have to have more courage, more spirit . . .

VERONICA   Probably.

FYODOR   Forgive my saying so, but . . . you ought to be doing something.

VERONICA   I can't.

FYODOR   Just overcome that "I can't."

VERONICA   I'll think about it.

FYODOR   And have patience . . . A letter will come. . . . And everything will be fine, you'll see.

VERONICA   Will you never forgive what I did to him? [*Cries.*]

FYODOR   I love you, silly girl.

[ANNA MIKHAILOVNA *comes in.*]

ANNA   Left my glasses some place. [*Looks for them.*]

FYODOR   But I never delivered lectures, I was scared of large audiences. Though, generally speaking, I could have. Did the papers come?

ANNA   I put them on your table.

FYODOR   Thank you. [*Goes out.*]

ANNA   [*finding her glasses*]   Here they are. [*To* VERONICA.] Mark Alexandrovich asked me to tell you that he'll be home early.

VERONICA   [*looking for something*]   Where did I put my little squirrel? . . . You didn't see it, did you, Anna Mikhailovna?

ANNA   Mark Alexandrovich took it with him.

VERONICA   Mark took it? Where?

ANNA   To give to some little boy.

VERONICA   My squirrel! . . . For some boy! . . .

ANNA   Don't get upset, Veronica.

VERONICA   Where did he go?

ANNA   He has a concert in the food-workers' club.

VERONICA   [*running to the phone*]   The club? Tell me, what time does your concert begin? Is this the food-workers' club? No, you're supposed to have a concert today. The day off? [*Hangs up.*] The club is closed today; it's their day off.

[IRINA *enters.*]

IRINA   What were you shouting for?

VERONICA   Where's Mark?

IRINA   At a concert.

VERONICA   I called—it's their day off.

IRINA   So, he must have gone to see somebody.

VERONICA   Where?

IRINA   I don't know.

VERONICA   You're keeping something back from me. He took my squirrel away to somebody.

IRINA   What of it? You're raising a cry over a little toy?

VERONICA   Who did he take it to? You know, don't you?

IRINA   Well . . . yes, I do.

VERONICA   Who?

IRINA   Antonina Nikolayevna Monastyrskaya.

VERONICA   What Monastyrskaya? What for?

IRINA   Ask Mark.

ANNA   Irina Fyodorovna, since you've started telling the truth . . .

VERONICA   [to IRINA, shouting]   Tell me!

IRINA   Don't you give orders. Well, Mark goes to this Monastyrskaya . . . often. . . . Well, you understand?

VERONICA   You're telling me that on purpose.

IRINA   What purpose?

VERONICA   Out of spite. You envy me—I'm loved, I have a husband, but you . . . you're an old maid!

ANNA   Veronica, shame on you!

IRINA   Monastyrskaya lives on Gogol Street, by the central delicatessen, on the second floor, I think—you can check. [Goes out.]

ANNA   You be calm, Veronica.

VERONICA   Something has to be done . . . something has to be done . . . something has to be done. . . .

ANNA   Of course . . . Mark Alexandrovich will come home, you'll settle things. Don't get upset now, you have to wait a little. . . .

VERONICA   Wait! Again, wait! All I do all the time is wait, wait, wait. . . . No more! I don't want any more of this! I don't want anything—I don't want these walls, or Mark, or Irina, or you, or anybody! I know, you all put the blame on me, you just pretend to be nice out of pity. I don't want that! I don't want it! [Puts her coat on.]

ANNA   Where are you going?

VERONICA   There . . . to him.

ANNA   It won't be right.

VERONICA   Everything's right! Boris wouldn't have done this . . . he would have taught me things . . . he'll come and forgive me everything, everything. . . . He loves me, loves me, loves me! [*Runs out.*]

ANNA [*calling*]   Irina Fyodorovna! [IRINA *enters.*] She ran out, going over there.

IRINA   Oh, damn me for ever getting mixed up in this business. . . . Nothing will happen, she'll raise a fuss—and that'll be all. She's spoiled things now. . . . And I was feeling so fine.

ANNA   Still, you're too harsh on her.

IRINA   Yes, I know. But I can't help myself.

ANNA [*looking at the time*]   It's time for me to go.

IRINA   Are you in a great hurry, Anna Mikhailovna?

ANNA   No, I'll go slowly and quietly. Why?

IRINA   Tell me, am I an old maid, really?

ANNA   What are you talking about, Irina Fyodorovna, you're only twenty-nine.

IRINA   And don't you think, well—I'm not hard-hearted and it's not that I can't love. I loved once, honestly, I did . . . very deeply. . . . It was back in school, in the last year. . . . He was so soft-spoken, so good—Grisha. . . . Only, please don't tell anybody. . . .

ANNA   I'm as silent as a strong-box, Irina Fyodorovna, a strong-box you can count on.

IRINA   He even walked me home several times. . . . But then he moved to Sverdlovsk. . . .

[FYODOR IVANOVICH *enters.*]

FYODOR   They sent us new instructions; have you read them?

IRINA   No.

FYODOR [*waving sheets of paper*]   Poke your nose into this!

ANNA   We'll finish our conversation later, Irina Fyodorovna.

IRINA [*hurriedly*]   Yes, sure.

[ANNA MIKHAILOVNA *goes out.*]

FYODOR   Three kopeks' worth of sense and forty pounds of red tape. Bureaucratic nonsense, bureaucratic nonsense!

IRINA   Don't growl. Let's see what it says.

[IRINA *takes the papers from her father, sits down at the table, reads.* FYODOR IVANOVICH *goes to the map on which little black flags mark the front line. He stands looking at it.*]

FYODOR   What a snake it is. [*A knock on the door.*] Come in.

[VOLODYA *enters, his sack over his shoulders.*]

VOLODYA   Does Anna Mikhailovna Kovalyova live here?
IRINA   She does. Only, she's teaching at the night-school now.
VOLODYA   Where's her room?
IRINA [*pointing*]   That one.

[VOLODYA *goes towards* ANNA MIKHAILOVNA'S *room.*]

FYODOR   Young man, just where are you going?
VOLODYA [*smiling*]   Home. I'm her son.
IRINA   Volodya!
VOLODYA   Yes. And you're Veronica, I guess.
FYODOR   And I'm Mark Alexandrovich.
VOLODYA [*laughing*]   Irina Fyodorovna!
FYODOR   You'll figure things out gradually.
VOLODYA   So it's you!
FYODOR   You approve? Come, dear visitor, drop your things. [VOLODYA
   sets his sack down.] Anna Mikhailovna has just gone out, so wait
   a little. Irusha, let's have what's on the special shelf. Meanwhile,
   we'll chat. You do drink?
VOLODYA   Sure.
FYODOR [*to* IRINA]   You hear how proudly he said that? [*To* VOLODYA.]
   How old are you?

[IRINA *goes out.*]

VOLODYA   Twenty-one.
FYODOR   But, you know, I was twenty-five before I tried vodka.
   Had no time. The World War, the Revolution, the Civil War . . .
   in short, I never got a chance.
VOLODYA   All the same, I was at the front.
FYODOR   I understand. On leave or discharged?

[IRINA *comes in.*]

VOLODYA   Discharged.
FYODOR   How did you get that?
VOLODYA   There's a bullet in my lung. It's not painful. Only, don't
   tell my mother—it's there and let it stay there, but we'll tell her
   they took it out.
IRINA   Why didn't you write you were coming?
VOLODYA   On purpose. Today is my birthday.
FYODOR   A surprise?
VOLODYA   Yes. Only I don't have much of a holiday look.

FYODOR Indeed, what the storekeeper foisted on you wasn't his best quality.

VOLODYA I took what he offered just to get out as fast as I could. And I got covered with dirt and dust on the road. It's already hot in Asia.

IRINA But why did you decide I was Veronica?

VOLODYA Mother wrote she was cute.

FYODOR Irina, your chances are improving!

IRINA You funny man, she wrote that about Veronica.

VOLODYA She also wrote good things about you.

FYODOR [to IRINA] Where is Veronica?

IRINA I don't know.

FYODOR [raising his vodka glass] Well, young hero, you're the first harbinger in our house. [They clink glasses.] And God grant not the last!

VOLODYA [clinking glasses] Yes, as the saying goes.

IRINA He didn't mean it in that sense, Volodya.

VOLODYA [gravely] I know.

SCENE 2 *Antonina Nikolayevna Monastyrskaya's room.*
Antonina Nikolayevna and Varya are setting the table.

ANTONINA So you see, Vavochka, how one's whole life can be turned upside down.

VARYA Cheer up, Antonina Nikolayevna. It's coming out really wonderful, just like before the war.

ANTONINA You should have seen my apartment in Leningrad. What furniture! . . . A wardrobe of bird's-eye maple! And just think, I nailed it shut with huge nails; my china's in there. The crystal I put in the bathtub. Do you really think they'll steal it? And the people that met at my place that day! Noise, laughter . . . Toward the end of the evening we just had to take a car and off we went around town. From one end to the other! To Vasily Island, to the Petrograd side, out to the islands—everywhere! Riding around in cars on that night was a tradition. But now . . . How terrible this war is! It has sort of knocked me out of that life with one stroke, one blow. . . . And you know, Vava, what the most terrible thought is? Suddenly nothing will be the way it used to. Nothing, ever!

VARYA It will be, Antonina Nikolayevna, it will be. I'll come visit you in Leningrad yet.

ANTONINA   That would be nice. I'm so grateful to you for taking
me in with you.

VARYA   Oh, don't think of it, don't. So many people descended on
our town—we found a place for all of them. We understand what
grief is, you know. And you're from Leningrad, one who has
suffered the most. Instead, look how I've done the salt-herrings:
pickles, a little onion, and egg sprinkled on top, as you suggested.

ANTONINA   Thank you.

VARYA   But I didn't sell your georgette crepe blouse, I simply traded
it directly for this meat. It had a bone, too, I cut it out—tomorrow we'll make soup.

ANTONINA   But why did you bring my wool skirt back, won't they
take it?

VARYA   They offered very little, and the skirt is good. Why let it
go for so little?

ANTONINA   If you want it, take it yourself, if you like it.

VARYA   Oh, no, how could you! Something so lovely!

ANTONINA   Take it, take it. I owe you so much.

VARYA   Now let me tell you this, Antonina Nikolayevna: once you
get rid of everything you own, what then? It's war, and it'll go
on and on. . . . Better if I go back to work in the soap factory.
I'll have money and a worker's ration card. . . . It was a mistake
for you to get me all confused then.

ANTONINA   No, no! What do you mean! I'll perish without you.
And who'll start doing everything: going to the bazaar, doing the
cooking?! Patience, Vava. I'll think of something.

VARYA   Yesterday I ran into the girls from the factory—Varvara,
they said to me, have you turned into a housekeeper? What a
time you picked! They made fun of me. . . .

ANTONINA   They envy you. What are they so busy with down there
at the factory? Boiling dead cats into soap?

VARYA   Oh, now, Antonina Nikolayevna, we never did anything like
that, you don't know our factory at all.

ANTONINA   I still have some pieces of material in my suitcase; I
haven't shown them to you yet. We'll be living in clover, you'll
see. You're so good, so kind. . . . Don't spoil today by talking like
that, all right?

VARYA   All right.

ANTONINA   I'm going to cry anyway. Oh, what a life, what a life!
[Cries.]

VARYA   Now, don't be so sad. You have some nice guests coming
today—that Mark Alexandrovich, how he plays the piano. He just

breaks your heart. . . . Comrade Chernov is a fine man, too. Nyura's coming. . . .

ANTONINA You don't understand a thing, Vava. Nyurka the bread cutter is coming, but why have I asked her? I can't do without her, she brings the bread. And not only bread, remember, but she has brought cheese, sausage, even found some pressed caviar somewhere.

VARYA In the commercial network they have good connections.

ANTONINA She'll be queen of the ball! I must pay court to her! . . . How repulsive! . . . How repulsive!

VARYA Nyurka is bad, that's true. I'd tell you where this Nyurka gets the bread and how she weighs it, but I don't want to make you angry.

ANTONINA Don't tell me, Vava. I don't want to know all the dirt, all this abominable business.

VARYA Is the student coming?

ANTONINA Misha? Yes, yes, he said he would. And bring his fiancée; I insisted he show her to us.

VARYA He's good—high-minded.

ANTONINA You know, when he talks about the universe, he fills me with awe. Without end and without limit, just think. What a nightmare! Only, he's not very high-minded. You know why he comes here?

VARYA Why?

ANTONINA To fill himself up. He lives badly, in great poverty. So, let him come, because having Nyurka alone would suffocate you. Vava, go dress a little better.

VARYA I put on my best dress, Antonina Nikolayevna.

ANTONINA Put on one of mine, any one.

VARYA It'll be too big.

ANTONINA Take it in.

[*The doorbell.* VARYA *opens the door.* CHERNOV *enters.*]

CHERNOV Congratulations, Antonina Nikolayevna. [*Gives her several boxes of candy and another little box.*] Vavochka, greetings.

VARYA Hello, Nikolai Nikolayevich. You're the first.

ANTONINA Go see if it won't fit, Vava.

VARYA I'll try. [*Goes out.*]

ANTONINA [*opening the little box*] Oh, how generous!

CHERNOV I can't stay—philharmonic business, sending brigades out into the district and to the troops. I won't be free until midnight.

ANTONINA   And you won't miss a thing—it'll be only an illusion of a holiday.

CHERNOV   I simply find being with you very pleasant; I couldn't care less about the others.

ANTONINA   [*laughing*]   That's the way I feel, too.

CHERNOV   About Borozdin, also?

ANTONINA   Will you keep bringing him up to me even when I have become, let's assume, your wife?

CHERNOV   No, only so long as he comes to see you. I could do something that would stop his coming here, but I know what a woman is like: to take a man away from you by force means raising his value and increasing your attachment to him. The natural course of events is the most reliable.

ANTONINA   How practical of you!

CHERNOV   I'm close to fifty, and I don't want to seem either better or worse.

ANTONINA   That's dull and disappointing but appreciated. Did you write your wife in Tashkent?

CHERNOV   Not yet. Naturally, I'll be sending her support for the younger boy. The older is already getting on his own feet; he, too, has to help his mother. Everything there will be quite regular and according to the letter of the law. Just you say "yes." [ANTONINA NIKOLAYEVNA *is silent.* CHERNOV *glances at his watch.*] The car is coming from the military sector to pick up the actors—I mustn't keep it waiting. And then I have to send a bus out into the district. . . . A big job, sometimes I feel just exhausted. . . . [*Smiling.*] Well, but that's something I wasn't supposed to let on to you.

ANTONINA   You'll be free around twelve? Listen, let's go for a drive, come pick me up in your car.

CHERNOV   I used the car to send the Moscow actors out to the collective farm.

ANTONINA   Well, come in something, even a bus. Why not? We'll drive around town together in a bus; that's marvelously out of the ordinary!

CHERNOV   We've only one bus; it goes out into the district at nine.

ANTONINA   Oh, get something. Please! Anything—a fire engine, an ambulance, it makes no difference what. . . . Get something!

CHERNOV   This is a whim of yours, Antonina Nikolayevna.

ANTONINA   So what if it is! . . . Come, please give me undreamt-of pleasure. . . .

CHERNOV   I'll try. Good-bye. [*Starts out but stops.*] I love you deeply.

[CHERNOV *goes out.* VARYA *enters wearing* ANTONINA NIKOLAYEVNA'S *dress—on her it looks ridiculous.*]

VARYA   I purposely didn't come in; it wouldn't have been right, would it?

ANTONINA   Clever girl.

VARYA [*looking over her outfit*]   I saw something like this in a magazine once. . . .

ANTONINA   In *Crocodile.*

VARYA   Yes, exactly, that was it.

ANTONINA   You didn't find anything that would fit?

VARYA   Nothing. I'll put my own on—it would be better, wouldn't it?

ANTONINA   Absolutely.

VARYA   What did Nikolai Nikolayevich give you?

ANTONINA   Here. [*Shows her the boxes of candy.*] And this. [*Hands* VARYA *the little box.*]

VARYA [*opening the little box*]   A lettered ration card. And the coupons for fat aren't cut out! Don't tell me he gave you his own! There's a generous man! Why didn't he stay?

ANTONINA   He couldn't, he had work to do.

VARYA   A busy man, obviously, gets things done. [*Bell rings.*] Open the door, Antonina Nikolayevna. I'll frighten the guests to death looking like this.

[VARYA *runs out.* ANTONINA NIKOLAYEVNA *opens the door.* MISHA *comes in, wearing thick glasses, with* TANECHKA, *a skinny girl with a pointed little face.*]

ANTONINA [*pointing to her apron*]   The guests are on time, but the host and hostess are late.

MISHA [*handing a package to* ANTONINA NIKOLAYEVNA]   Congratulations.

ANTONINA   What is this?

MISHA [*opening it up*]   A fig-plant. One is supposed to give flowers on such a day.

ANTONINA   What a funny fellow you are, Misha! Thank you.

MISHA   Tanechka, let me introduce you: this is Antonina Nikolayevna herself with whom we lived in the same entryway in Leningrad. There we only said hello at a distance, but here we got to know each other.

TANECHKA [*to* ANTONINA NIKOLAYEVNA]   How do you do, my congratulations.

ANTONINA [*greeting her*]   Thank you. Let me see you, let me see you—I want to know Misha's taste. He has talked about you so much.

TANECHKA   Do forgive him: I kept saying, don't get the fig-plant, but he kept saying, why not, it's silly. You know, he cut up half a cord of firewood for his landlady to get it.

MISHA   Since when do people say how much a present costs!

ANTONINA   You're very wonderful. Misha, I approve. [*To* TANYA.] Let's be gay today. We can dance and sing.

MISHA   Tanechka is one from our amateur group who even appears in hospitals. Solo. What a voice, a mezzo.

ANTONINA   I'm sure she has all kinds of virtues.

MISHA   And she studies absolutely brilliantly. . . .

TANECHKA   Misha, don't exaggerate.

MISHA   Tanechka, it's the truth.

TANECHKA   Misha! . . .

ANTONINA   Excuse me, I'm going to leave you for a moment. [*Goes out.*]

TANECHKA   Misha, why do you always keep on talking about me? It's embarrassing.

MISHA   But you're really a remarkable person.

TANECHKA   We won't stay here long, will we?

MISHA   Say when.

[*Bell rings.* VARYA *runs to answer.*]

VARYA   Hello, Misha. [*To* TANYA.] Hello. [*Opens the door.*]

MISHA [*to* TANYA]   Her name is Varya. She's a little strange—doesn't work and doesn't study.

TANECHKA   Then what does she do?

MISHA   Works for Antonina Nikolayevna.

TANECHKA   And where does Antonina Nikolayevna work?

MISHA   Nowhere. They sort of, you see, work for each other together.

[MARK *enters. At the same time* ANTONINA NIKOLAYEVNA *comes in.*]

ANTONINA   Mark Alexandrovich!

MARK   Many happy returns. [*Gives her the present.*]

ANTONINA   Thank you. Let me introduce you.

TANECHKA [*saying hello to* MARK]   Misha and I have heard your concerts.

MISHA   Your playing reminds one a little of Sofronitsky.

MARK   I take that as a compliment.

ANTONINA [*opening the package, seeing the toy*] I'm ten years
  younger!
TANECHKA Oh, what a wonderful toy!
MISHA [*to* TANYA, *quietly*] I'll get you one like it, if I have to dig
  it up out of the ground. [*To* MARK.] Where did you buy it?
MARK It was made to order.
MISHA Where?
MARK Sent from Moscow.
MISHA Ah! What a shame!
ANTONINA Comrades, be patient just a few more minutes. You
  young people, go pick out some records—there's Leshchenko and
  Shalyapin. Vava, show them. . . .
MARK Unfortunately, I'm not one of the young.

[VARYA, TANYA *and* MISHA *go out.*]

ANTONINA You brought a box of candy which you bought from
  Chernov.
MARK What do you mean!
ANTONINA Don't make up a story. Look how many he brought!
  Oh, don't be embarrassed, I love you for it—you child. He did
  it to try to put you in an awkward position.
MARK Yes, he's frightening.
ANTONINA I'm afraid of him myself.
MARK Tonya, go slowly with him. . . . I'll soon be leaving my wife.
ANTONINA If it's on my account, please don't. I don't want to sow
  the seeds of dissension in your house.
MARK There'll be no dissension—after all, she and I never filled
  out the official forms. I can tell you frankly: I don't love her,
  she doesn't love me. You know, I took on a burden that's more
  than I can carry, have worn myself out with her. She lives on old
  memories, doesn't say a word, but I see it all, understand it all.
ANTONINA You're jealous!
MARK How can I be jealous of what isn't there! My cousin has
  been killed, that's obvious. They all lack the courage to admit
  it. . . . Of course, it's hard, but it's war!
ANTONINA I'll be frank with you, too, Mark. There *is* a war on
  now; it'll take away a lot of men; and there'll be more and more
  young girls. Well, who will be tempted by me when there's such
  choice? I haven't rushed to get married, but now it has to be done.
  And rather soon, or else I run the risk of being left empty-handed.
  Will it be Chernov? Possibly. He always has money. And money,
  no matter what you say, is a great thing.

MARK He'll end up in prison soon; his money is stolen.

ANTONINA What can I do! Unfortunately, swindlers are frequently richer than honest men. His business won't involve me. I would be delighted to marry a rich, honest man, but where is there one? They are birds of a different feather from us. You're not some young Misha, you must understand all this. And we'll remain friends. . . .

[*Bell rings.* VARYA *runs through to the door.*]

MARK Listen to me, Tonya.

[NYURA *comes in. When she takes off her coat, we see she has on a very expensive but monstrously tasteless dress. She carries a shopping net.*]

NYURA Congratulations, Antonina Nikolayevna, on your name-day! Here are some canned goods, three kilos of flour, some hard poppy-seed rolls—you haven't tasted anything like them since before the war. . . . I've brought some lard. . . . Empty it out, Vavka, give me back the net. Mark Alexandrovich, hello there!

[VARYA *goes out with the shopping net with the things.*]

MARK Hello, Nyura.

NYURA [*glancing over the table*] What a spread! The little decanters are gurgling. And there's my little caviar peeping at me. I saved you for a special day, instead of eating you.

MARK Nyura, the young people are picking out records in the other room.

NYURA Oh, the heck with them. [*Sits down.*] And you drop your conversations, too. Petka and me, too, the minute we start petting and cooing there's no stopping. I tried to bring him along, but he wouldn't come, stubborn and pouting. A shy man I have. Are we waiting for somebody?

ANTONINA No, Nyura, you're last of all.

NYURA Not last of all, but last in line.

ANTONINA [*calling*] Misha, Tanya, come to the table.

[MISHA *and* TANYA *come in. A little later,* VARYA.]

NYURA I've already had a nip—the inspection committee was in today. I'm tired. They sent in these two girl-scout types, what do those stupid things understand? They stuck their noses under the counter, ran off to the bookkeeper. . . . Up-to-date all around.

ANTONINA Misha, the first toast is yours, as the most educated.

MISHA With pleasure.

NYURA [*to* ANTONINA NIKOLAYEVNA] What a nice little ring. Are you willing to sell it?

ANTONINA Later, Nyura, later.

MISHA Comrades, Antonina Nikolayevna will pardon us if we drink our first toast not to her . . .

ANTONINA [*laughing*] But to Tanechka.

MISHA Not even to Tanechka. To the soonest possible end to the war! To victory!

NYURA Ah, if the war would end sooner from the vodka that's downed, I'd drink a bucketful myself. But I have nothing against it; maybe it'll help.

[ALL *drink.*]

MISHA You're right, Nyura. Of course, the most important thing is that each and every one of us now work with all his strength. . . .

NYURA We're trying.

MISHA Only by concerted efforts . . .

TANYA Misha, don't.

MARK Let's forget everything that's going on outside.

VARYA Yes, forget that I went down to the market—they were bringing wounded from the station again.

ANTONINA Enough, enough. No gloomy conversation!

NYURA Here's what we'll drink to: our daily bread which feeds us.

MISHA Which nourishes us.

NYURA That's just what I'm saying.

MARK To Antonina Nikolayevna.

[ALL *drink.*]

NYURA How come nobody has said anything about my dress?

MISHA Nyura, it's stunning!

NYURA I have a panne one, too, oh so long. I was going to put it on but the tail sticks out under my coat.

VARYA How much white bread did you give for that?

NYURA You get plenty, living here off someone else, you're not one to start counting.

ANTONINA Comrades, no arguments. Tanechka, sing us something. Mark Alexandrovich will accompany you.

TANECHKA I don't want to.

ANTONINA It's not good to be obstinate.

TANECHKA [*with sharpness in her voice*]   I simply don't want to.

MARK   Antonina Nikolayevna, don't rush things. Let's wait for the
moment of inspiration.

NYURA [*taking the squirrel*]   I've eaten everything in the world, but
I've never cracked gold nuts. I'll just break a couple.

ANTONINA   We'll divide them evenly. Whoever wants to can keep
them as a souvenir of this evening. [*Parcels the nuts out, finds a
note on the bottom. To* MARK.] What's this, a note of congratulations? [*Opens the note, reads.*] "My one and only! . . ." Mark
Alexandrovich, your one and only should be your wife. . . . "Congratulations to you on your happy, joyful birthday!" You confused
it, Mark; it's my name-day. . . . "On this day you came into the
world. What happy fortune, my love and my life. Leaving you is
hard, but staying is impossible. . . ." There's something mysteri-
ous. . . . "I can't go on leading my old life, being carefree and
light-hearted, in a time when death roams our land. You'll understand this, my darling little Squirrel. There are days and minutes
when our private life, very happy as it may be, becomes as nothing
before the life of us all, of all the people, of the whole country.
I love you and believe in you. Your Boris." [*A pause.*] What's
this? Whose note is this?

MARK   I bought the thing in the market.

ANTONINA   What an awful thing to do, buying second-hand things
and, on top of that, giving them as presents! Maybe it's infected.

TANECHKA [*rising*]   Misha!

[MISHA *gets up and with* TANYA *goes toward the door.*]

ANTONINA   Where are you going? [MISHA *and* TANYA *put their coats
on without speaking.*] Leaving, you pure and upright man! Heard
the order! . . . Stuffed yourself full?

MISHA   What?

ANTONINA   Stuffed yourself full, I said?

TANYA   You ought to be ashamed of yourself! Misha sends his scholarship money to his mother and everything he earns on the side.
She's sick, you know. . . . I told him we shouldn't come to your
place, but he thinks everybody is good. . . . In our house he won't
even eat crumbs, but keeps going hungry all the time, I know. . . .
We'll get married soon, and then he'll be with us completely, be
his own. . . .

MISHA   Tanechka, don't think that I . . .

TANECHKA   Don't say a thing here, don't! [*They go out and in the*

doorway run into VERONICA.] See, even without us things will keep
going here. [*They go out.*]

MARK   What are you doing! What did you come for?

VERONICA   What did you take my thing for?

MARK   Veronica, you should be ashamed of yourself!

VERONICA   *I* should?

MARK   Have you any idea what you're doing?

VERONICA   Where is it?

MARK   What's the matter with you? [*Goes up to* VERONICA.] Well,
what's the matter with you?

VERONICA   Don't touch me.

MARK   Just don't make a scene. And don't, please, think anything. . . .

VERONICA [*seeing the squirrel*]   Pick it up from the table.

MARK   Don't behave stupidly, Veronica.

VERONICA   Wrap it up; there's wet snow out on the street.

MARK   All right, all right, I'm going with you.

VERONICA   What for?

MARK   I understand you . . . but calm down. . . . I'm visiting someone else—what's so special about that?

VERONICA   Hurry up.

MARK [*picking up the squirrel, gathering the nuts*]   Antonina Nikolayevna, forgive . . .

ANTONINA [*to* VERONICA]   Please, please do. There's also a note for
you here, from some Borya or other.

VERONICA [*forgetting everything, dashes to the note*]   From Borya! . . .

MARK   It's an old, old one . . . [VERONICA *reads the note.* MARK *goes
up to her, takes her by her shoulders.*] Now, why did you get all
excited and upset, silly? [VERONICA *looks at* MARK *and then suddenly as hard as she can hits him in the face.*] What are you
doing? What's that mean? What are you doing? . . . [VERONICA
hits him again, and again and again. She goes to the door.] I'm
going with you. [*To all.*] Forgive me. . . . You understand, naturally. . . . [*To* VERONICA.] I'm coming. [VERONICA *has gone out.*
MARK *follows her.*]

NYURA   Got a jealous girl—he'll not run away from one like that.

ANTONINA   What a disgusting scene. I was even frightened.

NYURA   Oh no, she means well. If ever I found my Petka with some
dame, I'd finish them both off on the spot.

VARYA   Antonina Nikolayevna, what did you insult Misha for? How
wrong of you to say that he stuffed himself full. It actually made
me blush.

ANTONINA   Leave me alone; all I need is you joining in, too.

NYURA   Sure, even without you there's been plenty of people shooting off their mouths.

VARYA   He has always discussed things with you so nicely. . . .

NYURA   Lay off it, you heard her!

VARYA   Shut up yourself. I know the way you weigh bread and how
much you take out the back door.

NYURA   Now, this isn't the first time we've heard talk like this. Consider yourself lucky you're not in the store in front of the counter.
I'd answer you, all right—I know how, I've learned the trick.

VARYA   You ought to leave my place, Antonina Nikolayevna!

ANTONINA   You're out of your mind! Where would I go?

VARYA   I'll go back to the factory. I was called Varya there. But
you thought up Vava. Just the way dogs bark: va-va. . . . Your
life is cultured, maybe, but then you live that way; I can't, it
doesn't work out. . . .

ANTONINA   Stop that, you hear. The district executive committee
assigned me here, filled out papers, and don't you go pretending
you're the landlady.

VARYA   All right . . . I'll go over to the dormitory, join the girls,
they'll let me. . . . Pa and my brother keep writing from the
front: Varvara, how come you're all by yourself? But I reassure
them. . . . When he was leaving, Pa said to me . . . [Cries.]

NYURA   Well, now she's made everything sad on a bright and cheerful day. [Goes over to ANTONINA NIKOLAYEVNA, takes her hand.]
I'm on my way. The evening has busted up. You don't get the
right people, I can tell you. Not the right ones. Weak sisters. But
now there's a war on—you have to have strong people at hand,
your own sort. That little ring shines so! . . . What do you need
it for, you're a beautiful woman anyway. Let it go, huh?

ANTONINA   Lord, if only Chernov would come soon. I'd hide myself
behind him and be quiet. I'm so exhausted, Nyura, so worn
out. . . . I just want quiet, peace and quiet.

NYURA   I hanker for peace and quiet myself. You're all raw nerves,
you know, Antonina Nikolayevna, raw nerves! I bring bread but
I keep looking back as if I was some kind of a thief. . . . I'll save
up five hundred thousand and quiet down. Vavka, don't sob. We
want quiet. Quiet, you hear? Stop sobbing!

ACT III

SCENE 1 *The setting of Act II, Scene 1. Fyodor Ivanovich and Volodya are in the room. They are sitting at the same table and continuing their conversation.*

VOLODYA . . . The Germans are coming at our hill in a crazy attack. . . . We've hidden ourselves in the trenches. . . . Up above the bombers are howling. . . . On the left, by the forest, a tank battle is raging. . . . Mines are whistling. . . . Everything all around, see, is screeching and thundering. . . .

FYODOR You write poems?

VOLODYA How did you guess?

FYODOR Had a sense of it.

VOLODYA Well, so . . .

FYODOR I look at you—and men like you have come into my hands, too, in a very sorry state—and I think: holy mother of god! Look at all the trouble that maniac of a private first-class has caused! Why, you know, it makes me want to believe in god.

VOLODYA Why?

FYODOR So there'd be hell. And so that there he'd be boiled and roasted and chopped up. . . . And once he's dead, what's it to him—peace and quiet! But a chance for us to live and eat our groats. Oh, it's a grievous thing, you know, and after the war how many years will its echo rumble across the earth.

VOLODYA After the war we'll start to live!

FYODOR We'll win the war and start to dance.

VOLODYA And when do her lectures finish?

FYODOR Depends. Listen, hero, let's call her up, because after her classes she has a habit of walking home. And that takes forty minutes. [*Goes to the phone.*]

VOLODYA Why does she?

FYODOR Time goes faster. [*Into the phone.*] The technicum? Kovalyova, Anna Mikhailovna, please. Aha! Well, as soon as her classes are over tell her to get a ride straight home. Her son is back. Yes, yes, Vladimir. [*Hangs up.*]

VOLODYA   Now you've spoiled everything—now she'll know.

FYODOR   What, you want to surprise her so she'll faint right there in the doorway? Even the secretary gave a shriek. . . . She'll be free soon; it's her last class now. Say, hero, I have something in the way of a uniform here—make yourself handsome, get changed. No matter how you look at it, it's your birthday, a special day. [*Gets* BORIS's *clothes.*] It will fit you. Mine's probably too wide in the shoulders.

VOLODYA   Here you are talking to me but thinking about him all the time.

FYODOR   About everyone.

VOLODYA   Especially about him.

FYODOR   Don't start philosophizing, hero.

VOLODYA   Don't call me that—I'm no hero.

FYODOR   You put your chest in the way of a bullet—that's enough, my friend.

VOLODYA   Oh, what miraculous things they do there!

FYODOR   I've read about it.

VOLODYA   But I've seen them.

FYODOR   Pick out a tie you like. You probably were something of a dandy?

VOLODYA   A little. [*Begins to change; a photograph falls out of his pocket on to the floor.*]

FYODOR   Something flew out of your pocket.

VOLODYA   [*picking it up*]   A snapshot. [*Sticks it into his pocket.*]

FYODOR   Oho, a lady. Clear enough.

VOLODYA   Not that at all.

FYODOR   Be modest! You're all experts in that field!

VOLODYA   Word of honor, it's not that at all.

FYODOR   Spill it, out with it!

VOLODYA   Well, I'll tell you, but keep it a secret: there was none of that at all.

FYODOR   Why keep it a secret?

VOLODYA   It's embarrassing, somehow, improper.

FYODOR   You funny boy, it's very proper. To come out of a war like this pure and clean isn't easy at all.

VOLODYA   [*showing the photo*]   It's Mama.

FYODOR   [*looking at the photograph*]   As a young girl?

VOLODYA   Why so? That was taken in forty-one.

FYODOR   You don't say!

VOLODYA   Isn't it like her?

FYODOR   Yes, yes, I recognize her. [*A knock on the door.*] Come in.

[CHERNOV *enters.*]

CHERNOV   If I'm not mistaken, Fyodor Ivanovich?

FYODOR   Himself.

CHERNOV [*greeting him*]   I'm the business manager of the philharmonic where your nephew, Mark Alexandrovich, works. My name is Chernov, Nikolai Nikolayevich.

FYODOR   Glad to meet you.

CHERNOV   I'm doubly glad.

FYODOR   [*to* VOLODYA]   Change in the other room. [*Softly.*] My nephew's boss—you understand, awkward to send him away.

[VOLODYA *goes out.*]

CHERNOV   I've heard so much about the marvelous things you do in your hospital. . . .

FYODOR   Sit down, please.

CHERNOV   Thank you. [*Sits down.*] Forgive me, but I've come to you to ask a favor. It's not quite proper, on the first day we've met. . . .

FYODOR   No matter, no matter, please.

CHERNOV   You're the chief surgeon at the hospital; I suppose they wouldn't refuse you a hospital car for a short time?

FYODOR   If it were necessary, I don't think they would.

CHERNOV   Be so kind as to get it for me. All the philharmonic cars are being used. It's very urgent.

FYODOR   That's not so easy. Somehow it's not right. . . . Cars are now worth their weight in gold, every liter of fuel is sparingly used. . . .

CHERNOV   I'll get the fuel, return it all to you. I can do that easily. I can get some for you, too, it's not expensive.

FYODOR   No, actually I don't need any.

CHERNOV   I've come specifically to you, Fyodor Ivanovich, as one comrade to another. I know it's difficult—it's a devilish time. Everything is difficult. A while back I, too, was running all around for Mark Alexandrovich. . . . Why, once you had asked a favor, I laid myself out, as the saying goes! . . . Your name! Oh! . . . You probably aren't even aware how highly they speak of you in town, both in the upper circles and among ordinary people. And let me beg one other thing of you, Fyodor Ivanovich: urge Mark Alexandrovich to work harder. Forgive my saying so, but he's turning into a regular, mediocre pianist. His special deferment is up in three months; the army is taking more and more—pulling in even those with a permanent deferment. [*Confidingly.*] You know the losses we've suffered; it's not for me to tell you. They say you're even putting them in the corridors. To get him a deferment this time will be, well, simply impossible. [*Offering* FYODOR IVANOVICH *a cigarette.*] Do you smoke? [FYODOR IVANOVICH *is silent.* CHERNOV *raises his eyes to look at him.*] Fyodor Ivanovich, what's the matter with you? Fyodor Ivanovich? . . . Who's there? . . . Who else is in the house? [VOLODYA *runs in. He hasn't completely changed.*] Don't worry for a minute; not another soul knows a thing about this . . . I know—your name . . . [*Looks at* FYODOR IVANOVICH.] Don't tell me Mark Alexandrovich deceived both me and you; that's not the way to do things! It was so hard for me. . . . No, how could he have: he said you were even offering to pay. Of course, I didn't take it. . . . In fact, it wasn't actually I who arranged the deferment. . . . Excuse me. . . . I'll have a talk with Mark Alexandrovich. . . . This is wrong, very wrong. Keep well, Fyodor Ivanovich. [*Disappears.*]

VOLODYA   Any unpleasantness? [FYODOR IVANOVICH *paces the room with heavy steps.*] But don't you get upset. Let's have a drink together to calm down.

FYODOR   Hero, never mind the bravado [*pointing to the decanter*], or it will get stuck in you and you'll make a fool of yourself.

VOLODYA   I was just suggesting.

FYODOR   Indeed!

[VOLODYA *goes out into the other room.* IRINA *enters.*]

IRINA   He's resting now. He's scared and fussing. I gave him an injection. Let him sleep—that's better, isn't it? Where's our warrior?

FYODOR   Changing. I gave him Borya's suit, he looked so drab.

[VOLODYA *comes in.*]

VOLODYA   It fits.

IRINA   Well, turn around. [VOLODYA *turns around.* IRINA *speaks to her* FATHER *quietly.*] You shouldn't have, it gives me an empty feeling in my stomach.

FYODOR   Nonsense.

IRINA   What are you, angry?

[VERONICA *and* MARK *come in.*]

MARK   Uncle Fedya, help me, please; it's as simple as that. You know what she has just done?

FYODOR   What?

MARK She flew over to somebody else's house—I had dropped in
there for a minute—she screamed and shouted like an old woman
in the marketplace. It almost came to a scuffle. Can you imagine?

FYODOR She didn't hit anybody?

MARK Uncle Fedya, this is no time for joking. There were other
people there; now there'll be gossip; it's a nasty little town. I'm
known to the public, and you are, too.

FYODOR Indeed, I'm not going to let anybody shame me.

MARK [to VERONICA] You hear that?

FYODOR And what next?

MARK Uncle Fedya, I know you love her. I feel sorry for her, too.
But my marriage is a failure—we all see that, but somehow in an
intellectual way we avoid the problem. Still, we have to make a
decision. Let's get a corner for her; maybe we could find a whole
room; I'm prepared to pay for it, to help. After all, she herself
has to learn to work and earn something. There's a war on—
everybody is working. This is all very unpleasant, but we have to
make a decision. You see what's happened: at one time you feel
sorry for a person . . .

VERONICA Liar! You're the one soiling yourself again!

MARK There are other people here; have a sense of decency. . . .

FYODOR It's all right; this is his home, too.

IRINA This is Anna Mikhailovna's son.

MARK Perhaps he could go into his room?

[VOLODYA starts to leave.]

FYODOR Stay.

IRINA [to MARK] Don't you dare talk about Veronica like that.

MARK You haven't liked her much either up to now; did something
happen?

IRINA Nothing's happened, but I know my own business, too. . . .

MARK Why are you flying at me on account of her? Well, I made
a mistake. . . . And she's not a little girl, either. . . .

FYODOR Don't dare compare yourself to her! She made a mistake,
and she's paying for it by punishing herself, hardly alive at all. . . .
But you do dirty, mean things and try to appear clean and pure!
I've just heard some news about you.

MARK What?

FYODOR Very nice. Maybe you will tell us about your brilliant move
yourself?

MARK I don't know what you're talking about.

FYODOR Do-on't kno-ow?

IRINA   Mark, don't make Papa angry, speak up!

MARK   I have no idea what he's been told.

FYODOR   Try to remember!

MARK   Maybe it's about my taking medicines from your medicine cabinet? I was asked to do it for a sick man. . . . What about it?

IRINA   Why did you take them, for whom?

MARK   The business manager of our philharmonic, Chernov, is sick.

FYODOR   You'll pay!

MIRK   What do you mean?

FYODOR   You'll pay, I warn you! In my name you asked that swindler to fix you up with a deferment so you wouldn't be drafted. And you still have that deferment!

IRINA   Mark!

VERONICA   Coward, coward, coward! But Borya . . . Borya went—himself!

IRINA   Papa, it can't be true; somebody was slandering him to you.

FYODOR   [to MARK] What were you thinking of? Did you think it was a light and easy prank? Allegro? . . . Scherzo? . . . Or what would you call it down there? . . .

IRINA   You mustn't get so upset. . . .

FYODOR   Leave me alone, please, nothing's going to happen to me. [To MARK.] How could you do it? Who in our family gave you an excuse for doing a thing like that? Me, Irina—or maybe Boris?

IRINA   Stop right now, you hear me! Sit down! [Forcibly seats her FATHER in a chair. To MARK.] I'll make you remember what you've done to my father, you'll see!

FYODOR   So now, Mark . . .

IRINA   Be quiet, I said!

FYODOR   I'll speak quietly, Irina. [To MARK, indicating VOLODYA.] That young fellow there caught a bullet with his chest. For me, for them [indicating IRINA and VERONICA], for everyone . . . including you. . . . If we live through it, we'll be in their eternal debt . . . eternal. . . . I don't even know how to talk to you, Mark. . . . If you had gone into the army, we would have waited for you, too . . . waited in a frenzy . . . and believed . . . worried, talked about you every day. . . . Irina there would have cried at night. . . . [To IRINA.] Because sometimes I hear it, you know. . . . [To MARK.] You think anybody likes sending his son off to war? . . . It has to be! . . . What, you think that for you and your well-being somebody ought to lose his arms, legs, eyes, jaw, life? But you not for anybody, nothing!

IRINA   Papa!

FYODOR [*more softly, pointing to* VOLODYA.]   Just you look, look at
that boy. . . . [*To* VOLODYA.] Forgive me, hero, I think he'll be
especially shamed by your presence. . . . Tell him something, even
just a word or two. . . .

VOLODYA   What for? [*A long pause. In the room, everyone has moved
apart.* VOLODYA *starts talking, wanting to break the heavy silence.*]
It's wrong of you to behave like a coward. . . . Sure, it's frightening. . . . But what can you do? . . . I don't regret all the things
I saw. I think maybe I got a little wiser. What did I know before
the war? Home, and school . . . And sports, too. I was just a mama's
boy. . . . But there, you know, there are men, really special. . . .
One taught me how to wrap on all the foot-cloths; a collective-
farmer, middle-aged. . . . He had real patience . . . taught me. . . .
And when we got surrounded, the Siberians fought off the attack
on our unit . . . saved us, or else we would all have been in the
soup. . . . No, I don't regret it. . . . And then when I was wounded,
they pulled me back. . . . [*A pause.*] It was so lively, really. . . .
We were out on reconnaissance, in pairs. . . . But somehow we'd
gotten separated. . . . I was heading back—open field all around,
snow had fallen, you could see easily. . . . They started shooting
at me. . . . Well, of course I dropped flat on the ground. But it
was so cold. . . . I wanted to get up, but over my head–zzip! zzip!
I lay back . . . for a long time. . . . Then I feel I'm starting to get
stiff. . . . I see someone crawling up to me, one of ours. . . . "Lie
flat," he says, "keep your head down," he says, "this is a dead zone,
here," he says. . . . That means you can't move back or forward.
. . . The both of us are lying there. . . . A ridiculous position! . . .
He was stronger than me, and I feel I'm freezing to death. We
were supposed to lie there till dark fell; it's easier once it's dark;
but that was a long way ahead then. . . . He started rubbing my
face with snow. . . . Probably he'd noticed that my nose had turned
white. . . . And suddenly I felt like going to sleep. . . . He knew
that would be death. . . . Unbuttoned his sheepskin-coat, pressed me
against his body . . . it was warm . . . and all the time he kept
talking about how he lived, where he worked. . . . Suddenly started
talking about his girl, how pretty she was, how she loved him,
how he'd go back and marry her. . . . It's a pretty popular theme
out there. . . . His face flushed all over, and, you know, I got
warmed up, too; I could feel his excitement. . . . And it was if
he could see this girl, kept calling her Squirrel. . . .

IRINA   What was his name?

VOLODYA   Boris. Just like your brother.

IRINA   And his last name?

VOLODYA   I don't know. He wasn't from our unit.

IRINA   And you didn't meet again afterward?

VOLODYA   Unfortunately not.

IRINA   What happened next, Volodya?

VOLODYA   We kept lying like that, and then it barely started to get dark. He was cold, too, and frozen through. . . . And I was already falling off. I remember he hit me hard with his fist, I woke up, once again realized everything that was going on, couldn't help it and jumped to my feet. . . . And then I got hit . . . here [*indicating his chest*] . . . I went down. . . . He swore, cursed me out. . . . But that didn't make any difference to me then. . . . Suddenly he jumped up, grabbed me around the body, and started running. . . . They were shooting at him, but he kept running over the frozen field. Didn't have to run far, just to the edge of the woods. . . .

IRINA   Did you make it, Volodya?

VOLODYA   He did. He set me down in the snow and had just gotten up himself when those bastards opened fire again and killed him, so that he fell right on top of me.

IRINA   Killed him?

VOLODYA   Automatic rifles, probably. So, actually, there's nothing for me to say.

IRINA   Who was it, you really have no idea?

VOLODYA   No. All hell broke loose then. . . . When ours came up, I was put on a poncho and carried back, and they started digging a grave for him.

IRINA   You didn't see his papers?

VOLODYA   He was out on reconnaissance, too, and when you go out on reconnaissance you're not allowed to have anything with you. . . . All they found in his pockets was some sort of a button. . . .

IRINA   [*goes quickly to the wardrobe, gets Boris's photograph, shows it to* VOLODYA.]   Doesn't this look like him?

VOLODYA   [*after a long pause, hesitantly*]   No.

IRINA   [*loudly*]   It *was* him!

VOLODYA   [*softly*]   Yes. [FYODOR IVANOVICH *goes out into the next room.* IRINA *quickly follows him. Then* MARK, *also, leaves.*] That's what happened. . . . You know, there was a junior lieutenant from Pskov lying in our hospital ward, looking for his wife, looking and looking for her, writing letters to the ends of the earth, and, it turned out, she was a nurse on the fourth floor, in the very same hospital. . . . And one man told me . . .

VERONICA   Volodya, didn't he say anything before . . . ?

VOLODYA   No, he died right away.
VERONICA   And they buried him there?
VOLODYA   Yes.
VERONICA   Where is it?
VOLODYA   The western outskirts of Smolensk, near Height zero six.

[FYODOR IVANOVICH *comes in followed by* IRINA *and* MARK.]

IRINA   Papa, don't you go anywhere right now.
FYODOR   I'll go, Irina. . . .

[*The door is flung open,* ANNA MIKHAILOVNA *runs in out of breath, throws herself on* VOLODYA.]

ANNA   Vovochka! Vovulka mine! Fyodor Ivanovich, Irina! Comrades! What joy! Oh, what joy! What joy!

SCENE 2   *A room at the Borozdins' in Moscow. After re-evacuation. Anna Mikhailovna and Varvara Kapitonovna are in the room.*

VARVARA   You're not going anywhere.
ANNA   The institute will assign Volodya dormitory space, and I'll find something for myself.
VARVARA   You'll be separated?
ANNA   We've crowded Fyodor Ivanovich too long already.
VARVARA   Well, go off wherever you like yourself, but he still won't give Vladimir up to you; he'll hold him by force. He's stern.
ANNA   He has become gentler now.
VARVARA   I noticed. And absent-minded: yesterday he brought home the keys to the operating room and today he left his gloves. [MARK *enters.*] Well, how are things, Markusha?
MARK   No different. You haven't seen my suitcase, have you?
VARVARA   It's probably in the corner room. [MARK *goes out.*] Look, there's a man they didn't shoot at but killed him, killed him on the spot. I don't know that he'll ever wake up. [MARK *comes in, a suitcase in his hand.*] Where did that flat-footedness of yours come from?
MARK   I was born with it, they say.
VARVARA   They won't take you?
MARK   No.
VARVARA   What bad luck. [*To* ANNA MIKHAILOVNA.] And he was such a good boy growing up, dreamy, courteous . . .

MARK   All right if I take two sheets?

VARVARA   Take them, Markusha, take them. But the others are probably still clean. [MARK *goes out*.] He walks around like a lost soul, troubled and tormented.

[FYODOR IVANOVICH *enters*.]

FYODOR   Where is everybody?

ANNA   Volodya went off to the institute. It's the last days of registration, and there are all kinds of forms and questionnaires.

VARVARA   Veronica hasn't been home since this morning. I said they had to be back by supper. They promised.

FYODOR   Yes, yes, sure, this is the third day we've been lounging about in Moscow, and we haven't once sat down to table together. And where's Irina?

VARVARA   You're the one should know that; we don't.

FYODOR   Ah, yes! . . . She went to see to something about her doctorate. Well, let's wait. Moscow is still the same: bubbling, noisy, people cursing each other. I was so squeezed in the street-car, I almost died with delight.

ANNA   Delight?

FYODOR   Of course. Squeezed in exactly as I used to be. Something that seems part of me, something I know! The first few days I'll watch closely, be delighted, and then I'll start pushing myself!

VARVARA   [*softly*]   Fedya, Mark's here.

FYODOR   Ah!

VARVARA   They rejected him; they won't let him atone for his sins.

FYODOR   Did the books come?

VARVARA   Two boxes in your study.

FYODOR   I'll have to begin excavations.

[IRINA *comes in*.]

IRINA   The street lamps are lit! They're faint, but they're lit, the lovely old lamps! Soon Moscow will be sparkling in light such as the world has never seen.

VARVARA   You haven't seen the salutes yet. That's tomorrow.

ANNA   Why do you think tomorrow?

VARVARA   According to my calculations, tomorrow.

FYODOR   Commander-in-chief!

IRINA   Even our radio isn't working.

ANNA   Volodya tried to fix it this morning, but he didn't have time.

VARVARA   It was working very low for me; he ruined it.

ANNA   Wait till he comes, he'll fix it; he knows how.

IRINA Our darling Moscow apartment, how shabby you are!

VARVARA And how do you comfort the wounded? If the bones are solid, the flesh will grow back. [MARK *enters. A pause.*] Fedya, Anna Mikhailovna says she doesn't want to stay here. . . .

FYODOR [*frowning*] As she likes.

MARK Stay, Anna Mikhailovna. I'm leaving.

FYODOR Where, if it's not a secret?

MARK To a friend's.

FYODOR Who's that?

MARK You don't know him. We studied together. Recently got out of the hospital.

FYODOR A pianist, too?

MARK He was.

FYODOR Nobody is chasing you out.

MARK I know.

FYODOR Well, whatever you like. I hope you'll drop in once in a while?

MARK Sure.

IRINA Stay for supper.

MARK No, he told me to come over right away. Good-bye.

[ALL *respond.* MARK *goes out.*]

FYODOR Unbearable for him . . . So, Anna Mikhailovna, decide for yourself. . . . We have lots of room. Irina, help me open up the boxes.

[FYODOR IVANOVICH *and* IRINA *go out.*]

VARVARA I wanted Mark to stay here, but it's hard for him, everyone knowing. . . . I'll go warm up supper, or the gas may stop working again.

[VARVARA KAPITONOVNA *goes out.* VOLODYA *runs in.*]

ANNA Well?

VOLODYA All's in order!

ANNA They accepted you?

VOLODYA I'll say! We veterans come first. Is Veronica home?

ANNA No, she hasn't come yet. Volodya, Fyodor Ivanovich has suggested settling in with them, but I think I ought to say no.

VOLODYA Why so?

ANNA It's not right. . . .

VOLODYA Now, what are you inventing! We can't go back to Leningrad right now, the blockade is still on; you know that yourself. . . .

ANNA   I do, Volodya, I do.

[VERONICA *enters.*]

VERONICA   Irina hasn't promised to kill me?
ANNA   No.
VERONICA   She threatened to, if I were late for supper.
ANNA   Varvara Kapitonovna has gone out to warm it up.
VOLODYA   You might help her; after all, she's old.
ANNA   Now why didn't I think of that myself. . . . [*Goes out.*]
VOLODYA   I'm in.
VERONICA   I should think! You veterans are getting in everywhere at the head of the line.
VOLODYA   That's the law.
VERONICA   In what department?
VOLODYA   Electromechanics.
VERONICA   Do you like the institute?
VOLODYA   It's all right; the building looks nice.
VERONICA   A long, sharply pointed iron fence and stone gates with lovely molding . . .
VOLODYA   Yes.
VERONICA   I used to wait for him at those gates, and he would run out, waving his books . . . and always laughing. Did you mean to pick that department?
VOLODYA   Yes . . . I love electronics.
VERONICA   You all want something technical.
VOLODYA   Naturally—not medical . . . Oops! Not a word in this house . . .
VERONICA   You remember which place it was, Volodya?
VOLODYA   The western outskirts of Smolensk.
VERONICA   Once the war is over, I'll go there.

[*A short pause.*]

VOLODYA   Did you get a job?
VERONICA   Yes. I went to three different building offices, grabbed the boss by the tail. I caught one of them. They're building some little thing, a nursery or a milk station or something.
VOLODYA   He didn't hire you?
VERONICA   I left my work-book. For the time being I don't care where I work.
VOLODYA   Will you study?
VERONICA   Afterwards.

VOLODYA   That's sort of silly.

VERONICA   Mind your own business.

VOLODYA   Look what I brought you.

VERONICA   What is it?

VOLODYA   [*unwrapping a lump brought wrapped up in newspaper*] Clay.

VERONICA   You can't do anything with that kind.

VOLODYA   [*disappointed*]   What do you mean?

VERONICA   I'll get some myself. . . . Afterwards!

[IRINA *enters.*]

IRINA   You could have said you were here. Father wanted to eat a long time ago, but he waited.

VERONICA   And you?

IRINA   Oh, me, too. [*Calls.*] Grandma! [GRANDMA *comes in.*] Are we going to sit down or not?

VARVARA   Now that's funny, Irina, as if I were holding you up.

[FYODOR IVANOVICH *and* ANNA MIKHAILOVNA *come in.*]

FYODOR   Everyone here? Well, then, sit down.

VOLODYA   I'll change, Mama. [*Goes out.*]

FYODOR   For a gala supper gala dress? Black tie, I wonder, or just a suit? Irusha, in the cupboard on the shelf . . .

IRINA   Already got some?

FYODOR   Ahha! [IRINA *goes out and quickly returns.*] At last I've sat in my own seat. Grandma, in your gala chair—time has left its marks on it. . . . Anna Mikhailovna, here. Irina, your chair should have been tossed into the attic long ago, but, to tell the truth, I don't much want to. . . .

IRINA   [*smiling*]   It looks as though I won't let you down.

FYODOR   You often used to sit here, Veronica, and so here you stay.

[VOLODYA *returns in uniform.*]

ANNA   Why are you wearing that?

VOLODYA   I just want to, Mama.

FYODOR   [*pointing to the place between himself and* VERONICA]   You sit here.

VOLODYA   Why such solemnity? [*Understands; goes and sits in Boris's place.*]

FYODOR   Let's drink silently to those who are silent, having had their say.

[*A volley.*]

VOLODYA   The salute!
VARVARA   It came, sweet sound, ahead of time!
ANNA   Let's go out on the street; let's see.
VARVARA   And we'll open the window; it's as bright as broad day-
light out.
IRINA   I wonder what's been captured?
VERONICA [*to* VOLODYA]   Oh you, promising to fix the radio!!

[VOLODYA *is busy with the radio.*]

IRINA   I'll find out from the people next door. [*Runs out.*]
VARVARA   From two hundred twenty guns, I can hear it.
FYODOR   They've started speaking.
ANNA   Alive and dead.

[IRINA *dashes in.*]

FYODOR   Well, what is it?
IRINA   Smolensk.

[*A pause. Outside the window, rockets. A volley. The radio breaks
in. A march. On stage, dark. The march fades into symphonic music.*]

SCENE 3   Finale   *The music of the preceding scene continues. The curtain rises on a field of grain. On the left,
a young forest. In the distance, on the horizon, a village. On
the edge of the forest, a wooden fence, a small obelisk, with
names inscribed in gold letters—a soldiers' grave. Evening is
coming on. It is quiet. Fyodor Ivanovich enters. A water can-
teen hangs over his shoulder; in his hand he carries a dry
branch as a walking stick. He goes up to the monument,
silently reads the names. Irina comes in, some field flowers
in her hands.*

IRINA   Not this one?
FYODOR   No.

[IRINA *tosses two or three flowers over the fence.*]

IRINA   Of course, all this is whimsical, Papa. How can we possibly
find him—so many years have gone by. . . . Aren't you tired?

FYODOR   A little. Yes, the war see-sawed back and forth here in this region; nobody will ever find him. . . . But it's a pleasant trip, and the walk, too. . . . A nice change.

IRINA   You know what your dear Bobrov announced to me yesterday during a five-minute break?

FYODOR   I don't.

IRINA   Well, listen . . .

FYODOR   I won't. Nature is making me lazy.

IRINA   He's angry at me, because I'm the one who's going to the congress.

FYODOR   Stop complaining. Let's listen to the quiet. [*After a silence.*] How good!

IRINA   [*after a short pause*]   It's time to go back, or we'll be late for the train.

FYODOR   Let all the trains go. I'll walk around here with a stick and enjoy myself. Like a poet, free and unfettered!

IRINA   Don't be an idiot. [*Shouts.*] Veronica! . . . Volodya! . . .

VOICES *of* VERONICA *and* VOLODYA   Oho—ho-ho! Coming!

IRINA   She's forgotten why she came. You might point out to Vladimir that he's following at her heels. He simply doesn't see a thing around; it's uncomfortable to watch him.

FYODOR   Well, now, don't you pay any attention. If he is, let him do it. . . . He won't crush her heels.

IRINA   Still, she's funny. . . .

FYODOR   That's natural, Irina. Nature—well, you know, nature abhors a vacuum.

[VERONICA *runs in. She has a huge armful of flowers: yellow snapdragons, clover, cornflowers, daisies.*]

VERONICA   Here I am! [*Notices the obelisk, goes over to the fence.*]

FYODOR   Other lads here. Voldemar has led us on a wild goose chase.

IRINA   It's time to head for the station. By the time we get there . . .

FYODOR   I think I'll stretch out for a minute. [*Lies down on the grass.*] Have we time?

IRINA   I'll give you five minutes for bliss. Oh, it really is good here. [*Pointing to the forest.*] What's that, aspen?

FYODOR   Alder. [IRINA *goes into the woods.*] Well, are you disappointed?

VERONICA   No.

FYODOR   Neither am I.

VERONICA   He seems alive forever.

FYODOR   They all are, all alive forever inside us. . . . Here, Veronica, come sit beside me.

[VERONICA *sits down beside* FYODOR IVANOVICH.]

VERONICA   What?

FYODOR   You mustn't torment a young man like that.

VERONICA   Are you talking about Volodya?

FYODOR   Yes. Either say yes or say no politely and firmly and completely. What are you waiting for?

VERONICA [*after a pause*]   A miracle.

FYODOR   There are no miracles.

VERONICA   Alas. Don't hurry me.

[VOLODYA *runs in.*]

VOLODYA [*giving flowers to* VERONICA]   Here! Such big ones. I went into the oats and picked them.

FYODOR   If the farmers had seen you they would have given you something to remember!

VERONICA   But what will I do with them! I have no more room.

VOLODYA   We'll take them home to Mama and Grandma.

FYODOR   So, now, my hero, you've led us on a wild goose chase. Let's go back.

VOLODYA   Everything is somehow changed here. . . . Before, there was a charred forest and snow—everything was dead. . . . We should have come here right after the war.

FYODOR   The business of daily living, hero, the daily business! Veronica had her exams to prepare for, and you had a bullet to be taken out, and Irina had her dissertation to defend. . . . [*Calls.*] Irina! [*No answer.*] She's gone farther in. I'll go find her. Don't you move from this spot. We'll head home right away. Oh, what beauty all around! [*Goes off into the forest.*]

VERONICA   And so we made our dream come true: we've come here.

VOLODYA   You know, I'm probably a scoundrel, but right now I feel sad and at the same time so good inside. There's some kind of absolutely incredible flow of strength. . . . I'll pick you up in my arms right now and carry you far, far away, you want me to?

VERONICA   Thanks, I'm not tired—I can go by myself. Pick up Irina and carry her to the station.

VOLODYA   Oh, you! . . .

VERONICA   Listen, Volodya, I want to talk to you seriously.

VOLODYA [*on guard*]   What?

VERONICA   Don't look for an answer from me.
VOLODYA   But I'm not asking you anything.
VERONICA   You are. All the time.
VOLODYA   Then don't answer. I'm not asking for a favor. I've waited and I'll keep waiting. . . .
VERONICA   You'll finish the institute in a year, and I'll finish my construction institute in two. . . .
VOLODYA   It's hard for you to work and study. . . .
VERONICA   No, it's easy. . . . Maybe because I feel myself indebted eternally.
VOLODYA   But what about me?
VERONICA   Of course, and you, too . . . And everyone who remains. . . . Borya used to say he had to be where it was most difficult. . . . And I'll always be there. . . . Know that. . . .
VOLODYA   I do, and I'll be there, too. . . . Everyone must . . .
FYODOR [*rapping on a tree with his stick*]   May I come in?
VERONICA   Do.

[IRINA *and* FYODOR IVANOVICH *enter.*]

FYODOR   Well, let's be on our way.
VERONICA   It's time.
VOLODYA   Let's go.
IRINA [*looking up*]   Look, some birds are flying, a whole flock.
FYODOR [*looking up*]   Ah, those are cranes. . . .

[ALL *look up.*]

VERONICA   I've never seen live ones before.
IRINA [*shading her eyes with her palm*]   Hard to see them.
FYODOR   Yes, they're flying right into the sun.
VERONICA   They're big. . . .
FYODOR   What a good world! Let's be off.

[ALL *set out.*]

VERONICA   I'll catch up, go ahead. [FYODOR IVANOVICH, IRINA, VO-LODYA *go out.* VERONICA *remains alone.*] Borya! . . . I so much want to talk to you. . . . And I do . . . In the evening, when everyone is asleep and the day has gone, I talk to you . . . ask you questions, ask for advice, and you always answer me. Your face fades from my memory, and I try to catch its features and keep them, and I do. . . . It's all right! You're becoming even handsomer than you were. . . . I love you! . . .
IRINA'S VOICE   Veronica!

VERONICA   You're like a legend to me . . . and I want to live my life well, very well, although it's already not so pure and clean as yours. . . . I haven't done anything yet. . . . I'm studying, studying and working. . . . It's all I can do for the time being. . . . But I think a great deal, Borya. I think about what I'm living for . . .

FYODOR'S VOICE   Veronica!

VERONICA   . . . what all of us are living for, for whom you and the others gave up your unfinished lives. . . . How do we live? What does each of us each day of his life add to the general happiness? Where's your drop? And is it tar or dew and honey?

VOICES *of* FYODOR, IRINA, *and* VOLODYA *together*   Ve-ron-i-ca!

VERONICA   You're mine, Borya, mine forever. And I'm taking your life with me! [*Tosses the flowers over the fence toward the obelisk, falls to the earth and kisses it. Shouts.*] Coming! I'm coming! [*Runs out.*]

CURTAIN

a Petrarchan sonnet

A DRAMA IN THREE ACTS

BY NIKOLAI POGODIN

CHARACTERS

Dmitry Alexeyevich Sukhodolov [*a construction engineer, a party member*]

Kseniya Petrovna [*his wife*]

Yakov Eduardovich Armando [*their friend, a concert violinist*]

Pavel Mikhailovich [*Sukhodolov's superior, head of the Regional Committee*]

Afanasy Kuzmich Dononov [*an engineer, Sukhodolov's colleague*]

Maiya [*a young library worker*]

Clara [*her roommate*]

Marina [*Sukhodolov's old housekeeper*]

Ternovnikov [*a friend of Maiya's*]

An Ice-Cream Vendor, *a woman*

A Fat Couple, *man and wife*

A Drunkard

Girls, *in gray and blue*

A Ferryman

A Waiter

A Mailman

A Secretary

ACT I

SCENE 1   *A cliff above a huge river. Forests stretch into the distance on the opposite shore. A city boulevard is in the foreground of the stage. Twilight in May, with a splendid sunset behind the river. Sukhodolov and the Ice-Cream Vendor are on stage.*

VENDOR [*offering her wares to passersby, timidly and cheerfully turns to* SUKHODOLOV]   Citizen, sir, may I— By the way, I've wanted to ask you, but all this while I haven't yet dared. . . . Maybe you're not in the right mood?

SUKHODOLOV   Oh, no; I am . . . very much in the right mood. Go ahead.

VENDOR [*having loudly run through all the flavors of ice-cream*]   I've been watching you, by the way, for a whole hour. Can a person really sit and wait for somebody for a whole hour? It's amazing!

SUKHODOLOV [*astounded*]   Waiting?! I'm not waiting for anybody. . . . No; why did you think so?

VENDOR   The expression on your face gives it away.

SUKHODOLOV [*cheerfully*]   Gives it away?

VENDOR   Definitely.

SUKHODOLOV   How?

VENDOR   There's something sad and lonely about it.

SUKHODOLOV [*more gravely*]   Sad and lonely . . . maybe so.

VENDOR   You have a very interesting expression. Sort of—aquiline.

SUKHODOLOV   Aquiline . . . That's good.

VENDOR   Definitely. But, also, melancholic.

SUKHODOLOV [*in feigned distress*]   A-ah, my dear! What kind of expression can it be! Neither flesh nor fowl nor good red herring.

VENDOR   And you don't wait the way everybody else does. You hope and you don't hope; you think and you don't.

SUKHODOLOV   You ought to be a mind-reader in the circus.

VENDOR   Don't be offended. I've been watching you because you're a very interesting man. . . . I can't help wanting to look.

SUKHODOLOV [*mischievously*]   Handsome, perhaps?

VENDOR   What about it? Handsome, too, even. But not so much handsome as attractive. Drive a girl wild.

SUKHODOLOV   Thank you, thank you, my dear. A pleasing portrait . . . Very clever.

VENDOR   You probably know lots of girls. . . . You've already lost count.

SUKHODOLOV [*turning back*]   One. And she, as you see, didn't come. Didn't come because I didn't call her. . . . But I waited, although I knew she wouldn't. You have a very sharp eye. Let me shake your hand and congratulate you. [*Starts out.*]

VENDOR [*after him*]   What a man, ah! . . . No denying it. No wonder people say everybody is a riddle. Now, if he'd just say to me, "Marusya, follow me," I'd throw everything to the winds and . . . Ice cream, vanilla, chocolate, fruit flavors! . . .

[*At the other end of the stage,* SUKHODOLOV *notices* ARMANDO.]

SUKHODOLOV [*enthusiastically*]   Armando? It is! Yakov Eduardovich, have you come here for a concert, have you really?

ARMANDO   Yes, I have. I'll be touring Siberia all summer. How are you, Dmitry Alexeyevich? You look splendid. Sun-tanned. But you . . . you . . . here on the street!

SUKHODOLOV   What's so surprising about that?

ARMANDO   Why, you know, you run into important people on the street only at summer resorts, whereas at home you all live apart from each other and rather gloomily at that.

SUKHODOLOV   At home we may be important, but at a resort we're vacationers.

ARMANDO   Have you been in Siberia long?

SUKHODOLOV   Today is May first. . . . Let's see: exactly six months.

ARMANDO   And you've already managed to do so damned much along the banks of this great river. How we've learned to build!

SUKHODOLOV   It's not me who has done it, old friend, but thousands of men with machines. That would be more accurate. And we haven't yet learned all there is to know about building. . . . We're still learning.

ARMANDO   The same old Sukhodolov, restless and always dissatisfied about something! No, of course not the very same. You look wonderful, young, radiant. . . . Not like me . . . I'm fading completely.

SUKHODOLOV   How nice that we met! Every so often I think of inviting you to my place, but where will I find the old violinist, I wonder. You know, you've spent your life on tour.

ARMANDO   Are you bored? Haven't you found friends in the new place?

SUKHODOLOV   It's not easy . . . making friends. Let's go to my place, or shall we walk along the river? The sunset today is unmercifully beautiful.

ARMANDO   Magnificent! There is real open space here. What a mighty land!

SUKHODOLOV   Siberia, the East . . . It's an unusual spring. Generally there are huge forest fires.

[A DRUNKARD *comes up, halts, sings.*]

DRUNKARD   Hardly managed to get married
Ere the wife took someone else,
All because I am a cripple
With a broken leg.

Noble colleagues, give something to a crippled man for sunflower seeds, a man who has suffered in two wars.

ARMANDO   This must be the tenth time I've seen you in town, my friend. You're lying. . . . Your leg is fine.

DRUNKARD   And all for three kopeks you'd let a cripple with a wooden leg stay wretched and miserable? Shame on you.

ARMANDO   Good-bye, good-bye. Good luck.

DRUNKARD   But for seeds? Why else did I sing you the song?

SUKHODOLOV   Here. [*Gives him money.*] Now don't bother us.

DRUNKARD [*to* ARMANDO]   Look, see what's inside me, in my heart. Even cows have legs, too. Can you understand a man driven to despair over women? They . . . you know . . . those stockings . . . ruined my sensitive soul! 'Cause once I was an artist just like you. [*To* SUKHODOLOV.] Thanks for the honorarium, colleague. [*Goes out.*]

ARMANDO   I can't stand these street Mephistos. A typical drunkard.

SUKHODOLOV   I can't believe my ears! Yasha, you haven't quit, have you?

ARMANDO   But I'm not a drunkard.

SUKHODOLOV [*affectionately and ironically*]   No, old friend, no . . . You're a pure priest of art. A virtuoso on the violin, and a virtuoso in the field of ladies' hearts . . . of myocarditic, adipose, bedridden hearts . . . of, in short, hearts that are tired out.

ARMANDO   What are you driving at?

SUKHODOLOV   Oh, only how you seduced my wife.

ARMANDO   I never did!

SUKHODOLOV   You did.

ARMANDO No, no . . .

SUKHODOLOV What do you mean, "no, no"! You played my wife
heart-rending tunes on your violin, and she slept in the chair.
From the time we first knew each other, you started courting my
wife licentiously. But I'm fond of you with all your faults, just as,
generally speaking, I take life as it comes.

[A FAT COUPLE *passes.*]

WIFE What are you looking at, Vasenka? Oh, how impertinent all
our husbands are. Out taking a walk with his own wife and keeps
looking to this side and that. Never a word, no point talking. . . .
Oh, we know, we do, where you all keep looking.

[*They pass on.*]

ARMANDO But what about Kseniya Petrovna—isn't she coming?

SUKHODOLOV The same old story: an apartment in Moscow, a summer house. She's supposed to come for six weeks or so.

ARMANDO What are you putting up over here?

SUKHODOLOV We're putting up . . . You know, I've been in construction for twenty years, but I've never been in charge of work
like this. Never dreamed of it.

ARMANDO Listen, when will we finish?

SUKHODOLOV What a ridiculous question! As if musicians could be
responsible! Have you ever had any political education?

ARMANDO I'm studying . . . I'll pass. . . . How do you feel?

SUKHODOLOV Fine, as you can see. Glad I met you. You're interesting to talk to . . . when you're sober, of course. . . . Now, take
my Party organizer, a friend of long standing, well, he can talk
endlessly about who, when, and why was or will be or wasn't and
never will be a minister. I have no use for conversations like that.

ARMANDO There's always something or somebody you have no use
for.

SUKHODOLOV I never have any use for petty middle-class people no
matter what their shape or form.

ARMANDO Then don't have middle-class friends.

SUKHODOLOV He and I used to be friends, some twelve years ago.
Then he was a different man. But the bumpkin in him came out
after all. Dononov is his name . . . actually, should be Dumbdunsov.

ARMANDO Interesting friends . . .

SUKHODOLOV All his reminiscences begin with his mama who used to fry him pancakes. From pancakes to the petty middle class isn't far but, what's important, it's a straight line. Anyway, I hope he gets lost in a swamp. I'm fed up.

ARMANDO Well!

SUKHODOLOV Why "well"?

ARMANDO Let me ask you one question.

SUKHODOLOV Even two.

ARMANDO Why are you so changed that I hardly recognized you?

SUKHODOLOV You ask interesting questions, friend. Let's move on a little, shall we? There, you see those masts in the distant, smoky haze? That's "Old Harbor." The sort of thing you like, a poetic place. Shall we go?

ARMANDO Wait, let me finish. Once again they've saddled you with something really important, but you're cheerful, relaxed . . . even younger.

SUKHODOLOV Ah, Yakov Eduardovich, is it so obvious?

ARMANDO And to approach fifty without your hair turning gray! In this day and age! A giant of a man! But I'll bet all my concert fees you've fallen in love with someone here.

SUKHODOLOV Shhhh. Don't shout.

ARMANDO You're even afraid.

SUKHODOLOV The least hint! . . . For you know how people here look on us. They'll make up a whole story.

ARMANDO But I'm not going to start it. I'm not middle-class, and no philistine, either.

SUKHODOLOV No, you're no philistine. . . . That's why I'm glad to see you.

ARMANDO You want to let me in on it? I'm not insisting. Go tell your secrets to your Party organizer.

SUKHODOLOV Oh you, Yasha . . . Yakov Eduardovich . . . friend of mine! The things that happen in our lives! There I am, out on a construction site in the taiga, sitting in a tent on the bank of this same great river. . . . Our site is upstream, there beyond "Old Harbor." There I sit, planning a running start on the summer. . . . The work is hard as hell, trying to look ahead accurately, make the right projections . . . drives you wild. And at that point, lo, in my tent there appears . . . I hardly know how to tell you. . . . Suddenly there is that miraculous moment, or vision, which must come in every man's life. I'm dumbfounded. I can feel how my heart has skipped a beat and then started pounding, face to face with this girl I don't know. I'm simply speechless from her look-ing at me. . . . Though I receive my visitor completely properly, officially. Her inquiry was nothing, something about organizing traveling libraries. I wrote her a memorandum, and she left. She left, and I went on with my work on projections for the summer. In sum, I had a glimpse of a face which I felt was unusually precious to me, and then it disappeared forever.

ARMANDO   Disappeared?

SUKHODOLOV   Wait, I haven't finished.

ARMANDO   Very interesting!

SUKHODOLOV   One day goes by; another; a week; but the image I have of the young girl remains vividly before my very eyes. Her slim figure, and young eyes squinting in the sunlight. I'm a strong man, energetic and assertive, some people even say I'm coarse, and I find it hard to go through a silly, childlike encounter. . . . I'm too old for it; it doesn't go with my position! . . . But I sense that an inexpressible calamity has occurred. I've lost my head. Over what? It's embarrassing; it's absurd. And I decided: it'll pass and be forgotten. I began to feel easier. I actually began to forget about the vision. So, one day, being in town, feeling light and easy inside, I thought, "Why not go see her where she works? Just like that . . . No special reason . . ." Well, believe it or not, I made up my mind, and off I went. She works in the library, does some kind of scholarly research. She was alone, and a bit frightened at seeing me, she became confused. But I . . . On the street afterwards, I understood what I had said to her.

ARMANDO   Which was?

SUKHODOLOV   Like a little boy, I told her straight from my heart that I had come on no business at all, I didn't need anything, I had come for *no special reason.* And I remember how those intelligent and timid eyes of hers glanced up at me attentively and sadly. She said very softly, but also frankly: "I understand." That's all. The end. A giant moment passed, a moment that has become part of my life forever. What I said after that I don't remember. It doesn't matter. . . . I left her and went outside. There was spring slush on the street; it was drizzling, but I left my car behind and walked along the sidewalk. I have no idea how many years it's been since I wanted to walk around alone, but I especially liked that rain and slush. In short, walking along the streets that rainy evening, I had a feeling of complete happiness. There in a nutshell is the whole story of my love.

ARMANDO   [*after a moment's reflection*]   Which means that you, Sukhodolov, are still human.

[*The same* FAT COUPLE *go by.*]

WIFE   Are you going to tell me again that you're not looking anywhere? Shameless, that's what you are. Maybe you don't turn
your head, but your eyes keep looking right and left. Shut up.
We know where you're always looking.

[*They pass on.*]

ARMANDO   I wish you success.

SUKHODOLOV   In what? . . . Dear friend, you don't understand. I
haven't the least thought of being successful in any sense. It's
something else entirely—really, you must understand me.

ARMANDO   Then you're doubly human.

SUKHODOLOV   Ah, Yakov Eduardovich, I haven't told you anything,
really. I've confided secrets, that's all! But watch out: if you give
me away, I'll kill you. . . . So, I went home to my little vacant
shelter and at night, in that same wonderful frame of mind, wrote
her how I had wandered along the street and what I had thought
about. You don't understand? I wrote a letter.

ARMANDO   Very clearly . . .

SUKHODOLOV   You won't believe me, because I myself sometimes
think that I've gone mad, starting to write her letters. We don't
see each other; that's impossible; and there's no point to it, anyway. Haven't seen each other since then. I just write her. I,
Sukhodolov, known all around, a construction engineer, a Party
member, call this girl my song. It's awful to admit, but I want
that person to know that she's like a song to me. . . . The last,
I suppose.

ARMANDO   It's marvelous. You've just reminded me of Laura. Exactly like Laura. Marvelous.

SUKHODOLOV   What Laura?

ARMANDO   You don't know about Laura, about Petrarch?

SUKHODOLOV   Petrarch? . . . What should I know about them?

ARMANDO   You should know about them because you're an educated man. . . . And secondly, you yourself are Petrarch, the
Renaissance poet who in courtly fashion revered Donna Laura
and wrote her a mass of sonnets. Really, haven't you ever read
him?

SUKHODOLOV   I never happened to.

ARMANDO   I will so mightily acclaim my love
              That I will stir a thousand sweet desires

In noble breast and set the blood on fire
By a thousand reveries of active love.

You and your letters are a Petrarchan sonnet. Mitya Sukhodolov,
if up until now you've merited my warmest respect, from now
on I take off my hat to you in admiration.

SUKHODOLOV What do poets . . . They're all like that! But I'm
ashamed . . . even terrified. . . . Let me continue. . . . There came
a change in my life. Breathing is easier now, I treat people better. . . . My work has become inspired. . . . A Petrarchan sonnet,
you say, Laura . . . Well, maybe, all right . . . A man doesn't have
many of these sonnets in his life.

ARMANDO What's her name?

SUKHODOLOV Maiya.

ARMANDO A modern name.

SUKHODOLOV Yes, modern.

ARMANDO Oh, what open spaces! . . . Mighty May! . . . How I
envy you. It has been a long time since I loved anybody; I drag
along, earning my living.

SUKHODOLOV It's something I hold sacred. . . . It's good. Though
sometimes alarming, scaring. [*A pause. A large steamer passes on
the river.*] Oh you alluring lights! How happy I would be to go
off on that ship down to the ocean. Impossible, of course; I would
be sent back . . . and people would say that Sukhodolov had gone
mad.

ARMANDO Send her your letters, Mitya. Sing your song and don't
be afraid that it's either tragic or the last. . . .

SCENE 2   *A corner of the foyer in a concert hall during intermission. Kseniya Petrovna and Pavel Mikhailovich.*

KSENIYA A colossal success! Now, there's a musician . . . What
power! Pavel Mikhailovich, how do you like our violinist?

PAVEL A great success. Really! Too bad he has such seedy features.

KSENIYA An artist.

PAVEL They don't all have to look seedy.

KSENIYA He travels a lot.

PAVEL Probably drinks a lot.

KSENIYA It's not his fault; he lives in hotels.

PAVEL But do . . . ?

KSENIYA Yet when he plays, he's a different man.

PAVEL   That, to be sure, is very true.

KSENIYA Plays so powerfully.

[*Two* GIRLS *go by, one in gray, one in light blue.*]

GIRL IN GRAY   Music has a negative effect on me. . . . It deactivates me.

GIRL IN BLUE   It's impossible to go anywhere with you. You're always thinking only about what activates you and what deactivates you.

GIRL IN GRAY   Strange, but what is art for? To activate people.

GIRL IN BLUE   I won't ever go to another concert with you.

[*They pass on.*]

PAVEL   Where's Sukhodolov? With the violinist?

KSENIYA Of course! They're old friends. What do you want?

PAVEL   I have to say two words to him.

KSENIYA Business? Let the man relax. I forbid you to.

PAVEL   Do you order everyone around like that? Your husband, too?

KSENIYA Certainly. What about it? Keep in mind that I'm a Cossack born and bred . . . from the Urals. We Shmyriovs are all like that.

PAVEL   You Shmyriovs? Why Shmyriovs?

KSENIYA It's my maiden name, my own name. . . . In Moscow I go out to Khimki to swim in the canal until October. Feel my arm here, above the elbow, and don't dare pinch me.

PAVEL   You're powerfully built, Kseniya Petrovna, handsomely built.

KSENIYA All of us Shmyriovs are. And, generally speaking, in a broad sense, I'm no petty middle-class woman in private life. I'm a progressive woman. Yes, yes I am, Pavel Mikhailovich.

PAVEL   But still, I beg you, let me tell Sukhodolov one little piece of news that will interest him greatly.

KSENIYA What news? Tell me.

PAVEL   He's had some disagreements with one of his workers. . . . A chance has come up to separate them.

KSENIYA Oh, those disagreements . . . He's too independent. I keep telling Sukhodolov all the time: They'll break your back.

PAVEL   You disapprove? "Break your back." . . . But why "break your back"?

KSENIYA In our life, you mustn't be different, you mustn't stand out. I keep repeating that.

PAVEL [*all the time he speaks to her, he suppresses a smile*] But
look at you, for example: you stand out . . . your height . . . slim-
ness . . . figure . . .

KSENIYA Oh, figure; why, figure even helps. But let's change the
subject. Look how stirred up the audience is.

PAVEL That's what surprises me—how many music-lovers there are
in our town. And lots of young people. I had no idea.

KSENIYA You go to concerts regularly?

PAVEL To tell the truth, we listen to music only after ceremonial
occasions. Shameful, but true.

KSENIYA Personally, I adore the violin. In the first excitement of
our acquaintance, Armando used to play for me personally. I
was simply overcome with delight. Show me your manners, Pavel
Mikhailovich; I'd like something to drink.

[*They go toward the buffet.* MAIYA *and* CLARA *come in.*]

CLARA It's a pity he's not alone. I had to see him about something.

MAIYA Who are you talking about?

CLARA The man who went into the buffet with the tall woman.
Pavel Mikhailovich. Our regional boss. Are you looking for somebody?

MAIYA Yes, I'd like to see a certain man, but he's not here.

CLARA Who? Not a secret, is it?

MAIYA It is.

CLARA Even from me?

MAIYA From the world.

CLARA Really?

MAIYA From the universe.

CLARA Must be love.

MAIYA No, not love.

CLARA Then what?

MAIYA What was just played.

CLARA For heaven's sakes, what subtleties.

MAIYA Clarochka, angel, after all, music is pure emotion.

CLARA We're close friends, you and I, but I think you hide all
your feelings from me.

MAIYA There are things in life which you can't talk about at all.
They're almost fantasies. They exist, and yet they don't. All a
dream.

CLARA More subtleties and fancies.

MAIYA Not fancies, but fact.

CLARA Careful, my dear, or I'll expose you.

MAIYA   For what sins and crimes?

CLARA   You're on the lookout for someone.

MAIYA   Don't be silly. If at twenty-five you can't look, when can you?

CLARA   That depends . . . depends on who . . .

MAIYA   You don't think our eyes themselves find what they need?

CLARA   That's mysticism.

MAIYA   Maybe. You wouldn't understand.

CLARA   Oh, so that's it. . . . You think I've never had any success in this kind of thing.

MAIYA   You . . . you're simply being ridiculous. Very ridiculous.

CLARA   [*crudely pressing* MAIYA]   Maika, silly, how I love you! But you're keeping everything to yourself! Somebody told me you're planning to leave soon.

MAIYA   I am. I think I'll go away.

CLARA   Without a word to me.

MAIYA   I hate this pointless work here, and suddenly I long to go home to wise old Leningrad.

CLARA   Studying the Soviet reader is pointless work? Do you understand what you're saying?

MAIYA   But studying for what?

CLARA   What do you mean, for what, for what? You're joking. For some time now you've been very gay and scatter-brained. Isn't there something you want to confess to me?

MAIYA   I have nothing to confess. You tell me why there has to be something to confess. That's not friendship but probation.

CLARA   No, Mayechka dear, we must, we must pay very close attention to each other . . . or we may skim over a lot of things.

MAIYA   I don't understand.

CLARA   Because you have a lot of the individualistic, of the subjective in you. . . . And I think that sometimes it's no sin to keep an eye on a comrade in order to help him in good time.

MAIYA   Literally keep an eye on him?

CLARA   What's strange about that? Nothing unusual at all. But excuse me, darling, I still have to go see that comrade there. [*Points to* PAVEL MIKHAILOVICH.] One of our chief leaders . . . The chief. [CLARA *starts toward* PAVEL MIKHAILOVICH.]

KSENIYA   I'll go see Armando. He adores the way I inspire him.

PAVEL   Go be inspiring, be inspiring.

[*She goes out.*]

CLARA   [*timidly*]   Hello, Pavel Mikhailovich. I'm Clara Mulina. The

Society for Disseminating Cultural and Political Knowledge. Do you remember me?

PAVEL   Why belittle yourself, Clara Mulina? I know you very well.

CLARA   There are thousands of us, but only one of you.

PAVEL   Again, that's not the thing to say.

CLARA   It's hard to reach you, so I finally made up my mind to bother you here. Just a little thing; won't take a minute.

PAVEL   Go ahead.

CLARA   I consider it my direct responsibility to give you personally some papers . . . which disgrace . . .

PAVEL   Papers? . . . I see. Disgrace whom?

CLARA   Comrade Sukhodolov.

PAVEL   Who? Who?

CLARA   Sukhodolov.

PAVEL   How do they disgrace him?

CLARA   You'll see from the papers themselves.

PAVEL   But before I take your papers, I have a right to know what they are.

CLARA   They're letters.

PAVEL   Whose?

CLARA   His . . . written in his hand.

PAVEL   To whom?

CLARA   Letters to a certain girl.

PAVEL   Who is the girl?

CLARA   A researcher, a research assistant from Leningrad . . . she works in the regional library. Her name is Maiya.

PAVEL   And what's in those letters?

CLARA   Well, if, let's say, an elderly man in a responsible position calls a girl, who is a stranger to him . . . well, what would you think?

PAVEL   I'm afraid to think about it, because I myself am an elderly man in a responsible position. What does he call her?

CLARA   He calls her his song.

PAVEL   What?

CLARA   See, it's incredible . . . His song.

PAVEL   Hm, yes; a very poetic epithet. And how did you get hold of these letters?

CLARA   By chance.

PAVEL   They showed them to you?

CLARA   Why would anyone show such letters! I found them accidentally.

PAVEL   And took them?

CLARA   Why? I made photostats of them. The letters are still where
they were.

PAVEL   Why did you put them back in place?

CLARA   That's an odd question. Let them pile up.

PAVEL   Hm, yes; I didn't think about that. Well, what about it?

CLARA   I don't understand you.

PAVEL   What do you want me to do?

CLARA   I want you to read these letters.

PAVEL   Well, you see, the thing is: you want me to, but I don't
want to.

CLARA   [*astounded*]   Seriously?!

PAVEL   Yes.

CLARA   You won't take them?

PAVEL   No, I won't.

CLARA   In that case . . . I don't understand . . . Who should I give
them to?

PAVEL   Why do you have to give them to anybody? Sukhodolov
isn't writing to me, or to you, but to the girl. And the girl, as I
understand it, is keeping them. So let them remain with her.

CLARA   Is that a directive?

PAVEL   There's the bell, you hear it? Let's go listen to the music.

CLARA   No . . . what'll I do? If it is a directive, then I'll have to
draw corresponding conclusions . . . general conclusions.

PAVEL   What sort of directive could it be?! Simply, I think it's
wrong to steal a girl's letters . . . photostat them. . . . Perhaps
the girl is even your friend? As you please, but I think it isn't
right. [*Goes out.*]

CLARA   He's playing the liberal. I can mail them. . . . He'll read
them then.

[MAIYA *runs up.*]

MAIYA   Clara, let's hurry in; the lights are about to go down.

CLARA   Go by yourself. I don't feel like . . .

MAIYA   Don't feel like what? What happened?

CLARA   I don't feel well. I have a headache. Good-bye. [*Goes out.*]

MAIYA   Strange and pathetic. [*Having noticed* SUKHODOLOV.] You're
here, too. Hello.

SUKHODOLOV   Hello, Maiya Sergeyevna. The things I send you don't
seem ridiculous? You're not annoyed at me?

MAIYA   I treasure them. There's nothing ridiculous about them.

SUKHODOLOV   Farewell, my angel.

MAIYA   Greetings to your . . . Greetings.

SUKHODOLOV [*turning around sharply, in a low voice*] Be sure to destroy the letters.

MAIYA What do you mean? Why?

SUKHODOLOV Simply into the stove . . . And then there'll be nothing.

MAIYA What can there be?

SUKHODOLOV All kinds of things!

MAIYA The letters are pure poetry.

SUKHODOLOV Poetry isn't for me. . . . Don't you understand?

MAIYA Then don't write.

SUKHODOLOV [*having looked around, insistently, firmly*] No, I will write . . . I will. But, at least hide them in a safer place.

MAIYA Don't worry. Nobody in the world will ever find out.

SUKHODOLOV What enchanting delight merely to look at you. . . . [*Goes out.*]

MAIYA The man can't hide the truth from me or from himself. . . . He's in love.

SCENE 3 *Sukhodolov's apartment at night. Marina and Sukhodolov.*

SUKHODOLOV Go to bed, my dear, it's late.

MARINA That's it, it's late . . . or I'd tell you everything I know about you.

SUKHODOLOV All right, go ahead.

MARINA I will. You don't love your wife. And she doesn't love you. Or you wouldn't have started giving me that nonsense about your life being over. But I remember you never were very fond of each other. And once you had made your two ways in the world, why, each of you started living his own separate life.

SUKHODOLOV Why are you telling me all this?

MARINA I'm cross. . . . I can't stand false living. His wife off somewhere, who knows where, and he's babbling on about old age. That's not the trouble.

SUKHODOLOV [*bantering*] What is?

MARINA That violinist loomed up on the horizon.

SUKHODOLOV Marina Gerasimovna, how intellectually you've learned to talk. Horizon . . . What's a "horizon," come on, tell me?

MARINA Traipsing all over Russia for fifteen years with an educated employer, I got educated myself.

SUKHODOLOV Never mind that, what's a "horizon"?

MARINA Just what . . .

SUKHODOLOV You don't know; you're stalling. The horizon is a great thing. . . . And when it disappears . . . and it's pitch dark . . . then everything's rotten.

MARINA But you're in no mind to pay attention to the truth. Maybe you can tell me where your wife is.

SUKHODOLOV Leave me alone; go to bed.

MARINA Ah, you . . . Haven't you slept away your life; haven't you?

SUKHODOLOV I have—and you can't get it back.

MARINA And aren't you sorry?

SUKHODOLOV Ah, you . . . kind friend and comforter of my poor youth . . . That's poetry.

MARINA You're a kind man, you are. It's surprising, really.

SUKHODOLOV What's surprising?

MARINA That you're kind; obliging, so to speak.

SUKHODOLOV Come, sit down.

MARINA And all the same doesn't mind talking to an ignorant old woman, even if she doesn't understand about horizons. Go on.

SUKHODOLOV No, why do you think I'm obliging, so to speak? It matters a great deal to me.

MARINA Because for a long time you weren't.

SUKHODOLOV I wasn't what?

MARINA So . . . so . . . obliging.

SUKHODOLOV Obliging, obliging . . . As if I had been attacking people and biting them.

MARINA Attacking them or not, I don't know, but you were very unfriendly. That didn't bother me, you know, but it was terrible for an outsider.

SUKHODOLOV You're pretty smart, old woman. Where do you get it from?

MARINA [pretending surprise] What, how's that?

SUKHODOLOV Yes, really . . . smart and wise. Because, for example, from the time I was a young boy I learned to hate. . . . Remember the revolution, the Chapayev years.

MARINA I can't forget them; so?

SUKHODOLOV So, once that feeling is lost, that's the end. I wasn't a Party member yet, back then, only serving in the ranks. So I thought class hatred a sacred and noble feeling. But nowadays we really have no hostile classes. Who is there to hate? Scoundrels, the dregs of society, robbers . . . They deserve scorn, perhaps, but sometimes pity. I'm talking now about great, purifying hatred. Who am I supposed to hate in our country? Maybe it's time to learn to love. . . .

MARINA   Now wouldn't that be good . . . ?

SUKHODOLOV   [*reflectively*]   The things I used to love. [*Pause.*] I used to love to start work on a site, to live in a new place, to surprise people by the scale on which I did things, used to love fame. . . .

MARINA   Nobody's asking you to die, and here you've launched into a full confession.

SUKHODOLOV   No, don't interrupt, or I'll lose the train of thought.

MARINA   Well, don't say "used to love."

SUKHODOLOV   Sure, I admit, I still love fame, love the future, love my Party, love my son, love you, the people. . . . But, you know, I don't love the ordinary, everyday man-in-the-street. I'm mistrustful of him, I treat other men like strangers. What do you say to that?

MARINA   What do I say? What nonsense! All that's just talk. You've always worried about other people. But as for your character, well, you've softened.

SUKHODOLOV   Maybe something has started to stir. You're not the only one who has noticed it. But I'm talking about the problem in the broad sense . . . philosophically.

MARINA   That, too . . . that philosophical . . . that's nonsense. If you didn't like people, you'd never get the idea that you don't. You going to wait up for your wife?

SUKHODOLOV   What's the point? She's hale and hearty.

MARINA   In the old days, in my time, treating people like that was called a dog's life, but in your time, now, in this new life, it's called comradely. Good-night! [*Goes out.*]

SUKHODOLOV   You say frightening things, old woman. Up until now, I myself hadn't realized that I didn't love my wife, wanted her without even a shadow of feeling. . . . That old woman knows, and I don't. It's crazy. What in particular, though? Habit. But I—that's what's so crazy—I didn't know it was simply a habit. What misery! . . . It's too late to make discoveries like that, you can't correct things. Maybe it's all merely cold rationalizing. Maybe I simply have no feeling for Kseniya because of her hopeless middle-classness, her loud manners, her petty mind, the fact she seems to be a stone statue. . . . Somehow, a lot of things have piled up. And I should have seen it all twenty years ago. Too late now to see through things, old man. The light has fallen across your meager life—and now you've started looking inside. The light . . . It's strange. I've seen the person three times, and I'm in love. No, it's not love, but the need for love . . . a desire to love . . . a dream of some extraordinary girl whom you've never had and never will. Maiya herself may be a very ordinary and primitive girl. . . . What if she is! Let the dream stay a dream. Just so my wife doesn't get mixed up in it. Then there'd be music! No, Armando won't tell; he's a man of great ideals. So, that's settled. My wife will know nothing about it; indeed, there's nothing to be known; and from day to day I'll have only the vision. . . . It doesn't bother anyone; it will never cause anyone even a moment's sadness. . . .

[KSENIYA PETROVNA *appears in the door.*]

KSENIYA   Well . . . why don't you say something? Curse me, insult me. . . . Swear at me.

SUKHODOLOV   Why do that?

KSENIYA   To prove that I'm your beloved wife.

SUKHODOLOV   That's stupid.

KSENIYA   But on the other hand I have a clever husband who in his heart thinks I'm a petty middle-class woman and I don't know what else. . . . He won't try to understand his wife fully, the way others will, and to see that she's a progressive, modern woman. He thinks of her as his slave.

SUKHODOLOV   His what?

KSENIYA   I said his slave. . . . What, isn't that true? It's true a million times over!

SUKHODOLOV   Kseniya, what happened? My wife comes home after midnight and raises a row!

KSENIYA   Well, you tell me who I've been in your eyes all my married life! Not a word! Caught red-handed! And I doted the best years of my life to you, my whole self I doted to you.

SUKHODOLOV [*getting angry*]   Not doted; devoted.

KSENIYA   I don't stew around in books; I lead a regular family life. And I don't give a damn whether it's doted or devoted. For a long time now I've been waiting for you to show me some gratitude for all my years of suffering. . . .

SUKHODOLOV   What suffering? What are you talking about?

KSENIYA   Couldn't I have chosen a different, more vivid fate for myself? I certainly could. We're Shmyriovs, we're not just anybody! My grandfather, may he rest in peace, used to say, "You'll never find us salted and pickled." All my brothers, sisters, too, all have good places. Nikifor is a general, covered with medals. . . .

SUKHODOLOV   My dear, I see, you're overexcited.

KSENIYA   Now, that's the first thing you saw. . . . She treated her-

self to a minute of freedom, and right away you started making
something of it. But the fact she doted her whole self to you . . .

SUKHODOLOV   Excuse me, I must get some rest. This is a senseless
conversation.

KSENIYA   No, wait! It's not senseless at all. . . . You're not going to
get away from me now with your high-and-mighty manners. Tell
me, honey, what's the little doll you've latched on to here? Whose
is she? Cost a lot? Where does she sleep? What, I really got you?
You didn't expect questions like that?

SUKHODOLOV   [*gravely, threateningly*]   Who told you?

KSENIYA   The one man who knows all about it. What's the matter? . . . You look shaken. You didn't think that Yasha Armando
values my friendship more than yours.

SUKHODOLOV   The one man . . . Yes, sure, he's a man, too.

KSENIYA   I should say so! . . . To give you away like that, what a man
he is! Ah, you . . . Look at yourself; what kind of a man are you!
A scoundrel, that's what; a scoundrel.

SUKHODOLOV   Please . . . can you stop talking?

KSENIYA   A libertine.

SUKHODOLOV   Shut up!

KSENIYA   I've been shut up. Now I'm through. I'll talk all I like.

SUKHODOLOV   [*slowly*]   I can . . .

KSENIYA   What can you do? Nothing now. You can't do a thing. But
I can. Until you start begging me for forgiveness and escort that
bathing beauty of yours out of town, I won't give you a moment's
peace, my dear. What, fed up, Mitenka? We Shmyriovs are very
tough people . . . and don't you expect any other treatment from
me now. My day has come. At last, *my* turn.

SUKHODOLOV   [*in anger*]   Your turn?! All right, take advantage of it!
I'll forgive many things, but not this. [*Goes out.*]

KSENIYA   You? . . . Forgive? . . . Me? Stop! You've been caught;
confess; repent. You know jokes can be very dangerous. Come
here, I say, Dmitry; there'll be no peace in this house today!

[MARINA *enters.*]

MARINA   Why are you shouting?

KSENIYA   Go away. I want my husband.

MARINA   He left.

KSENIYA   Where did he go?

MARINA   Out.

KSENIYA   Out? What do you mean, out? Even though I was so up-

set! One more excuse for going to see his mistress. Tell me, does
he often spend the night out?

MARINA   You're making a fuss over nothing, Kseniya Petrovna.

KSENIYA   He bought you off, too?

MARINA   Child . . . really . . . now . . .

KSENIYA   No "really now" at all.

MARINA   I mean it seriously. Come, my lady, let's go to bed.

KSENIYA   Would you ever betray him? You never have. He's given
you lots of presents. But the boil has burst. . . . Just you wait, my
pets; I'll fix you. . . .

MARINA   [gaily]   What will you do?

KSENIYA   I'll find a way.

MARINA   But still?

KSENIYA   I'll fix it so that the both of you are as quiet and meek
as mice. And none of this "Marina Gerasimovna!" "Marina Gerasimovna!" Gave you the big title of "domestic manager." He
can't get on without you. Now we know why you're so important to him. Don't shake your head; you can't get out of it. Who's
been coming into my place, tell me! Won't tell me? Then tell the
court. . . . Wait; he really did leave? Really?

MARINA   Go see for yourself.

KSENIYA   Really went out and left me? [Tearfully.] You know,
Marina, I've had my fortune told many times by celebrated Moscow fortune-tellers, and many times they've predicted a hard
knock. Is it really beginning to come true? What bad luck! Who
needs me at my age! The children are grown up; I'm alone and
can't justify having an apartment in Moscow. Marina, you listening?

MARINA   I am, I am. . . . It's not the first time you've cried. And
it's always the same.

KSENIYA   But there wasn't anything then.

MARINA   And there isn't now.

KSENIYA   Tell me.

MARINA   I'll tell anybody you like.

KSENIYA   Could you swear to it?

MARINA   I could.

KSENIYA   You're blind.

MARINA   So I'm blind.

KSENIYA   Because it's true. . . . A man I trust told me everything.
It's terrible to think about what he told me! Oh, so frightening. . . .
It's not just some little affair. . . . You could forgive that. . . . This
is love with a capital L. But it won't come to anything; no; I
won't let it. I don't care if he pounds the wall, if he hates me like

a viper, I won't let him go; I won't give him a divorce. What's mine is mine, and there's no point in pretending to be noble. Against this disease you need plain, harsh medicines.

MARINA The woman is mad.

KSENIYA And what would you do if you were a forty-year-old wife?

MARINA But, look, you're being told reasonably and sensibly that there's nothing to it.

KSENIYA So what if there isn't!

MARINA Then what are you torturing yourself and others for?

KSENIYA I have to . . . I have to!

MARINA She's absolutely mad.

KSENIYA Even if, in fact, there's nothing, if it's only fantasies and day-dreams, it makes no difference; I have to. I hope they rub themselves raw, like with sandpaper. Let him learn to be afraid of day-dreaming. Nowadays in a solid Soviet family nobody is going to delight himself with day-dreams like that! I'll show him his Laura!

MARINA Even told you her name? The things they make up . . . Laura . . .

KSENIYA That's what the violinist calls her, in honor of something or other. But actually her name is Maiya. I'll show her, the little sweetie, I'll show her Maiya and Laura! These poets . . . I'll show you some poetry!

ACT II

SCENE 1   *In a tent at a construction site, afternoon. Sukhodolov is on the phone.*

SUKHODOLOV [*continuing*]   Thanks, Pavel Mikhailovich. I appreciate your thoughtfulness. I feel fine, first rate. I've got a long way to go before a heart attack. But you know what bit of scientific information I heard recently on the Moscow plane? If you take a normal, healthy monkey and treat it roughly, oppress and frustrate it in all sorts of ways, shout at it and so on, in two months it will have a heart attack. A monkey! Can you imagine! Interesting. I think so, too. Interesting. [*Pause.*] I live out at the construction site now. Oh, there are special reasons for it; no point going into them; but out here in this tent on this wooden platform I feel like a fish in water, I feel wonderful. . . . Old habit. Yes, in a tent. Thanks for thinking of me. My best to you. [*Hangs up.* DONONOV *enters.*] Comrade Dononov, hello; haven't seen you in a long time. I had even begun to miss you.

DONONOV You're joking, chief. . . . You joke a lot. But you keep avoiding me. You know I've told you many times that you and I ought to have a chat about your private affairs. . . . Well, it can't be helped—if Mohammed won't come to the mountain, then the mountain must come to Mohammed.

SUKHODOLOV Who is the mountain and who is Mohammed?

DONONOV You're the wise man; you ought to know.

SUKHODOLOV Why me? You called yourself a mountain. But don't forget: there are different kinds of mountains, sloping and low, steep and terrifying. . . . And just what is a mountain? A dead body.

DONONOV You're a master of wit . . . but it's not always apt.

SUKHODOLOV Don't be annoyed, Afanasy Kuzmich. . . . A bad habit. Want some tea?

DONONOV Tea in this heat?

SUKHODOLOV Think of it . . . The Kazakhs in Turksib taught it to me.

DONONOV You've really been everywhere! Well, so, shall we talk?

SUKHODOLOV Let me make a general resolution: personal affairs are to be discussed in off-hours, at night. Nights are by their nature meant for personal affairs. Again, another economy for the government! It would immediately reduce personal affairs by ninety percent! But—go ahead. No, wait a minute. As long as the line is working, I better call civil aviation. [*While talking to the operator.*] I want to get rid of the mosquitoes.

DONONOV I think that's impossible.

SUKHODOLOV I did something like it once before.

DONONOV You've really done everything!

SUKHODOLOV Twenty-five years of doing things. [*He is connected.*] Civil aviation? Hello. Sukhodolov speaking. Could you send a plane up here to get rid of the mosquitoes? We have a huge project here, involving millions. Send a plane. Thanks. Regards.

DONONOV How easily you decide about projects involving millions!

SUKHODOLOV You know what Mohammed did, don't you? Established Mohammedanism.

DONONOV   You're playing with words. Now, what are mosquitoes, after all? Who do they bother? We've become very soft.

SUKHODOLOV   With them around, you get one level of output; without them, an entirely different level.

DONONOV   You figured that out?

SUKHODOLOV   Everything is always calculated, Comrade Dononov! Even such an elusive thing as our relationship . . . how much it costs the government, down to the last kopek. You've heard about electronic machines? They compute everything.

DONONOV   What about our relationship? If we criticize each other, it's only to guard against unhealthy assimilation. Our relations are perfectly normal.

SUKHODOLOV   People have heart attacks from such normal relations. But let's go out to the other sections today. You've never once been in the Kedrovo mill. The boss there is no damned good. Have to get him moving. The Kedrovo mill has a great future.

DONONOV   I've heard about it; I know; yes, let's go. But, Sukhodolov, I came to see you about your personal problem.

SUKHODOLOV   Sorry; spill it.

DONONOV   What does that mean, "spill it"?

SUKHODOLOV   A verb, imperative mood. We have a lot of things to do, Afanasy Kuzmich; don't dawdle.

DONONOV   Things to do, things to do. A person mustn't become a thing-doer, either. Sometimes there's no harm in stopping and looking around to see what's happening to you. For example, for a long time now I've been wanting to ask you why you don't go home at night.

SUKHODOLOV   You've noticed?

DONONOV   How could I help it?

SUKHODOLOV   Well, what's the difference?

DONONOV [significantly]   You don't know?

SUKHODOLOV   No.

DONONOV   If I must, I'll explain. But what's your answer?

SUKHODOLOV   What's my answer? No answer.

DONONOV   I mean, answer my straightforward question.

SUKHODOLOV   I don't wish to.

DONONOV   What? What?!

SUKHODOLOV   That's right. I don't want to, and I won't.

DONONOV   You consider it beneath your dignity?

SUKHODOLOV   Beneath yours and mine.

DONONOV   What foolishness. Why?

SUKHODOLOV   It's not up to you, in your social and official posi-
tion, to ask such questions, nor do I have to answer them.
DONONOV   Now, you know, friend! . . . [*A pause, full of ill-will.*]
SUKHODOLOV   No, I don't know. Tell me so I will.
DONONOV   Other men—men whom you can't be compared to, way
above you—also were ruffled, but then they softened and answered.
SUKHODOLOV   So, I can't be compared to them.
DONONOV   That's just your trouble! Dmitry Alexeyevich, you're a
great man, and they're right to think so well of you in higher
circles, but you suffer from colossal conceit.
SUKHODOLOV   What the hell! What conceit!? I don't understand—
and I don't want to understand—why I have to give you an ac-
counting of where I sleep. Wherever I feel like it—that's where
I sleep.
DONONOV   Stop that; don't, don't try to get out of it. Your wife has
come. Everybody knows that.
SUKHODOLOV   She's here. . . . What's that got to do with you?
DONONOV   What's happened between you two? Be frank, Dmitry
Alexeyevich. It'll make things better.
SUKHODOLOV   My dear Afanasy Kuzmich, even if you were my
closest friend, I couldn't always be frank with you. But who are
you to me? An official colleague. . . . How can I include you in
what's most precious to me? I'm sorry, but it's humanly repug-
nant and senseless. Nobody can help me. Even the cave men
didn't interfere when couples squabbled.
DONONOV   But we're not cave men, but a modern, socially orga-
nized society. I want to help you. . . . I owe it to you; I'm called
on to! I can see you've gotten into a mess.
SUKHODOLOV   You see that, but I don't. I can give you an affidavit.
DONONOV   Stop it. . . . Everything has been obvious for some time.
SUKHODOLOV   What has?
DONONOV   Your ardor.
SUKHODOLOV   I don't understand.
DONONOV   Cut it out. What are you, illiterate? A lady after your
heart . . . a mistress. . . . Don't pretend. We're adults.
SUKHODOLOV [*agitated*]   So that's it, Dononov. . . . That's how it's
going to be between us. . . . I'm ready and willing to talk to you
on any subject, you can lecture me on construction, but I won't
take this. Let me tell you, on my honor and conscience as a com-
munist, that I'm doing nothing which would disgrace my Party.
So, I indignantly reject statements like "gotten into a mess."

DONONOV   How great and mighty you've become! Amazing.

SUKHODOLOV   And where did you pick up this priest-talk?

DONONOV   Your talk smacks of petty-bourgeois anarchism.

SUKHODOLOV   Learned your lessons at our expense! You really are
a biblical dogmatist, aren't you? What has anarchism got to do
with this? And if you came here to hold forth on where I sleep,
then forget we even had a conversation. They're calling me from
the launch—hear them? Some geologists are waiting on the other
side; they have to make a decision about the greatest dam in the
world. The greatest . . . [*Goes out.*]

DONONOV   Stupid man. A child. You would think that, as an old
communist, he would understand that I'm trying to protect him
from serious trouble. You idiot, why provoke unhealthy curiosity
about your private life? I can't stop the gossip. It has sunk in;
it's spreading. . . . Word came round to me, too—anonymously, to
be sure. Of course, we know all about these slanderers who defame
honest people by anonymous letters; but here's confirmation for
you: Sukhodolov refuses to carry out his conjugal responsibilities.
Very well. Fine. That means there's something to it. . . . He had
a fight with his wife. But why? He could have a fight merely because of his own quick temper. He often follows his heart, not
his head. Who objects to that? We can't take away a man's right
to be quick-tempered. But Party members keep asking me: why
doesn't the director live at home? Undoubtedly, there's a pinch
of philistine inquisitiveness in that, too. We all like to peek through
the crack into the neighbors' apartment. There's that about it, of
course there is. Have to check these leftover, bourgeois habits. . . .
But on the other hand, try to meet a man halfway or give him his
head. . . . Sukhodolov himself, with his looks, would become dis-
sipated in a moment. Silly man! Thinks he can get free of all this
by noble indignation. You don't get out of things like this by being noble.

[KSENIYA PETROVNA *enters.*]

KSENIYA   I'm not mistaken, am I? Comrade Dononov? I'm Sukho-
dolova . . . his wife.

DONONOV   Pleased to meet you, though it's unexpected. Sit down.

KSENIYA   We must become acquainted. [*Handshake. She repeats
her name.*]

DONONOV   Very pleased indeed. You came to see me?

KSENIYA [*very cautiously*]   And why do you think that?

DONONOV [*also cautiously*]   I could be wrong.

KSENIYA   No, no, you're not. But I have the impression you were waiting for me.

DONONOV   Yes and no . . .

KSENIYA   Yet you immediately guessed that I came to see you.

DONONOV   There was a reason.

KSENIYA   What? You must realize how important it is to me.

DONONOV   Just now your husband and I exchanged views about what everybody can't help noticing.

KSENIYA   Yes . . . can't help . . .

DONONOV   And where there's smoke . . .

KSENIYA   Yes, yes . . . yes, indeed.

DONONOV   But if the tumor isn't malignant, then, as the doctors say, it must resolve.

KSENIYA   You think so?

DONONOV   Why draw hasty conclusions?

KSENIYA   But immediate steps?

DONONOV   Steps are steps, but conclusions are conclusions.

KSENIYA   But sometimes you can stumble.

DONONOV   And if you do? It's something that can be corrected.

KSENIYA   Depends where you fall. . . . If it's on a steep slope, head over heels—what then?

DONONOV   Well, then . . . It's clear what will happen.

KSENIYA   Do you understand what I'm talking about?

DONONOV   I think so.

KSENIYA   Should I file charges against my husband?

DONONOV   I refuse to give advice—or even a hint of advice.

KSENIYA   Why?

DONONOV   How can you ask? You're rather naïve. Let there be a complaint, let there . . . but without any prompting.

KSENIYA   It's terrible.

DONONOV   Have things gone so far?

KSENIYA   No, I mean it's terrible trying to get all this straight.

DONONOV   Then let's clarify matters first.

KSENIYA   Let's. Alone, I'm out of my mind.

DONONOV   What are you afraid of, basically?

KSENIYA   Stumbling, as I said before.

DONONOV   But suppose, for example, there's nothing to it, and you've raised a tempest in a teapot?

KSENIYA   Exactly.

DONONOV   I must tell you, though, that there have been warning signals.

KSENIYA   You don't mean it! That's awful. So, there were, after all.

DONONOV   Initial ones.

KSENIYA   Everything is clear to me. He has a second family here.

DONONOV   Don't be too hasty. And let's calmly ask ourselves what we're after. I'm for . . . I'm fighting for Sukhodolov's integrity and authority. His authority is the authority of our leading circles.

KSENIYA   That means filing a complaint?

DONONOV   Wait a minute. . . . When a man has gotten into a mess once and for all, it's too late to fight for him.

KSENIYA   You think he hasn't yet?

DONONOV   Honestly speaking, I don't know.

KSENIYA   But the signals?

DONONOV   Anonymous.

KSENIYA   Really! Anonymous! That means that even strangers . . . or maybe people we both know . . . That means everybody knows, and I, wretched me, was the last to find out. But let nobody take advantage of that! [*Pulls out an envelope.*] Here's my complaint.

DONONOV   Now, dear Kseniya Petrovna, this whole delicate story takes on quite a different aspect. From the realm of speculation it passes into the realm of discussion and evaluation. Sukhodolov must now explain himself. In short, I would like to tell you, there's no pulling back now.

KSENIYA   I'm not planning to.

DONONOV   Well, you know, it happens . . . a woman's heart . . . old attachments . . .

KSENIYA   You don't know the Shmyriovs.

DONONOV   Who are they?

KSENIYA   We . . . I . . . We never sentimentalize. We never behave like that! My grandfather used to say . . . We never sentimentalize.

[SUKHODOLOV *appears in the doorway.*]

SUKHODOLOV   Dononov, are we going or not?

DONONOV   On our way, on our way. I'm ready.

KSENIYA   Dmitry, what are you doing? . . . Don't you want to see me? Here's a third party; I beg your forgiveness, as he is my witness. Forgive me.

SUKHODOLOV   You and I have both known for a long time that we don't love each other. But that is not a conversation for third parties . . . even if you've already gotten hold of everything you want. Go on with your business; I'm leaving.

DONONOV   Why am I a third party? I don't understand. You and I are communists, Sukhodolov; don't forget that.

SUKHODOLOV I'm ready and willing to give my life for a Party
comrade, though in personal terms that comrade may be an outsider and mean nothing to me.

DONONOV Now, stop such subtle distinctions. . . . You think you're
the only one who can talk dialectics; nobody else. The best of all
dialectics is for you two to make up. How long can a man talk of
love? Love is decisive at a certain age, but after that love not
only decides nothing but even interferes.

SUKHODOLOV [after a pause] The trouble, Dononov, isn't that you're
saying stupid things—though you're not a stupid man by nature;
the trouble is that you're delighted to be saying them. [Goes out.]

KSENIYA Now he's let the cat out of the bag, all right. Thinks he's
so smart! No, Afanasy Kuzmich, I won't take that complaint back.

DONONOV You, and you alone, are mistress of your actions. I didn't
prompt you at all. That must be made specific. Good-bye, Kseniya
Petrovna; we'll have many occasions to meet again. [Goes out.]

KSENIYA Doesn't want to see. . . . Doesn't have eyes but stones.
. . . What's the point in thinking about it now? Now I have to
think only about his crawling back to his family on hands and
knees. And he will.

SCENE 2 *Pavel Mikhailovich's office in the Regional Committee. Pavel Mikhailovich and Sukhodolov.*

PAVEL [after a painful silence; slowly] So . . . you won't say a
word! Don't want to. Don't like it?

SUKHODOLOV More than that.

PAVEL Do you think I like it?

SUKHODOLOV I don't know.

PAVEL [almost shouting] Well, listen! Day and night that Afanasy
Kuzmich of yours keeps coming to see me, curse his hide. Your
man; you can't get out of it; you were the one who brought him
in. He says in the presence of all the members of the Regional
Committee that objectively speaking it seems that I'm covering
up the improper behavior of Comrade Sukhodolov. You think I
like that? Do you think I like trying to straighten out your family
squabbles—reading and listening to your wife's disgusting charges?
You pull some of the stupidest, little-boy pranks, don't go home,
have an affair in town, set rumors flying, drive me wild, the whole
thing is your fault, you have a scandal raging, and still you don't

want to talk to me about it! Look at it soberly for a minute: aren't you crazy to do what you're doing?

SUKHODOLOV   I've thought about it.

PAVEL   You've thought badly then.

SUKHODOLOV   Pavel Mikhailovich, old friend, understand me . . . if my whole being protests, shudders all over . . . No, I can't talk to anybody about it.

PAVEL   Amazing! Makes no sense!

SUKHODOLOV   In a man's life there are things which are higher and more complicated than our ordinary concepts.

PAVEL   What is? What's more complicated?

SUKHODOLOV   Nothing.

PAVEL   We do something foolish, ruin our lives, then the complications start. Listen, friend, for the last time let me urge you to sit down and write out an explanation.

SUKHODOLOV   I won't write anything.

PAVEL   Well, look out. . . . But don't cry later.

SUKHODOLOV   A great Russian writer once said that even a father couldn't talk about his relations with a woman to his son—never mind you and me—and even if those relations were the purest. Why can't we follow the laws established by the highest morality?

PAVEL   Who said that?

SUKHODOLOV   Dostoevsky.

PAVEL   Avoid such relationships; don't touch a woman. Why won't you understand?! Because your refusal to explain yourself is going to be interpreted as disrespect, as a challenge, as something unthinkable, unheard of. It will be thrown back at you with a new, grave accusation. Who are you actually refusing to talk to? To the Party!

SUKHODOLOV   But you . . . you're a man with a good heart, intelligent. Understand, again, that there are things which you can't tell the Party. If it were something political, why then you could have my head. . . . But what's political about it?! I pledge my heart and soul to the Party; I'd lay down my life for it. . . . But still a man can have a private side to his life, a side which he'll let no one else into. He simply doesn't have to, and there's no law which says he does.

PAVEL   Maybe . . . there are unexpected things, subtle and delicate matters. . . . But what does it look like on the surface? On the surface it's an ugly business . . . twenty years of married life. . . . I'm sorry; I won't try to force you any more, but silence is a poor kind of defense.

SUKHODOLOV   It's not a question of defending myself, but of fighting . . . really fighting for it. . . .

PAVEL   Now that's something I'm ready to see!

SUKHODOLOV   But if it comes to fighting you, what then?

PAVEL   Fight.

SUKHODOLOV   I'm afraid I'm the one who will get the bruises.

PAVEL   And I thought you a brave man.

SUKHODOLOV   Well, that means I'm not.

PAVEL   I don't believe it.

SUKHODOLOV   As you like.

PAVEL   There was a chance to separate you and Dononov at different construction sites, but that's out now. We'll see how this business ends. Let me repeat, it's a painful business.

SUKHODOLOV   Are you pulling out of it?

PAVEL   I'd like to, but I can't. So, don't be offended, my friend, if ultimately I have to vote for harsh measures.

SUKHODOLOV   What am I in the Party? A miniscule, millionth particle. A tiny molecule. Can a huge, fiery substance be faulted for offending one tiny molecule?

PAVEL   Sukhodolov, stop it. The parallel is no good at all.

SUKHODOLOV   Vote for harsh measures. Offend me, insult me even— I won't complain.

PAVEL   You're that proud?

SUKHODOLOV   I am. In this instance, especially. [*Goes out.*]

PAVEL   The closer I look at that man, the more I like him. He has something of Kirov's spirit about him, something everlasting. And he's not easy. But what does it mean to call a man "easy"? God knows what the hell it does. Maybe things aren't easy for him? Maybe he himself can't make sense of what's happening to him? And we're making him responsible and getting ready to punish him. . . . I hate compassion, all those fine feelings, but how easily punishment suggests itself. Yet in every human error, drama, even crime, to what extent is some important thing hidden, something that punishment knows nothing about. Out of habit people rush to punishment first thing. And habit gives rise to trite ideas and laziness, as far as others are concerned. No, I'll find out about this business myself. No point in riding a man, tormenting him. I'll have to call Clara Mulina in. [*Dials a phone number.*] Clara Mulina? Recognized me? Well, good. Come in to my office. Letters? . . . Oh, what you told me about. . . . Bring them, too. [*Hangs up.*] Oh, the tragedy! Leo Tolstoy was right about tragedy when he said that there have always been and always will be

these tragedies despite any and all human earthquakes and revo-
lutionary upheavals. Am I really going to have to read his letters?
I'll have to. Others will read them and even make copies. I'll
have to.

[CLARA *enters.*]

CLARA   Hello, Pavel Mikhailovich. Well, here I am.

PAVEL   So you are. [*Pause.*] So, Sukhodolov comes calling on that
girl you were telling me about?

CLARA   At the concert you wouldn't even listen to me.

PAVEL   I heard you, all right, but I didn't take the letters. Now
those letters may be necessary.

CLARA   You see . . . That means there was some point in my making an effort.

PAVEL   Circumstances in the case have changed, but my view of
it won't change under any circumstances. However, since you
know everything about Sukhodolov from one point of view so
well, tell us: does he visit the girl he has been writing to, or not?

CLARA   No, he doesn't.

PAVEL   You're certain?

CLARA   I am.

PAVEL   Very, very strange . . . What you tell me has enormous,
decisive importance in the matter because, through anonymous
reports, formal complaints, and idle gossip, he has been accused
of gravely immoral behavior.

CLARA   I've kept my eyes open. They don't see each other. I
wanted to make sure whether my Maiya was lying to me or telling the truth. It turns out that she's been telling the truth.

PAVEL   She's a friend of yours?

CLARA   Yes, we're very fond of each other.

PAVEL   And she tells you everything about Sukhodolov?

CLARA   Well, you see, Pavel Mikhailovich, the thing is, she never
mentions him by name but talks about some man very precious
to her and very noble, and I understand clearly that this is Comrade Sukhodolov.

PAVEL   So, she loves him. . . . What do you think, Clara?

CLARA   She's very sensitive. . . . But I think so, yes.

PAVEL   What a strange relationship you have, though. . . . What's
her name?

CLARA   Maiya. She's from Leningrad. And I— Please excuse me,
but why did you cut me off so sharply at the concert? I have
nothing but the best intentions as far as the girl is concerned.

She's a promising young researcher, and suddenly Leningrad University will get a file very damaging to her.

PAVEL   Now, listen, Clara, what has he been writing to this Maiya?

CLARA   I have copies with me. Here, please, read them.

PAVEL   You made photostats?

CLARA   Well, yes . . . What about it? They're essential.

PAVEL   Oh, Sukhodolov, Sukhodolov . . . Well, let's have them! [*A long pause. Then he begins reading aloud.*] ". . . Sometimes, especially out on the river, I hear you as a song, but when I begin to listen closely, the song vanishes, and there's nothing. You see, my darling, how late in life and how uselessly what people call the poetry of life has come to me. And still, without bitterness or regretful sighs, I lightly ridicule myself. Then, when I've plunged into my work on the site, you again shout 'Hallo!' to me in a snatch of melody, and because of it I often feel a tenderness and ecstasy inside. That's why, in my last letter, I called you my song." [*To* CLARA.] You've read this?

CLARA   Of course!

PAVEL   And you find it abnormal?

CLARA   You don't?

PAVEL   I'll tell you in a minute. I'd like to know what you find in it.

CLARA   It is abnormal! Sukhodolov himself says that it's too late and useless. . . . Says and shows. Where are his Party scruples? What kind of example can he be to our young people? It's old, rotten stuff and nothing else.

PAVEL   You didn't happen to be in Moscow last summer, did you?

CLARA   I was.

PAVEL   Then maybe you saw the exhibit of pictures from the Dresden Gallery?

CLARA   I did, I did. . . .

PAVEL   And naturally you saw Raphael's "Sistine Madonna" there?

CLARA   The "Sistine Madonna"? Of course. A fabulous thing.

PAVEL   You didn't find it abnormal?

CLARA   I don't understand. What do you mean?

PAVEL   Showing the Virgin Mary with the infant Christ in her arms. . . . You didn't find this picture propaganda for religious hallucinations?

CLARA   What queer comparisons . . . I'm not such a . . . It's great art, poetry, and so forth.

PAVEL   So . . . You do understand. Excellent. But then Sukhodolov mustn't have even the least dealings with poetry? We, communists—and on top of it rather along in years and in positions of authority besides—we must be deprived of all poetry, of spiritual excitement, of song? You, a young woman busy disseminating culture and knowledge among us, saw in that little holiday of a man's spirit only papers for making a communist live up to his responsibilities! I say this to you with great sadness. But you may not agree with me. You also have the right of doing with these letters whatever seems necessary to you. . . .

CLARA I don't understand. Here you're reproaching me, but you can't give me any directives.

PAVEL No, I can't. It's not something you can give orders about. Here we are, two Party members, but in this case our views are different. We're working out a new communist morality, and it's a long-drawn-out, harrowing, even tragic business.

CLARA Haven't we worked it out already? This is the first I've heard about that. I thought everything about all this was clear.

PAVEL I don't know about you, but it isn't for me.

CLARA A person can't help being confused. . . . What am I supposed to do? How should I behave?

PAVEL Alas, I can't give instructions on that. May I ask your friend to come in?

CLARA As soon as you like.

PAVEL Good. Right now. Good-bye.

CLARA And the result? Honestly, I really don't know what I ought to think now.

PAVEL Thinking is one thing, but living off other people's thoughts is another. Try to think for yourself. You see, our Party's program allows great scope for independent thinking . . . and how much Lenin offers. . . .

CLARA No, you may think so, but I disagree. That causes complete confusion. To think individually on each issue, individually to come to a decision—you would go mad, first of all. You can't live without guide lines.

PAVEL You need guide lines for emotions, too?

CLARA Why not? Of course. Emotions, too, belong within definite frames. Pavel Mikhailovich, I bow to your authority, but you confuse me. After this conversation, I'm afraid I really will go out of my mind. I've never been so upset in my whole life. [*Goes out.*]

PAVEL How sad . . . Very sad! [*Calls his secretary.*] The violinist hasn't come?

SECRETARY [*a man*] He's here. He's waiting.

PAVEL   Send him in.

[ARMANDO *enters.*]

ARMANDO   Excuse my red and swollen face. I'm sick. Health and good fortune to you. May I sit down?

PAVEL   You've been visiting our district quite some time.

ARMANDO   I've been caught in some unpleasant business, I'm losing my best friend, and so I asked to see you.

PAVEL   What can I do for you?

ARMANDO   Nothing for me. I have only one request, concerning a certain Sukhodolov. If possible, help him. I beg you to believe that he has done nothing disgraceful and, in my opinion, never can. You must think my calling on you and my request strange, but in this damned business I'm suffering more than anyone. The thing is, Mitya told me everything, and I betrayed him.

PAVEL   How? To whom?

ARMANDO   His wife.

PAVEL   [*bursting out*]   Ah, you . . .

ARMANDO   It's so shameful . . . petty. I talked too much . . . actually slandered him, because in the eyes of a woman like Kseniya Petrovna it's infidelity and a liaison, but in the eyes of any thinking man it's a natural outburst of feeling. Now I sit in my hotel, I keep drinking, and I don't know how it will end.

PAVEL   Perhaps you need help to leave?

ARMANDO   Not financially, though. I have something . . . I wanted to get free of the moral burden. I made up my mind to tell you everything.

PAVEL   It's good you did.

ARMANDO   I could write. . . .

PAVEL   No need. They'll take my word.

ARMANDO   May I go with my mind at rest?

PAVEL   When all is said and done, nobody is going to punish him.

ARMANDO   But you see, I know how hard it is for him, if they're going to keep hounding him . . . and he's touchy, and proud.

PAVEL   A good lesson. His friend did wrong . . . was no friend.

ARMANDO   Oh, don't make it worse. I'm a man of art, I must be far above base reflexes . . . but I slandered for the sake of base aims. It was the fault of something outside us.

PAVEL   Why "outside us"? Everything is inside us.

ARMANDO   Oh no, no . . . Good-bye. I'll leave now with a clearer conscience. [*Goes out.*]

[*The* SECRETARY *enters.*]

SECRETARY Maiya has come to see you.

PAVEL What Maiya? Oh, she, yes . . . Ask her in. [SECRETARY *goes out.*] What will I talk to her about? What a business! [MAIYA *enters.*] Please be seated.

MAIYA Thank you.

PAVEL How do you do.

MAIYA In my nervousness I forgot. . . . How do you do, Pavel Mikhailovich.

PAVEL Nervousness? Why are you nervous?

MAIYA My humble job here . . . and suddenly I'm called in by the director. . . .

PAVEL The director . . . so . . . No, put your notepad away; I have no intention of giving you any instructions.

MAIYA No intention? How can that be? Oh, excuse me. Very well.

PAVEL You're from Leningrad?

MAIYA Yes.

PAVEL We're from the same place. I graduated from Leningrad University. Now . . . I'm not clear exactly what it is you do here.

MAIYA It's not clear to me, either.

PAVEL You have a special assignment?

MAIYA I'm supposed to do a scientific description of the typical Soviet reader.

PAVEL I suppose that's terribly interesting.

MAIYA No, it's terribly boring. Though perhaps that's because I don't like my work.

PAVEL So? You speak your mind.

MAIYA What can I do? I don't like philology. I could lie: "I'm ecstatic about the Soviet reader." But I don't know what he looks like. Nobody does. There are as many typical faces as there are readers. I can't possibly comb their hair and present them all neatly. They won't let me.

PAVEL [*laughing*] Won't let you! What impudent rascals! Someone has come here on an assignment to comb their hair and present them neatly, and they won't let her! Seriously speaking, though, what do you like?

MAIYA Dancing.

PAVEL Well, we-ll, so!

MAIYA [*frightened*] Don't be angry, I really mean I love dancing.

PAVEL That's getting even!

MAIYA Why?

PAVEL   My young daughter hops around day and night.

MAIYA   Don't stop her. They stopped me and made me miserable.

PAVEL   Still, dancing isn't work.

MAIYA   Nature herself taught man to express himself first of all in dance. Even before he could speak, man learned to dance. I could go on forever about it. You don't like dancing?

PAVEL   A strange question for you to put to a Party worker.

MAIYA   But you like working for the Party?

PAVEL   I do; can you imagine that?

MAIYA   Why are you annoyed? I'm asking seriously.

PAVEL   And I'm answering seriously. Noble Kirov taught me to love working for the Party and sent me as an instructor to the district committee on Vasily Island. . . . Incidentally I went somewhat reluctantly.

MAIYA   But working for the Party isn't a profession.

PAVEL   It was for Lenin.

MAIYA   Forgive me, I suppose that was awful, what I said. Lenin . . . Do you remember him? Did you see him?

PAVEL   No.

MAIYA   Were you fond of Sergei Mironovich?

PAVEL   If you only knew how he loved us . . . loved people.

MAIYA   I've come here. . . . And it's amazing. . . . Talking so easily. It's strange, but I'm not at all afraid of you.

PAVEL   Why should you be?

MAIYA   But there should be . . . some . . . uneasiness. . . .

PAVEL   Yet you feel none?

MAIYA   Not a bit. Still, you've surprised me so!

PAVEL   Not by saying that I love working for the Party?

MAIYA   Not by what you said, but because you really love it.

PAVEL   Oho! And how did you find that out?

MAIYA   Your eyes say so. Some times when a person talks to you about the Party, his eyes show no Party spirit.

PAVEL   [lightly]   Do eyes show absence of Party spirit?

MAIYA   Sometimes.

PAVEL   What does that look like?

MAIYA   Droopy.

PAVEL   Eh-eh, that's not so. What if a Party worker is droopy by nature . . . or if, say, he has liver trouble . . . what are you supposed to do: beat him until he cheers up?

MAIYA   Lack of Party spirit is complete indifference to everything in the world except your own self. And you can always see it in a person's eyes.

PAVEL   That's probably true. When are you leaving for Leningrad?
MAIYA   Soon, I suppose.
PAVEL   I'll send my daughter to see you.
MAIYA   How old is she?
PAVEL   Fifteen.
MAIYA   We'll get along fine.
PAVEL   Yes, obviously. [*Holds out his hand.*]
MAIYA   Good-bye. You're just as you were described to me.
PAVEL   By whom? If it isn't a secret?
MAIYA   By my friend Clara. A wonderful girl . . . though some of
the things she does are peculiar. [*Goes out.*]
PAVEL   Strange girl. Very forthright, but not simple-minded, not
naïve. She's cleverer than you think . . . leaves a vivid, clean
impression. A pure person must be forthright, clean, intelligent. I
understand Sukhodolov: ". . . like a song." That shows he still
has his youthful, pure spirit. How could I have given in to those
two wild women! "Crime, vice." There you have holdovers. And
what holdovers! Dononov, too . . . What about Dononov? . . .
Petty bourgeois. [*Takes a thick file of papers from the table.*] A
personal . . . affair . . . an affair prohibiting song. Into the archives.
The archives.

SCENE 3   *A room in an old hotel. Afternoon. Rainy. Armando and the waiter.*

ARMANDO   Shura, I beg you, one last decanter.
WAITER   And I beg you—don't ring; it won't help.
ARMANDO   You took the letter to Comrade Sukhodolov yourself.
Sukhodolov will pay.
WAITER   Who? Him? Never. And don't wait for him. He won't
come. He didn't want to touch the letter.
ARMANDO   But he asked how I felt.
WAITER   Nothing of the sort. Said three words: "Is he drinking?"
I said: "Yes." That's enough; I'm not giving you any more.
ARMANDO   You will! [*Gets his violin, opens the case.*] If nothing
else works, we'll distill this. Here, take this.
WAITER   Oh, no point.
ARMANDO   Something different!

WAITER This is giving in completely. Shameful, to my way of thinking.

ARMANDO None of your business. Shut up.

WAITER You ought to be thinking about how to get out of here.

ARMANDO Please, my friend! . . . Sasha . . . Sukhodolov will pay.

WAITER He won't come.

ARMANDO You don't know what a generous man he is.

WAITER He wouldn't even take the letter.

ARMANDO But I have faith in him. He'll come for sure . . . because his heart is a violin. He'll come. See? Go look. It's him. [SUKHODOLOV *enters. The* WAITER *starts out.*] Shura! . . .

WAITER As you like. [*Goes out.*]

ARMANDO Mitya, you've come to kill me?

SUKHODOLOV What's there to kill? Everything was killed long ago.

ARMANDO [*submissively*] Not everything . . . Don't say everything.

SUKHODOLOV [*ironically, reproving him*] The creative intellectual!

ARMANDO Mitya! Don't beat me to death.

SUKHODOLOV Are you drinking?

ARMANDO I'm finishing up.

SUKHODOLOV Why did you call me?

ARMANDO I went to the Regional Committee.

SUKHODOLOV What for?!

ARMANDO I told them everything.

SUKHODOLOV Did I ask you to?! What the hell was that for?

ARMANDO There's something in me . . . Oh, god, god, I don't know myself how I started it all. . . .

SUKHODOLOV One can guess. I've never liked so-called strong language, but now, when it's a question of . . . You really hit me below the belt! You . . . How I admired men like you! High priest of art! Intelligent man. Somebody wiggled a finger at you. . . . You sell yourself cheap.

ARMANDO But Kseniya Petrovna . . . she got hold of me.

SUKHODOLOV That shows you give in easily.

ARMANDO Are you convinced that I ruined you deliberately?

SUKHODOLOV I think a worm . . . even an earthworm . . . has a reason for crawling. And you can recite Petrarch by heart.

ARMANDO Pavel Mikhailovich himself gave me the impression that it's not so terrible.

SUKHODOLOV And you went crawling to him to rescue a friend. Idiot! What terrifies me is what I feel in my heart, which I ought to seal up with seven seals and never open to anyone. And you

think I'm afraid of the consequences. I'm not afraid of anything.
What grief you caused me! What grief!

ARMANDO I know. [WAITER *enters with a tray. A long silence while*
ARMANDO *drinks.*] And how did you want it to come out? Without any suffering?! [*To the* WAITER.] Alexander, tell our boss here
how much suffering [*points to the decanter*] *she* causes me. . . .
And what is she? Vodka! [*The* WAITER *goes out.*] The most repulsive
thing in the world, and the most natural for the man who wants
it. But you want to do without grief. You wanted some idyll? I
behaved foully toward you—but you, a serious man, really don't
you understand that your being carried away had two meanings
in a thousand different ways? It meant as much happiness as the
bitterest unhappiness. Is it hard for you now, Mitya? Well and
good. I'm not sorry for you. You know why not? Not so long ago
you were terribly scornful of emotional subtleties of this sort, but
now when it has turned out that they're within reach of reinforced-
concrete comrades, too, you're again sure that your experiences
are worth nothing. So, now learn this, my dear Dmitry Alexeyevich, that the world has not merely huge construction sites but
also huge emotions. . . . Huge, and terribly dear.

SUKHODOLOV What were you after? Don't forget, I know what you
think. Only you people can have those huge emotions; we can't.

ARMANDO Who is "you people"? Who's "we"?

SUKHODOLOV I was thinking that the artist, the poet . . . He knows.
What's the difference between you and Kseniya Petrovna? She
can be forgiven—she's a wife. But you . . . I haven't words! . . .

ARMANDO If you came to bail me out, don't. You can leave me.

SUKHODOLOV What, you were waiting for me to start drinking
vodka with you? [*Rings.*]

ARMANDO There was no Laura, Dmitry Alexeyevich. Petrarch made
her up. You understand? A symbol, a vast, pure symbol.

SUKHODOLOV I don't need you to tell me.

ARMANDO No, you wouldn't know if I hadn't told you.

SUKHODOLOV Much obliged.

ARMANDO So, what will you do? You'll marry your Laura. Same
old story, goddamn it. Go get married. I wish you luck. I don't
like thinking that everything will have to turn out as it did the
first time. In the beginning, under the veil of youth, we don't
notice the clichéd mind and the terrible middle-class pettiness
. . . and then suddenly, as if you were hit on the head by unexpected news, you shudder, "People, good people, what have I
done!" This Laura has turned out to be no different than the part-

ner I so ecstatically ran away from. I don't want to think about it, let me tell you, but you keep that in mind! Go ahead, get married. I wish you luck!

SUKHODOLOV Stop it. . . . Please, I beg you.

ARMANDO No more about that; something else now. . . . A sweet remembrance of myself. Armando could have become a great musician, but *she* came. [*Points to the vodka.*] And she came on the heels of my Laura. Maybe your choice is nobler and worthier. I don't know her.

[*The* WAITER *enters.*]

SUKHODOLOV Does the musician owe a lot? [*Takes out money, puts it on the table.*] Is that enough? [*The* WAITER *nods affirmatively.*] Buy him a ticket on the first through train and send him off. He's sick. [*Goes out.*]

WAITER Well, what a man! So solid, you know! But you've displeased him. Displeased him terribly.

ARMANDO Clear out. . . . [*The* WAITER *goes out.* ARMANDO, *tears in his eyes, picks up his violin.*] You're safe . . . you're with me. . . . O my muse! O my muse!

ACT III

SCENE 1   *In Sukhodolov's tent at the construction site, afternoon. Pavel Mikhailovich and Dononov.*

PAVEL [*on the phone*] Don't be delayed, Dmitry Alexeyevich, hurry up. . . . There's great news. [*Hangs up.*]

DONONOV News, news . . . and the heat here is still unimaginable. In general, the work has moved ahead only with difficulty. But please . . . tell me: who is being fired? Don't keep me guessing.

PAVEL Nobody.

DONONOV You're joking! Somebody has to be fired; they have to have a scapegoat.

PAVEL You, of course, were not set to be the scapegoat. Huh? Somebody else . . . Sukhodolov, myself . . .

DONONOV You? Why you?

PAVEL   So then, Sukhodolov. There it is, the secret longing!

DONONOV   Excuse me, Pavel Mikhailovich, I said nothing.

PAVEL   The clue is in what you didn't say. That's all you've been living for. How could you miss such a wonderful chance of taking a peck at a man!

DONONOV   Pavel Mikhailovich, I didn't.

PAVEL   The wife's complaint—who blew that up?

DONONOV   I'm sorry—I had to.

PAVEL   You had to understand what was happening and not spread a dirty story.

DONONOV   Pavel Mikhailovich, please . . . I didn't.

PAVEL   Stop right there, Afanasy Kuzmich.

DONONOV   Maybe I overdid it a little . . . but out of personal conviction, seeing as my wife and I live together. . . .

PAVEL   That's enough of your petty middle-class virtues!

DONONOV   You mean a sturdy family is petty middle-class? Interesting. We'll go far with opinions like that.

PAVEL   It's not the family that's petty middle-class, understand me, my dear comrade; it's your family virtues magnified into a social cult. That's what's petty middle-class. That way we condemn the women for adultery, for illegitimate children.

DONONOV   Well, as far as that's concerned, I read his letters to his mistress with my own eyes. . . . The things he wrote her! Shocking! About a song, and other things like that! And his wife sitting at home. I think that if a man is a double-dealer in private life, he's capable of deceiving the Party.

PAVEL   Of betraying it . . . of making himself an enemy of the people.

DONONOV   I don't say that.

PAVEL   Yes, you do.

DONONOV   Well, all right . . . There's a logic of action. . . . One thing follows inevitably from another.

PAVEL   That's it, that's it. . . . According to that logic of yours, the world consists of two antagonistic colors, black and white. All the rest is simply double-dealing, betrayal, and what have you. You can't understand or even imagine any other position?

DONONOV   I try to. . . . Nothing comes of it.

PAVEL   But there is a third . . . and a fifth, and a tenth. . . . There's a whole mass of positions which, to put it bluntly, refute our old petrified dogmas. According to dogma, Sukhodolov is a dishonorable man, but according to real life, he's fully reliable, holy. . . .

DONONOV   Don't joke. "Holy"!

PAVEL   What did he do?

DONONOV   Read the letters! You didn't read them.

PAVEL   Yes, I did . . . I did. And I assure you that, for him, the girl
is something holy and precious. And you're trying to have him
grilled, picked to pieces, practically tossed out of the Party! Wake
up!

DONONOV   I don't know . . . I'm used to thinking about things in
certain ways.

PAVEL   On account of those certain ways, men often used to be
sent to prison. But now it's beyond anyone to figure out who's
sent for a reason and who for none.

DONONOV   You came back from Moscow rather bitter. No good news
in that. Tell me frankly, who is being fired? Me?

PAVEL   I will tell you: Sukhodolov is staying on in his old job, and
you've been made head of construction at Kedrovo Mill.

DONONOV   And who is the Party organizer? A new man?

PAVEL   Yes, more or less . . . Me.

DONONOV   Well, that *is* news! Hard to make sense of right away.
What's so special about Sukhodolov? . . . Why, who would have
thought . . . I'm the scapegoat, and he's not touched. This hand
mine? It is. But where am I? I have no idea.

PAVEL   You reason penetratingly, Afanasy Kuzmich.

DONONOV   I reason in an everyday way, without blind staggers.
Without denying Sukhodolov his positive qualities, I say, nevertheless, that we've seen men like him before. Was he beaten? He
was. Did he happen to be hanging by a hair? He was. You see,
I looked into this personal affair of his very carefully . . . amazing
how he came through unscathed!

PAVEL   May I say something? Without the staggers, too?

DONONOV   Please; go ahead.

PAVEL   For you the strangest thing of all is that he was unscathed.
How well I understand you! You don't like Sukhodolov.

DONONOV   What does that make me? A misanthrope, perhaps; is
that what you think?

PAVEL   You grew up in a certain direction . . . all one-sided.

DONONOV   What do you mean?

PAVEL   Your mistrust of people, intolerance, anthropophobia. It's
all narrow-minded and one-sided.

DONONOV   Well, of course, my upbringing . . . was the school of
hard knocks. What sort of school did you have, Pavel Mikhailovich?

PAVEL   Communist . . . Lenin's school, like most of the people of
my generation.

DONONOV You worked with Kirov, you were lucky. . . . Ah, my
friend, you think I don't understand anything! . . . Leninist norms,
principles . . . How can that be alien to any real communist?
But it takes time.

PAVEL I know. You're still a young man; you have a great positive
quality: devotion to the Party. That's not what bothers me.

DONONOV Then what . . . Tell me.

PAVEL I'm afraid you'll feel offended.

DONONOV Oh, come. . . . We're talking seriously.

PAVEL You are a petty, middle-class man, Dononov. That's what's
so terrible.

DONONOV Forgive my laughing. It's ridiculous! Nonsense, Pavel
Mikhailovich! Not in the least insulting! That's what Sukhodolov
put into your head. Don't believe it. His head is forever full of
fantasies, turbulence. . . . In fact, I'm a cautious man, have a
definite sense of moderation. I like order. You're smiling skep-
tically. But, forgive me, I wouldn't be so stupid as to send letters
to some cheap little slut . . . especially when there was nothing
between them anyway. For shame! I'll say it a hundred times:
For shame!

PAVEL What is most terrible, Afanasy Kuzmich, is that you have
no idea of how to ennoble life. Probably you often say that life
is beautiful. But what does "beautiful" mean? As I understand it,
the most beautiful thing in life is man . . . and not every man. . . .
He can be disgusting and even unfit to live with others . . . but
when I meet a man, a contemporary Soviet man in our country,
endowed with great spiritual beauty, I feel even more delighted
to be alive. For a man, free from capitalism, new, purposeful,
and endowed with spiritual beauty, is for me a sort of perfection,
a delight. In him I see the future of the world, communism. But
communism isn't in stones; it's in people.

[SUKHODOLOV *enters.*]

SUKHODOLOV Glad to see you, Pavel Mikhailovich. I don't think
we've met today, Dononov; hello.

DONONOV You don't even remember whether we've met or not.

SUKHODOLOV But, you know, you spend more time with my wife.

DONONOV Can't be helped, since you don't.

SUKHODOLOV Maybe you're thinking of getting married. . . . I don't
recommend it . . . even for you.

DONONOV I live with one wife already . . . my own.

SUKHODOLOV What do you know about that! My wife also thinks of me as her property. . . . What are you? Both from the same village?

DONONOV   You brag about your proletarian origin.

SUKHODOLOV   I do. I didn't drink cabbage soup with a bast shoe.

PAVEL [*shouting*]   That will do! You should be ashamed! Adult men . . . [*After a brief silence.*] I'm empowered to inform you of a decision affecting you both. I wish to bring to your attention, Dmitry Alexeyevich, that you adopted an incorrect line as far as Party leadership was concerned. . . .

SUKHODOLOV   Me?

PAVEL   You! But it has been decided to consolidate the leadership by having a Central Committee Party Organizer. Comrade Dononov has been appointed chief of construction at Kedrovo Mill.

DONONOV   Rejoice and be glad!

SUKHODOLOV   And who's the Central Committee's Party Organizer? He hasn't been appointed yet?

PAVEL   No, he has been. It's me.

SUKHODOLOV [*to* DONONOV]   Aren't you glad?

DONONOV   When will we officially fill out the papers?

PAVEL   No time to lose; today if possible.

DONONOV   Right. Now, Comrade Sukhodolov, your private business will involve me least of all. You can sleep soundly. [*Goes out.*]

SUKHODOLOV   What a depressing man!

PAVEL   His trouble is that he himself can't understand what is genuine in him and what is ephemeral. In the nature of things, he has got to. What do you think: will he do all right in his new position?

SUKHODOLOV   It's been a long time since I felt such elation. You see . . . Understand me . . . Here on the table, in front of you, lie our scientists' projects. . . . They involve great risk but are a terrible temptation. . . . One would like to give the people the present of an unexpected saving of millions. . . . Real millions . . . But Dononov's and my relations became such that it was impossible to talk about serious problems. And, you know, he's an able, sensible executive and will show his real worth at Kedrovo.

PAVEL   Come to my place this evening.

SUKHODOLOV   I can't today. Tomorrow?

PAVEL   You're busy . . . doing what? No, it's none of my business.

SUKHODOLOV   Is my case closed?

PAVEL   We discussed it in the Regional Committee and decided to close it. Majority vote.

SUKHODOLOV   Dononov didn't withdraw his charges?

PAVEL No, and he never will. You can be sure of that. But your opponents have, in fact, rehabilitated you.

SUKHODOLOV Opponents . . . They're opponents of everything that doesn't fit into their bird-brained understanding. They cost me blood.

PAVEL A new world is only born in pain and struggle. I reiterate that simple truth to emphasize that it's being born. These petty middle-class people have to be fought. Why, they even want to see communism turned into a middle-class paradise. Comfort, satiety, and empty-mindedness.

SUKHODOLOV Now that we're not on official terms, when you . . . I mean, now, but not then, when you shouted at me . . . I'll admit to you something you'll never enter in any report. I really love a girl who is twenty-five years younger than I am.

PAVEL Since we're being frank, tell me honestly, how do you explain it? What has happened to you, Dmitry Alexeyevich?

SUKHODOLOV I don't know. Indeed, is it really love, in the accepted sense, seriously speaking? Or something else . . . perhaps just a dream.

PAVEL A dream . . . Clear enough. It's beautiful, noble. . . . But a dream of what?

SUKHODOLOV What do you mean, of what? Not of anything.

PAVEL That doesn't happen. A dream is the highest reaching of the soul for something missing. For what?

SUKHODOLOV I don't know. I'd like to grasp it, make it concrete, but I can't.

PAVEL A need for true love, if you've never known it?

SUKHODOLOV Probably . . . yes. Most likely.

PAVEL Perhaps because all your life you never had the deep affection of a woman's friendship.

SUKHODOLOV Yes, yes, I missed that very much.

PAVEL Some men are incurable romantics. Are you one?

SUKHODOLOV There's that sin, too.

PAVEL Or sometimes, you know, we've had something in childhood that was very precious but never became real, vanished without a trace, and then came back again in some other person.

SUKHODOLOV Vanished without a trace and came back . . . Also true.

PAVEL Well, so?

SUKHODOLOV Everything together, perhaps?

PAVEL Well, then your love is enormous.

SUKHODOLOV You and I have strange conversations in the office, don't you think?

PAVEL Look out the window. . . . The endless human torrent. Don't you think that all of them experience something similar? They do, one way or another, endlessly. No, Sukhodolov, what you and I are talking about right now is a very serious matter but one which you'll never talk out. The only thing I see is that it's very difficult for you.

SUKHODOLOV Your hand, Pavel Mikhailovich. I thank you. It's all difficult and enormous, and one little scratch can end everything. All I have to do is think that the girl can start thinking of somebody else and my whole magic world becomes a sordid anecdote. So, you must see why I don't strive for closeness, why it's only a dream.

PAVEL Mitya, do you know her personally, know her ways?

SUKHODOLOV No, I don't. And I don't want to. . . . Suddenly she'll turn out to be entirely different.

PAVEL I understand. But admit that age has something to do with it, too.

SUKHODOLOV It does.

PAVEL And since we're being so frank . . . Aren't you going to see her? Why?

SUKHODOLOV To say good-bye. She's leaving.

PAVEL You're a strong man. I wasn't wrong. It must be very difficult; tell me truthfully.

SUKHODOLOV It's impossible to express.

PAVEL But you're going . . .

SUKHODOLOV I am.

SCENE 2 *A room in the old wooden house where Maiya lives. Sunshine. Late afternoon. Maiya. Clara.*

MAIYA No, don't go. I wanted to tell you something, but I forget what.

CLARA You haven't forgotten. You don't want to tell me. You know how to keep secrets in your heart.

MAIYA A heart isn't a courtyard.

CLARA And you know how to think. Wonderful thoughts. They should be written down.

MAIYA Trivial ideas; no point in setting them down.

CLARA   I've always shared things with everybody, and now inside
there's a kind of awful emptiness.

MAIYA   You're developing self-criticism. Not long ago you were
terribly pleased with yourself. You've always expressed a passionate
desire to meet my admirer. Now be happy. He'll soon be here.

CLARA [*dumbfounded*]   Who'll be here? Who's coming?

MAIYA   What are you afraid of? He's an essentially lyrical admirer.
Anyway, all admirers are lyrical. What's the matter with you?

CLARA   I just can't control myself.

MAIYA   Clara, darling, have you really never seen a single, live
admirer?

CLARA   It's not that. . . . What's his name?

MAIYA [*cheerfully*]   Yura . . . Mitya . . . Seriozha . . . Ivan Ivanovich!

CLARA   How many have you?

MAIYA   A million!

CLARA   You're mad! How can you say such things?

MAIYA   Oh, Clara, what a literalist you are! Haven't you any sense
for symbols? I can imagine that million as being sweet, dear to
me, scattered all over the planet . . . and each could be my admirer, go through life with me, sing my songs.

CLARA   What are you saying! How can you say such things! It's
a nightmare.

MAIYA   You're my little middle-class girl. All middle-class people
are pious and well-meaning, neither fish nor fowl.

CLARA   You've said that a hundred times.

MAIYA   He'll be here in a minute. I can tell you everything he'll
do.

CLARA   But who is he?

MAIYA   One of the million. Somebody gray. In a minute he'll appear, shake my hand terribly correctly and certainly ask, "How
do you feel?" Then he'll ask permission to sit down, permission
to light a cigarette, permission to stay here a little while. I think
he lives in the world on somebody's permission, and once that
permission ends he'll die on the spot in fear. A fascinating person. Get ready to meet him. Here he is.

[TERNOVNIKOV *enters.*]

TERNOVNIKOV   May I come in? It's me, Ternovnikov.

CLARA [*in an outburst*]   But I expected . . .

MAIYA   What?

TERNOVNIKOV   Forgive me, Maiya Sergeyevna, you have visitors. I
can come another time.

MAIYA   This is my friend . . . incidentally, my only girlfriend. . . .
Say hello.
TERNOVNIKOV   [*shaking* CLARA's *hand*]   Ternovnikov. [*To* MAIYA.]
How do you feel?
MAIYA   Same as always.
TERNOVNIKOV   Haven't suffered any?
MAIYA   Illnesses? No, I haven't.
TERNOVNIKOV   May I sit down?
MAIYA   Please do.
TERNOVNIKOV   Thank you. May I smoke?
MAIYA   Do, please.
TERNOVNIKOV   There were deafening explosions on the construction
site. Did you hear them?
MAIYA   I did . . . yes . . . What about them?
TERNOVNIKOV   Well . . . I wasn't thinking of anything in particu-
lar. Oh . . . nothing.
MAIYA   An atmospheric oscillation . . . is a noise.
TERNOVNIKOV   I won't deny that, a noise . . . but very loud.
MAIYA   Have you never heard a louder noise?
TERNOVNIKOV   Noises, in my opinion, are harmful. . . . The nervous
system . . .
MAIYA   But some noises even kill . . . bombs.
TERNOVNIKOV   That hasn't fallen within my sphere. Have you ex-
perienced them?
MAIYA   I have. As a child.
CLARA   Where do you work, comrade, if I may ask?
TERNOVNIKOV   [*refractorily*]   What importance can that possibly
have? Work is work, but a man is a man. If you don't like me,
pay no attention. After all, nobody here does like me.
MAIYA   Comrade Ternovnikov, what's wrong? You've never before
brought up such bitter problems.
TERNOVNIKOV   But I have today. Insofar as I am an object of your
disregard, I bring them up. Everything is in the open! . . . And
my thoughts have become clear on this subject, so don't feel
offended. Important people interest you, Maiya Sergeyevna, people of national prominence. That's why I experienced your indifference to me for so long a time. An oppressive fact; let us
leave it there. I don't censure you, because I understand fully.
I not only resign myself to it, but I welcome it, the right choice.
I shall remain deaf and dumb to everything hereafter. May I stay
here, please, a bit longer?
MAIYA   No. You pretended to be downtrodden and inoffensive.

TERNOVNIKOV   But did you notice how Ternovnikov would come to you, having wiped his tears dry ahead of time? You didn't. For whom, do you think, did he sob so long? For himself or for the other?

MAIYA   Oh, stop!

TERNOVNIKOV   Why? The material at hand speaks for itself. But I repeat: let's leave it there. In your place I would have done exactly the same. There is no point in losing control. National prominence is superior to anything local.

MAIYA   Good-bye, Ternovnikov, I'm going home. We'll never meet again.

TERNOVNIKOV   You're joking!? But what about him? . . . Is he staying here?

MAIYA   We'll never meet again.

TERNOVNIKOV   Well, that makes the situation different . . . and perhaps . . .

MAIYA   Good-bye.

TERNOVNIKOV   But you won't give me your hand?

MAIYA   I will. You're not to blame at all.

TERNOVNIKOV   You're an incomprehensible girl. For that, indeed, I loved you. As we part forever, with the greatest anguish, let me tell you that I loved you as best I could. [*Goes out.*]

MAIYA   Finally I've remembered what I wanted to talk to you about. Two letters are missing from the papers in my suitcase.

CLARA   Are those letters valuable to you?

MAIYA   Very.

CLARA   Really?

MAIYA   Infinitely.

CLARA   But you won't share your secret with me?

MAIYA   Impossible.

CLARA   Tell me why!

MAIYA   Nobody sees how flowers bloom, how an ear of wheat grows, how a storm comes up.

CLARA   But if it isn't flowers? If it's toadstools?

MAIYA   I'm beginning to think that you've been keeping track.

CLARA   Here are your letters. . . . Look.

MAIYA   Where did they come from?

CLARA   You shouldn't scatter them around.

MAIYA   Did you read them? I beg you, don't tell a soul . . . even after I've gone. Maybe this is the first and the last in my life. . . .

CLARA   Are you really living with him?

MAIYA   How you . . . How unhappy you are!

[KSENIYA PETROVNA *and* DONONOV *appear in the door.*]

KSENIYA   Tell me, girls, which of you is having relations with my husband?

DONONOV   Kseniya Petrovna, I wouldn't like to . . . would much dislike . . . I'll be there, out in the yard. . . . Excuse me. [*Goes out.*]

KSENIYA   I repeat, girls, which of you is having relations with my husband?

CLARA   Who are you? What do you want?

KSENIYA   I want to talk to whichever of you is having relations with my husband Dmitry Alexeyevich Sukhodolov.

CLARA   What kind of relations?

KSENIYA   What kind! The obvious kind. A wife isn't deceived for nothing. . . . She's deceived for somebody else.

CLARA   What can we do, Maiya? Speak up.

MAIYA   I've had no relations of any sort.

KSENIYA   [*coming over to* MAIYA] Pleased to meet you . . . just to get a close look. Exactly as I imagined you. He's not indifferent to that type, the cute, pure type. What's this about no relations, huh? After all, you're ready to sink through the ground in front of me. When there's nothing between a woman and a man, she has the trump cards. But you played around with somebody else's husband, and now you feel terrible looking at his lawful wife. Don't be scared; I won't start pulling your braids. I'll handle you in a civilized way. Still, let's hear what you have to say.

MAIYA   I've had no relations of any sort.

KSENIYA   [*from the table, picks up a letter which she had noticed some moments previously*] What's this? Whose hand? [*Reads.*] "My song"! Heavens above! He calls her a song! What nonsense! He couldn't have thought it up sober, so that means he was drunk when he wrote. That's to be expected. Wherever there are sluts there's too much drinking.

CLARA   You, madam, may stop using such expressions.

KSENIYA   I'm sorry; I'll stop; I was carried away. So, my dear, you're called Maiya. Now, we'll consider ourselves personally acquainted. I'm not going to berate you, because you're an intelligent girl. It will be painful for you. But you must understand, as an intelligent girl, how painful it is for me to prove my rights to you. It would be best for us both to end this business peacefully and in a civilized way. If you don't want to be sent away in disgrace and have disgraceful references follow you, get your things together and clear out in twenty-four hours.

CLARA   You have no right. People used to be sent away, but now
such lawlessness isn't permitted.

KSENIYA   And who are you?

CLARA   Someone . . . Her friend.

KSENIYA   Oh, her friend . . . You aren't by any chance the friend
who snitched Sukhodolov's letters from her friend—from her—and
took them around town?

MAIYA   Clara! That's what I suspected!

KSENIYA   Why did you take other people's letters? And disgrace
Sukhodolov?

CLARA   I was motivated by high principles. I thought . . .

KSENIYA   Fighting to keep your husband isn't a high principle? She
thought . . . [To CLARA.] Keep quiet!

MAIYA   There was no reason for you to fight to keep your husband.
I don't think he ever planned to leave you.

KSENIYA   Are you trying to make yourself look like some holy innocent? Or to appear cute and pure? "Won't leave you." He
left me long ago.

MAIYA   I don't know if that's so; I never heard it. But the letters
. . . well . . . Does he really have no right to exchange letters?
Why don't you ask him what he's to blame for? Please, don't come
to see me again. I'll leave when I find it necessary. And in fact
. . . You ought to leave right now, please. I'll do something I
shouldn't, something awful, if you don't! Both of you . . . Both of
you . . .

[A MAILMAN *appears in the door.*]

MAILMAN   Maiya Sergeyevna, a letter for you.

KSENIYA   Local?

MAILMAN   Yes, local.

MAIYA [*taking the letter*]   Thank you.

MAILMAN   You're leaving us, Maiya Sergeyevna?

MAIYA   Tonight, on the express.

MAILMAN   Good luck to you. Maybe you'll come back and see us
[*Goes out.*]

KSENIYA   Read it, my dear. I won't leave until I've found out what
he's written you.

MAIYA   Yes, of course, I'll read it. [*Reads in silence.*] You want to
know?! Here you are! [*Throws the letter at her.*] And get out!

CLARA [*scared*]   Maiya!

MAIYA   Get out, both of you.

CLARA   Mayechka, forgive me.

MAIYA   Both of you . . . Both of you . . .

[MAIYA *goes out. Then* CLARA *after her.* KSENIYA PETROVNA *reads the letter for some time.*]

KSENIYA   So, she's really leaving. . . . A typical farewell letter. But is it really true? Did he really not have relations with her? That's something new! [*Almost shouting.*] What have I done, damned fool that I am!

[DONONOV *runs in.*]

DONONOV   What's the matter, dear Kseniya Petrovna?

KSENIYA   Read this! [*Tosses the letter to him.*]

DONONOV   This is amazing. I know Sukhodolov's handwriting from official resolutions.

KSENIYA   Read it!

DONONOV   I am, I am. . . . Not very interesting . . . "I give you my blessing on your pure, upright path through life. . . ." Gives her his blessing. . . . Right thing to do, of course. Means to love her . . . have a family. . . . Kseniya Petrovna, I don't understand any of this.

KSENIYA   Oh, my dear, what is there to understand? Sukhodolov is asking her to come to their first and last encounter. It's down there in black and white. He wants to see her for one last time before she leaves. That means that there was nothing between them! You understand that? It was something else . . . something more terrifying.

DONONOV   How so, Kseniya Petrovna? If there was nothing, all right. . . . As the young people say, we'll hush it up.

KSENIYA   It's easy enough to say that! But it was we ourselves who drove him into someone else's arms. . . .

DONONOV   What do you mean, we? Maybe some lines should be drawn?

KSENIYA   We drove him, we hounded him. . . . We, we, we! Now if you ask why we hounded him, there's nothing to say. To tell the truth, I, a plain and simple woman, got carried away by the way things were going at home. But you finished a school of political science; Sukhodolov was afraid of you. . . .

DONONOV   Easy . . . easy . . . Hounded him . . . Really! Let's put that in writing.

KSENIYA   "Put that in writing"! When all's said and done, I'm left alone. You know I followed you as a man of ideas.

DONONOV   My dear, not so much noise. Besides, it's far from clear

who followed whom. You followed me, and I, you. Don't cry;
he'll come back. We'll use our influence on him.

KSENIYA Thanks a lot for your influence! "He'll come back." . . .
He never will. Yes, I'm crying. . . . Should be sobbing, not crying. Roam the wide world . . . After all, he wasn't some old
foot-soldier, some old bum . . . but a great man.

SCENE 3   FINALE   *A vacant river bank called "Old Wharf."
A small, old ferry; masts of sailboats. Evening lights. Maiya
and a ferryman.*

FERRYMAN You out for a walk, girl, or you waiting for somebody,
somebody special?

MAIYA Waiting, officer, I'm waiting. Why do you ask?

FERRYMAN Our "Old Wharf" is a lonely place. I see you're alone.
It's clear you're lonely. I thought maybe you had to get over to
the other side. I'm no watchman. I'm the ferryman.

MAIYA Thanks, but I don't need anything.

FERRYMAN Well, I won't bother you. I'll light my pipe and clear
out of sight. Did the same thing in my day. It's hot nowadays
in summer. Feel how it blows in from the taiga? Something's
burning.

MAIYA No, I don't.

FERRYMAN I guess I'm the only one who smells it. . . . You do your
waiting, have a good time. . . . Some young fella you waiting for?
Shh, not a word!

MAIYA No, not a young fellow, but somebody else's husband.

FERRYMAN That happens, too. Understandable . . . if it's a real
love affair, of course. That him waving there? Look at him, how
he's hurrying.

MAIYA That's him, that's him.

FERRYMAN Him?! I know that fella. Well, that happens, too. Understandable. [*Goes out.*]

[SUKHODOLOV *appears.*]

SUKHODOLOV I ran as boys do. Felt ridiculous. But it couldn't be
helped. I started out to a rendezvous and then immediately had
to turn back. Had to send a plane out into the taiga. . . . There's
a forest fire somewhere. Hello, my dear friend, don't be cross with
me.

MAIYA I'm not, no, but turning back is a bad sign. Don't you believe that?

SUKHODOLOV Foolishness. I've been in a wonderful frame of mind
all day, and no sorts of signs can undo it.

MAIYA Why are you so cheerful?

SUKHODOLOV Because I've been waiting to see you, and now I do.

MAIYA Why see each other, though, Dmitry Alexeyevich?

SUKHODOLOV No reason.

MAIYA Like the first time . . . I'll remember it the rest of my life.
But it's impossible! Some place inside there has to be a wish of
some kind, some kind of goal. . . . I don't know what, but something.

SUKHODOLOV Oh, my darling, of course there is! The overwhelming
desire of seeing your eyes, of hearing your voice, of touching your
shoulder . . . and a thousand other things which make my heart
beat faster. But to put it simply . . . simply, I wanted to say good-
bye to you forever.

MAIYA Dmitry Alexeyevich, are you supposed not to see me?

SUKHODOLOV I don't understand the question. What are you talking
about?

MAIYA You've had some real difficulties . . . your wife . . . and
things in general. I heard about it.

SUKHODOLOV It's hard for any woman—my wife included—to understand everything that happens to me. No, Maiya, no difficulties
would keep me back, but the thing is that I myself couldn't long,
or rather, haven't longed for us to see each other. I don't want
anything.

MAIYA Yes, I know. . . . Just a song.

SUKHODOLOV Just a song . . . A sonnet . . . I wrote you.

MAIYA A Petrarchan sonnet . . . Dmitry Alexeyevich, you're amazing. You lifted me above the clouds, but I'm an ordinary girl, and
I have admirers. I mean to get married.

SUKHODOLOV All that shouldn't affect me.

MAIYA But your letters! . . . It's very complicated, extraordinary.

SUKHODOLOV No, my dear, it's all very simple. Listen. I ennobled
you, spiritualized you, and that pleases me, warms me inside, very
closely, and it will stay with me to the end of my life. No? Understand me. For if it were something else, something completely
ordinary, your first admirer would kill all my love. I'd start being
jealous; there would be reproaches, quarrels, and nothing would
be left of my Maiya. Oh, well I know the dubious happiness of
aging Romeos and young women.

MAIYA Don't make me protest. . . . You're not aging.

SUKHODOLOV Well, never mind, but Maiya . . . Don't be hurt; I don't in the least mean that you're a giddy girl. But we've started on a dangerous conversation. It's easy for us to hurt each other. Understand me in the sense that in my harsh, difficult life, you, Maiya, are my snowdrop.

MAIYA Being with you is terrifying. A person could go mad.

SUKHODOLOV My darling . . .

MAIYA Dmitry Alexeyevich, you mustn't.

SUKHODOLOV That, too, will pass, like a unique moment of enormous happiness.

MAIYA You've hypnotized us both by your letters. In the beginning you invented me, and then you believed in your invention.

SUKHODOLOV I love you.

MAIYA You mustn't, Dmitry Alexeyevich. I'm plain and earthbound.

SUKHODOLOV I love you.

MAIYA Your snowdrop will fade on first touch, and nothing will be left of Maiya.

SUKHODOLOV Oh, my dear, if you didn't fade, how sad it would be that it's all so late! What an old story, damn it all! I can't tell you often enough that I'd hang myself in grief if my Maiya only looked *that way* at someone else. . . . You're right, I mustn't. So vanish, my priceless sorceress! It's ridiculous, I suppose, if you look at it objectively.

MAIYA You're amazing. A person can make you a friend in spirit forever.

SUKHODOLOV What do I want? That's precisely what I long for— that we love each other as friends. I want to make an agreement with you that we write each other, not lose sight of each other, see each other from time to time.

MAIYA I'll have a husband, and he'll be angry at me if we do.

SUKHODOLOV You tell him it's only poetry.

MAIYA He won't believe it.

SUKHODOLOV You think so. . . . Sometime, when all this has healed over, I'll tell you how I was tormented by this poetry. . . . There's our plane in the sky. If he doesn't drop a message, I'm free for the whole evening. I know the ferryman here; let's get a boat.

MAIYA Even the taiga has to get in the way! But, anyway, it's for the best.

SUKHODOLOV [*looking up in the sky*] Come, boy, don't keep us in suspense!

MAIYA There'll be a message dropped. You want there to be.

SUKHODOLOV   What do I want? A fire? You can't imagine how dangerous a forest fire is for us.

MAIYA   There'll be a message. Your plane is circling.

SUKHODOLOV   What a nuisance!

MAIYA   There it is! Get it. . . .

SUKHODOLOV   Why are you delighted?

MAIYA   Am I? You think I am? I think I am, too.

SUKHODOLOV   So, now we have to say good-bye forever. . . . Who knows, maybe we'll never see each other again.

MAIYA   Now I'll tell you the whole truth! Only, for a few minutes forget about the message drop, the taiga, everything in the world. . . . Can you?

SUKHODOLOV   Probably . . . yes. Tell me.

MAIYA   In that "probably, yes," you, Dmitry Alexeyevich, just as you are, show yourself to be an endlessly purposeful man. I say that seriously and not merely out of affection for you. I'm purposeful, too. And I can tell you that I'd do everything for you which a person can do who is in love, who is filled with admiration. . . . No, don't correct me. I'm saying exactly what I mean, what's been lingering inside me. Because you wrote me, my darling, and asked for no reply. You sort of forgot about me completely. . . .

SUKHODOLOV   I? . . . How could I?

MAIYA   I mean, you remembered, but remembered me as a name, as a picture, an image, and forgot that that image also has feelings, has a heart full of real blood. . . . Darling, don't be hurt. This has been stored up and is now boiling over. Now I can say that you never dreamed of the height on which you exist in my imagination. What you've just said to me makes you even better, makes saying good-bye to you even more unbearable. It's terrible! Terrible that I'm not afraid of ruining my sunshine, but that you are. You're afraid of everyday life with me, yet I look on that life with you as a holiday. But I'm a young girl. . . . I was too brazen . . . and I lost all sense of proportion. I love you to distraction. But, my darling, exactly why you're so dear to me is that, for you, I'm only poetry, a snowdrop. . . . Now, good-bye . . . with tears. . . . And don't forget, I . . . if you call me, I'll drop everything and fly to you. [*Goes out.*]

SUKHODOLOV   Gone . . . Even the stars fall. It's hot. So, they'll say, he got involved, and they'll remember a humdrum affair. No, when thoughts and feelings get mixed up and you yourself don't know which is which, when your heart protests against what your

mind tells you . . . Oh, what am I muttering? Have to bring her
back. Call her right away. Maiya! Come back, Maiya!

[*The* FERRYMAN *appears.*]

FERRYMAN   She . . . that Maiya flew past me like a partridge, gave
a shout. You won't catch her. I couldn't even get out "good
evening." The taiga is on fire. You smell it, chief?

SUKHODOLOV   How could I not? I know it.

FERRYMAN   Hard thing for people to say good-bye for good.

SUKHODOLOV   You have a sense of that?

FERRYMAN   It's understandable. And that's what I wanted to tell
you. . . . Don't mind me talking peasant-plainly like this;° I'm
an old man. . . . No reason to hurry and part forever. You think:
I've busted my heartstring for sure; but no, it's there to stay. Too
early for you to be looking backward. You look ahead.

SUKHODOLOV   Too early, Siberian? You, too, say that! Go after her,
bring her back? Why don't you answer? Give me your advice.
I'm listening.

FERRYMAN   As you like . . . I'm saying, you've got more ahead of
you than behind. But you're in a rush. . . . And she flew off who
knows where with a shout. . . . Don't hurry. But I don't advise
turning around now. Let's cross over. Whatever you like, though.

SUKHODOLOV   You, too, believe in signs!

FERRYMAN   No, no. Look at the glow. The taiga is burning across
the whole sky.

SUKHODOLOV   Truly, Siberian, I follow you. You've said some wonderful things. It's wonderful when what's ahead is more than
what's behind. [*Shouts.*] Hey, over there, listen! Get everyone together on the dock! The taiga is on fire!

CURTAIN

°He apologizes for using the familiar form, *ty*, "as peasants do."

THE NAKED KING

THE NAKED
KING

BY EVGENY SHVARTS

CHARACTERS

Heinrich
Christian
The Princess
The King, *her father*
The King
Ministers
Ladies of the Court
Gendarmes
Ladies-in-Waiting
Soldiers
The Public

ACT I

A meadow filled with flowers. In the background, the royal castle. Pigs wander through the meadow. The swineherd Heinrich is telling a story. His friend, Christian, a weaver, lies on the grass, lost in reverie.

HEINRICH   So I'm carrying the suckling pig across the King's court-yard. It had had the King's brand put on it—a snout with a crown on top of it. The little pig is bellowing—something terrible! And suddenly a voice from up above says: "Stop torturing the animal, you so-and-so!" I was just about to curse back—because, you see, I didn't like the pig's bellowing, either—when I take a look up and lo! there's the Princess. So pretty, so sweet, my heart gave a leap. And I made up my mind to marry her.

CHRISTIAN   This is the thousandth time you've told me that in the last month.

HEINRICH   So white, you see! And so I says: "Princess! Come down to the meadow and see the swine grazing." And she says: "I'm afraid of swine." And I says to her: "Swine are gentle." And she says: "No, they grunt." And I says to her: "That won't hurt anybody." You asleep?

CHRISTIAN *[sleepily]*   As'eep.

HEINRICH *[turning to the pigs]*   And so, you dear little pigs of mine, I started going along this road right here every evening. The Princess was blossoming in the window there like a little flower, and I was standing like a post down in the courtyard, pressing my hands to my heart. And I keep telling her over and over: "Come on down to the grassy meadow." And she says to me: "What's there that I haven't seen?" And I says to her: "The flowers there are very beautiful." And she says: "We have them, too." And I says to her: "There are different colored little stones there." And she says to me: "Just think, how interesting." So I keep trying to talk her into it until I get chased away. But nothing will convince her! Finally, I thought of something. "Listen," I says, "I have a pot with little bells, which sings in a lovely voice, plays

141

the fiddle and the waldhorn and the reed-pipe, and, besides that
it tells you what anybody is fixing for dinner." "Bring it up here,"
she says, "bring up that pot." "No," I says, "the King will take
it away from me." "Well, all right," she says, "I'll come down to
your meadow next Wednesday at the stroke of midday." I dashed
off to Christian. He's got hands that can do anything, and we
made this pot with little bells. . . . Hey, pigs, little pigs, you've
gone to sleep, too! Sure, you're fed up. . . . It's all I've been talking about for days and days. . . . Can't be helped—I'm in love.
Oh, she's coming! [*Pushes the swine.*] Get up, Duchess; get up
Countess; get up, Baroness. Christian! Christian! Wake up!

CHRISTIAN   Huh? What?

HEINRICH   She's coming! Over there! So white, down the path
[HEINRICH *sticks his finger out to the right.*]

CHRISTIAN   What are you talking about? What's there? Hah, right—
she's coming! And not alone, with her whole train. . . . Stop you
trembling. . . . How are you going to marry her if you're so scared
of her?

HEINRICH   I'm not trembling from fear but from love.

CHRISTIAN   Heinrich, pull yourself together! Is it the thing to do
to tremble from love and just about fall on the ground?! You're
not a girl!

HEINRICH   The Princess is coming.

CHRISTIAN   Well, since she is, that means she likes you. Remember
how many girls you've loved—and always successfully. Maybe
she is a princess, but she's a girl, too.

HEINRICH   The main thing is she's so white. Let me have a swallow
from the flask. And so pretty. And so nice. You go up across the
courtyard and she's blossoming there in the window like a little
flower. . . . And I'm like a post down in the yard, pressing my
hands to my heart. . . .

CHRISTIAN   Be quiet! The main thing is to be firm. Now that you've
made up your mind to get married, don't fall back. Ah, I can't
count on you. You were a cunning, bold young fellow, but now . . .

HEINRICH   Don't scold me, she's coming over. . . .

CHRISTIAN   And with her whole train!

HEINRICH   I don't see anybody but her! Oh my sweet little darling!

[*The* PRINCESS *and the* LADIES OF THE COURT *enter. The* PRINCESS
goes up to the SWINEHERD. *The* LADIES OF THE COURT *stand up to
the side.*]

PRINCESS   Hello, swineherd.

HEINRICH   Hello, Princess.

PRINCESS   Looking down at you from the window, I thought you were shorter.

HEINRICH   But I'm taller.

PRINCESS   And your voice is gentler. You were always shouting up at me from the yard very loudly.

HEINRICH   But I don't shout here.

PRINCESS   The whole palace knows that I came here to hear your pot, you shouted so! Hello, swineherd! [*Holds her hand out to him.*]

HEINRICH   Hello, Princess. [*Takes the* PRINCESS *by the hand.*]

CHRISTIAN   [*whispers*]   Bolder, bolder, Heinrich!

HEINRICH   Princess! You scare me, you're so sweet and nice!

PRINCESS   Why?

HEINRICH   So white, so nice and kind, so gentle. [*The* PRINCESS *shrieks.*] What's the matter?

PRINCESS   That pig there is looking at us maliciously.

HEINRICH   Which? Oh, that one! Go away, Baroness, or I'll cut your throat tomorrow.

THIRD COURT LADY   Ah! [*Faints.*]

[*All the* LADIES OF THE COURT *surround her.*]

INDIGNANT EXCLAMATIONS
    The boor!
    You're not allowed to cut a baroness's throat!
    Churl!
    That's not nice—cutting a baroness's throat!
    What impudence!
    It's indecent—cutting a baroness's throat!

FIRST COURT LADY   [*solemnly going up to the* PRINCESS]   Your Highness! Stop this . . . this little pig from insulting Ladies of the Court.

PRINCESS   In the first place, he's not a little pig but a swineherd, and secondly, why do you offend my retinue?

HEINRICH   Call me Heinrich, please.

PRINCESS   Heinrich? How interesting. My name is Henrietta.

HEINRICH   Henrietta? Really? And mine's Heinrich.

PRINCESS   See, how nice. Heinrich.

HEINRICH   There you are! That happens . . . Henrietta.

FIRST COURT LADY   I make bold to remind Your Highness that this . . . this person you're talking to is planning to slit the Baroness's throat tomorrow.

PRINCESS   Oh, yes . . . Tell me, Heinrich, please, why are you planning to slit the Baroness's throat tomorrow?

HEINRICH   Well, she's already stuffed herself full enough. She's terribly fat.

THIRD COURT LADY   Ah! [*Faints again.*]

HEINRICH   Why is that lady doing somersaults all the time?

FIRST COURT LADY   That lady is in fact the Baroness whom you
called a pig and whose throat you're going to slit.

HEINRICH   Nothing of the sort. There's the pig I called the Baroness
and whose throat I'm going to slit.

FIRST COURT LADY   You called that pig the Baroness?

HEINRICH   And that's the Countess.

SECOND COURT LADY   Nothing of the sort! I'm the Countess!

HEINRICH   And that pig is the Duchess.

FIRST COURT LADY   What insolence! I'm the Duchess! Giving a pig
noble titles! Your Highness, kindly direct your attention to the
disgraceful conduct of this swineherd.

PRINCESS   In the first place, he's not a swineherd, he's Heinrich.
And in the second place, the swine are his subjects; he has the
right to confer on them whatever titles he pleases.

FIRST COURT LADY   And he behaves disgracefully in general! He's
holding your hand!

PRINCESS   What's disgraceful about that! If he were holding my
foot . . .

FIRST COURT LADY   I beg you, keep quiet. You're so innocent that
you can say absolutely terrible things.

PRINCESS   And don't you badger me. Tell me, Heinrich, why do you
have such strong hands?

HEINRICH   You don't like them?

PRINCESS   How silly! How could I not? Your hands are so very sweet
and nice.

HEINRICH   Princess, I've got something to tell you. . . .

FIRST COURT LADY [*determinedly*]   Your Highness! We came here
to hear the pot. If we're not going to hear the pot but, in extremely disgraceful attention, are going to keep listening to a
strange man, I will immediately . . .

PRINCESS   Well, then, don't listen to a strange man and go away.

FIRST COURT LADY   Why . . . but he's a stranger to you!

PRINCESS   How silly. I never talk to strangers.

FIRST COURT LADY   I give you my word, Princess, I'll call the King
this minute.

PRINCESS   Stop badgering!

FIRST COURT LADY [*shouts, facing toward the castle*]   Ki-ing! Hurry, come here! The Princess is behaving dreadfully!

PRINCESS   Oh, I'm so fed up with them. Well, show them the pot, Heinrich, if they care so much.

HEINRICH   Christian! Come here. Let me have the pot.

CHRISTIAN [*takes the pot out of a bag. Quietly*]   What a fellow, Heinrich! That's the way. Don't let go of her. She's up to her ears in love with you.

HEINRICH   You think so?

CHRISTIAN   There's no thinking involved. Now the main thing is: kiss her. Find the chance! Kiss her so she'll have something to remember you by when she gets home. Here, Your Highness, and you, noble ladies, is a remarkable pot with little bells. Who made it? We did. What for? For to entertain a princess of royal birth and noble ladies. It looks plain—made of copper, smooth, covered on top with a piece of ass's hide, and decorated on the sides with bells. But that's a deceptive plainness. Hidden behind these copper sides is the most musical soul in the world. This copper musician can play a hundred and forty dances and sing one complete little song, ringing its little silver bells. You'll wonder: Why so many dances? Because it's merry and gay, like us. You'll wonder: Why only one song? Because it's faithful, like us. And that isn't all: under its ass's hide this miracle-working, merry, faithful machine has a nose.

LADIES OF THE COURT [*in chorus*]   What?

CHRISTIAN   A nose. And what a nose, O beautiful Princess and noble ladies! Beneath the coarse ass's hide there lies concealed, like a gentle flower, the most sensitive, the keenest nose in the world. All you have to do is aim it at any distance at any kitchen in any house, and right away our great nose can smell what's being fixed for dinner there. And right away this nose will perfectly clearly, though with something of a twang, to be sure, describe that very dinner to us. O my noble audience! What will we start with? With the song, or with dances, or with dinners?

FIRST COURT LADY   Princess, what would you have him start with? Ah! I was having such a good time listening and didn't notice! Princess! Princess! Princess! I'm talking to you.

PRINCESS [*languidly*]   To me? Oh, yes, yes. Say anything you like.

FIRST COURT LADY   What are you doing, Princess? You're letting yourself be embraced around the waist. It's disgraceful!

PRINCESS   What's disgraceful about it? If he were embracing me by the . . .

FIRST COURT LADY   I beg you, keep quiet. You're so innocent that you can say absolutely terrible things!

PRINCESS   And don't you badger me. Go listen to the pot!

FIRST COURT LADY   But we don't know what to start with: the song or dances or dinners?

PRINCESS   What do you think, Heinrich?

HEINRICH   Ah, my sweet little darling . . .

PRINCESS   He says he doesn't care.

FIRST COURT LADY   But I'm asking *you*, Princess.

PRINCESS   I've already told you that we don't care. Oh, start with dinners.

LADIES OF THE COURT [*clapping their hands*]   With dinners, with dinners, with dinners!

CHRISTIAN   At your service, noble ladies. We'll set the pot on its left side and thereby get the nose working. You hear how it's sniffing and wheezing? [*Loud sniffing and wheezing.*] Those are its warm-up sniffs. [*A deafening sneeze.*] It sneezed. That means it will start talking in a moment. Your attention!

NOSE [*with a nasal twang*]   I'm in the Duchess's kitchen.

LADIES OF THE COURT [*clapping their hands*]   Oh, how interesting!

FIRST COURT LADY   But . . .

LADIES OF THE COURT   Don't interrupt!

NOSE   The Duchess has nothing cooking on the stove; she's just warming things up.

LADIES OF THE COURT   Why?

NOSE   Yesterday at the royal supper she stuffed into her sleeves nine caviar sandwiches, twelve sausage sandwiches, five chops, one rabbit, some Karsky-style shashlyk, a chicken in white sauce, eighteen various meat pies, tartar sauce with capers and olives, filet of beef Godard, fumet sauce, vanilla ice-cream with candied fruit, coffee parfait, and the crust of a small loaf of bread.

FIRST COURT LADY   You're lying, you impudent nose!

NOSE   There's no reason for me to lie. I'm an accurate instrument.

LADIES OF THE COURT   Bravo, bravo! How interesting. More, more!

NOSE   I'm in the Countess's kitchen.

SECOND COURT LADY   But . . .

LADIES OF THE COURT   Don't interrupt.

NOSE   The Countess's stove is so cold—ha-choo—that I'm afraid of catching a cold! Ha-choo!

LADIES OF THE COURT   But why?

NOSE   The Countess's stove hasn't been used for a whole month.

LADIES OF THE COURT   But why?

NOSE   She has been dining out all month. She's economizing.

SECOND COURT LADY   You liar, you shameless nose!

NOSE   Why should I lie? A machine doesn't lie. I'm at the Baroness's. It's warm. The stove is roaring for all it's worth. The Baroness has a wonderful chef. He's getting dinner ready for the guests. He's making chicken cutlets out of horsemeat. Now I'm on my way to the Marquise, and then to the General's wife, and then to the President's wife . . .

LADIES OF THE COURT [shouting in a chorus]   Enough, that will do, you're tired.

NOSE   I'm not tired.

LADIES OF THE COURT   No, you are, you are, that's enough, enough!

CHRISTIAN [turns the pot]   I hope you're simply delighted, noble ladies? [The LADIES OF THE COURT are silent.] If not, I'll set the nose out on its travels again.

LADIES OF THE COURT   We're very pleased, satisfied, thank you, bravo, don't!

CHRISTIAN   I can see you really are happy and satisfied. And since you are happy and satisfied, the only thing left for you to do is to dance. Now you'll hear one of the hundred and forty dances concealed within this pot.

FIRST COURT LADY   I hope—it's a dance without—without—words?

CHRISTIAN   Oh, yes, Duchess, it's a perfectly innocent dance. So, I set the pot on its right side and—can you hear it?

[Ringing its little bells, the pot starts playing. HEINRICH dances with the PRINCESS, CHRISTIAN with the DUCHESS, the COUNTESS with the BARONESS. The other LADIES OF THE COURT move in a circle around them. The dance ends.]

LADIES OF THE COURT   More, more! What a marvelous dance!

CHRISTIAN   Heinrich, do something. This is your chance.

PRINCESS   Yes, please, Heinrich, make the pot go again. I had no idea I love dancing so much.

CHRISTIAN   Your Highness, this pot has one awful thing about it.

PRINCESS   What?

CHRISTIAN   Despite its musical spirit, it doesn't do anything for free. The first time it played in thanks for your coming from the royal palace to our humble meadow. If you want it to play more . . .

PRINCESS   I must come again. But how can that be done? Because to do that I have to leave, and I don't want to at all!

HEINRICH   No, no, don't leave, why, it's still early, you've just come!

PRINCESS   But otherwise it won't play, and I so much want to dance with you again. What do I have to do? Tell me! I'm ready.

HEINRICH   You . . . have to . . . [*in a quick patter*] kiss me ten times.

LADIES OF THE COURT   Ah!

PRINCESS   Ten?

HEINRICH   Because I love you very much. Why do you look at me so strangely? Well, then, not ten; five.

PRINCESS   Five? No!

HEINRICH   If only you knew how happy I would be, you wouldn't argue . . . Well, then kiss me just three times . . .

PRINCESS   Three? No! I refuse.

FIRST COURT LADY   You are behaving absolutely correctly, Your Highness.

PRINCESS   Ten, five, three. To whom are you suggesting this? You forget that I am the King's daughter! Eighty, that's what!

LADIES OF THE COURT   Ah!

HEINRICH   Eighty what?

PRINCESS   Kiss me eighty times! I'm the Princess!

LADIES OF THE COURT   Ah!

FIRST COURT LADY   Your Highness, what are you doing? He's going to kiss you on the lips! That's disgraceful!

PRINCESS   What's disgraceful about it? After all, it's on the lips, and not . . .

FIRST COURT LADY   I beg you, keep quiet. You're so innocent that you can say absolutely terrible things.

PRINCESS   Don't you badger me!

HEINRICH   Hurry! Hurry up!

PRINCESS   Please, Heinrich; I'm ready.

FIRST COURT LADY   I beg you, Princess, don't do it. If you so much want to dance, let him kiss me even a hundred times. . . .

PRINCESS   You? Now that would really be disgraceful! He didn't ask you. You yourself are suggesting to a man that he kiss you.

FIRST COURT LADY   But after you, you, too . . .

PRINCESS   Nothing of the sort; he made me! I understand you—a hundred times. Of course, he's so nice, curly-headed, has such a lovely little mouth. . . . She's partly right, Heinrich. Kiss me a hundred times. And don't argue, Duchess, or I'll have you locked up in the dungeon.

FIRST COURT LADY   But the King can see you from the palace windows!

PRINCESS   Come stand around me! You hear me! Stand around! Shield us with your kerchiefs. Hurry up! It's unheard of—interfering with people about to kiss each other! Come here, Heinrich!

FIRST COURT LADY   Who will count, Your Highness?
PRINCESS   That doesn't matter! If we lose track, we'll start all over.
FIRST COURT LADY   Count, mesdames.

[HEINRICH *and the* PRINCESS *kiss.*]

LADIES OF THE COURT   One.

[*The kiss continues.*]

FIRST COURT LADY   But Your Highness, for the first kiss—that's really enough! [*The kiss continues.*] But this way we won't finish until tomorrow. [*The kiss continues.*]
CHRISTIAN   Don't upset him, Madame; he doesn't hear anything anyway; I know him.
FIRST COURT LADY   But this is simply dreadful! [*The* KING *leaps out of the bushes. He has on his crown and an ermine robe.*] The King!
KING   Who has a match? Give me a match.

[*General commotion.* HEINRICH *and the* PRINCESS *stand with their eyes lowered.*]

LADIES OF THE COURT   Your Majesty!
KING   Shut up! Who has a match?
CHRISTIAN   Your Majesty . . .
KING   Shut up! Do you have a match?
CHRISTIAN   Yes, Your Ma—
KING   Shut up! Let me have it.
CHRISTIAN   But why, Your Majesty?
KING   Shut up!
CHRISTIAN   If you won't tell me, I won't give it to you, Your . . .
KING   Shut up! I need a match to light the bonfire which I'm going to burn the Ladies of the Court on. I've already collected some brush in the bushes there.
CHRISTIAN   Why, certainly, Your Majesty, here are some matches.

[*The* LADIES OF THE COURT *faint.*]

KING   How terrible! My daughter kissing a swineherd! Why did you do it?
PRINCESS   I felt like it.
KING   Felt like kissing him?
PRINCESS   Yes.
KING   Really! Tomorrow I'll marry you off to the neighboring king.
PRINCESS   Not on your life!
KING   And who is asking you?

PRINCESS   I'll pull out his whole beard.

KING   He doesn't have one.

PRINCESS   I'll yank out all his hair.

KING   He's bald.

PRINCESS   Then I'll knock out his teeth.

KING   He has false teeth.

PRINCESS   And you would marry me to that toothless ruin!

KING   You don't live with teeth but with the man. Hey you, ladies!
[*Deafeningly.*] On your feet! [*The* LADIES *get up.*] Fine thing!
Very fine! Just because I was held up, couldn't immediately find
the safety pins to pin my robe on with, you arranged yourselves
an orgy here! No, it's not enough burning you on a bonfire! I'll
burn you first and then cut off your heads and then hang you all
by the highway. [*The* LADIES *cry.*] No wailing! No, even that's not
enough! I've thought of something else: I won't burn you and I
won't hang you. I'll leave you alive and your whole life long I'll
scold you and scold and nag and nag. Aha! Got you! [*The* LADIES
cry.] And besides that, I'll cut off your salaries. [*The* LADIES *faint.*]
On your feet! As for you, swineherd, I'll send you and your friend
out of the country. You're not much to blame. The Princess is
really so cute and wonderful that it's hard not to fall in love with
her. Where's the pot? I'll take the pot for myself. [*Grabs the pot.*]

POT [*begins to sing*]

> I wander through the wide, wide world,
> Full of fire, I.
> Henrietta is my love,
> And I'm the apple of her eye.
> As vast as the plains, as high as the trees—
> That's my love for you.
> Princess, I won't give you up;
> My love for you is true.
> We'll battle for our happiness,
> Then peacefully go home,
> You and I together, love,
> You and I alone.
> I gaily roam the wide, wide world,
> Full of fire, I.
> Henrietta is my love,
> And I'm the apple of her eye.

KING   The pot singing that?

HEINRICH   Yes, Your Majesty.

KING   It sings well, but the words are shocking. It's insisting that
    you'll marry the Princess all the same?
HEINRICH   Yes, I'll marry the Princess all the same, Your Majesty.
PRINCESS   Right, right!
KING [*to the* LADIES OF THE COURT]   Take her away.
PRINCESS   Good-bye, Heinrich. I love you.
HEINRICH   Don't worry, Princess, I'll marry you.
PRINCESS   Yes, please, Heinrich, be so kind. Good-bye, good-bye.
    [*She is escorted out.*]
HEINRICH   Good-bye, good-bye!
KING   Heinrich!
HEINRICH   Good-bye, good-bye!
KING   Hey, you, now listen!
HEINRICH   Good-bye, good-bye!
KING   I'm talking to you. [*Turns* HEINRICH's *face to him.*] Does your
    pot sing only one song?
HEINRICH   Yes, only one.
KING   It doesn't have a song like this? [*Sings in a very jarring voice.*]
    Nothing is going to come of all this for you; scram.
HEINRICH   It doesn't have a song like that and never can.
KING   Don't you make me angry. You've seen how angry I can be?
HEINRICH   I have.
KING   Shivered and shook?
HEINRICH   No.
KING   What did I tell you!
HEINRICH   Farewell, King.
KING   Where are you going?
HEINRICH   To the neighboring king. He's a fool, and I'll wrap him
    around my little finger. No man is bolder than me. I've kissed
    your daughter and now I'm afraid of nothing! Farewell!
KING   Wait a minute. I have to count the swine. One, two, three,
    fifteen, twenty . . . So. They're all here. Go on!
HEINRICH   Farewell, King. Let's go, Christian. [*They go out singing.*]

> As vast as the plains, as high as the trees—
> That's my love for you.
> Princess, I won't give you up;
> My love for you is true.

KING   I have a feeling that trouble is brewing. Well, and I'm no
    fool, either. I'll send for a foreign governess for my daughter, one
    as malicious as a watchdog. She'll make the trip with her. And
    I'll send a chamberlain with her. But not the Ladies of the Court.

I'll keep them for myself. Look how they prance and sing! Prance, go ahead, prance; nothing is going to come of all this for you!

CURTAIN

The Minister of Tender Feelings appears in front of the curtain.

MINISTER   I'm the Minister of Tender Feelings to His Majesty the King. Right now I have a terrible lot of work—my King is marrying the neighboring Princess. I've driven out here in order, first of all, to arrange the meeting with the Princess with the necessary pomp and solemnity. And secondly and thirdly, to solve two very delicate problems. The thing is that my Most Gracious Sovereign has gotten a terrible idea into his head. Gendarmes!

[*Two bearded* GENDARMES *enter.*]

GENDARMES [*together*]   What do you wish, Your Excellency?
MINISTER   Keep your eyes and ears open so that I'm not overheard. I'll be talking now about secret matters of national urgency.
GENDARMES [*together*]   Yes, sir, Your Excellency!

[*They separate in different directions and stand at the portals.*]

MINISTER [*lowering his voice*]   So: last Tuesday at lunch my Sovereign got a terrible idea in his head. He happened to have been eating a sausage—and suddenly froze with a piece of food between his teeth. We dashed to him, exclaiming: "Your Majesty! What does this mean!" But he merely groaned in a hollow voice without unclenching his teeth: "What a terrible idea! It's terrible! Terrible!" The royal physician brought the King to his senses, and we learned what indeed had the honor of causing his alarm. It's really a terrible idea. Gendarmes!
GENDARMES [*together*]   What do you wish, Your Excellency?
MINISTER   Stop your ears.
GENDARMES [*together*]   Yes, sir, Your Excellency! [*They stop their ears.*]
MINISTER   The King thought: what if Her Highness's mama, the mama of the King's betrothed fiancée, was in her time [*in a whisper*] a naughty girl! What if suddenly the Princess weren't the King's daughter but a girl of unknown parentage? That's the first problem which I must solve. And the second is this: His Majesty

was having a swim, was very gay and cheerful, giggling and saying playful things. And then suddenly he, the King, exclaimed: "I have another terrible idea!" and in a shallow place sank to the bottom. It turned out that the King had thought: what if the Princess, prior to their betrothal, [*in a whisper*] had also been a naughty girl, had had her little adventures, and . . . well, in short, you understand! We saved the King, and right there in the sea he gave me the necessary instructions. I've come here to find out the whole truth about the Princess's parentage and conduct and—I swear on my honor as a knight—I will indeed learn all the ins and outs about Her Highness. Gendarmes! Gendarmes! What's wrong with you, are you deaf? Gendarmes! Oh, yes! I told them to stop their ears. What fine discipline! The King sent into every village on the Princess's route the best gendarmes in his kingdom. They show the local populace how to stage triumphant welcomes. Hand-picked fellows. [*Goes up to the* GENDARMES, *puts their arms down.*] Gendarmes!

GENDARMES What do you wish, Your Excellency?
MINISTER Go see if the Princess is coming.
GENDARMES Yes, sir, Your Excellency! [*Go out.*]
MINISTER What difficult problems I have. Right? But I know exactly how to solve them. To help me I have one little pea and twelve bottles of choice wine. I'm a very clever man. [*The* GENDARMES *enter.*] Well?
GENDARMES Your Excellency. Far, far away, where the sky on the horizon melts into the earth, a high column of dust spirals above a hill. At times a halberd shines in it; at times, a horse's head appears; at times there flashes a golden coat-of-arms. That is the Princess coming to us, Your Excellency.
MINISTER Let's go see if everything is ready for her arrival. [*They go out.*]

The gentle slopes are covered with vineyards. In the foreground, a hotel. A small two-storied house. Tables are set in the hotel courtyard. The Mayor of the little village dashes back and forth across the courtyard together with girls and young men. Shouts of "She's coming! She's coming!" The Minister of Tender Feelings enters.

MINISTER Mayor! Stop being nervous. Come here.
MAYOR Me? Yes. Oh, there he is. What? No!

MINISTER   Make ready twelve bottles of the strongest wine.

MAYOR   What? Bottles? Why?

MINISTER   I need them.

MAYOR   Aha . . . I see. . . . To welcome the Princess?

MINISTER   Yes.

MAYOR   Is she an alcoholic?

MINISTER   You're mad! We need the bottles for supper, which you'll
serve to those accompanying the Princess.

MAYOR   Ah, those accompanying the Princess. That's better. . . .
Yes-yes . . . No-no . . .

MINISTER   [*laughs. Aside.*]   How stupid! I just love stupid people;
they're so amusing. [*To the* MAYOR.] Get the bottles ready, get
the suckling pigs ready, get the quarters of bear meat ready.

MAYOR   Ah, so. No . . . I mean, yes. Hey, you, get the keys to the
cellar! Let me have the keys to the attic! [*Runs.*]

MINISTER   Musicians!

CONDUCTOR   Present, Your Excellency!

MINISTER   Everything in order?

CONDUCTOR   The first violin, Your Excellency, ate too many grapes
and lay down in the sun. The grape juice, Your Excellency,
started fermenting in the first violin's belly and turned into wine.
We've been trying and trying to wake him up but he kicks and
twitches and goes on sleeping.

MINISTER   Scandalous! What'll we do?

CONDUCTOR   We've fixed everything, Your Excellency. The second
violin will take the place of the first, and the double-bass will
take the place of the second. We've tied the violin to a pole,
and the double-bass player will play it like a double-bass, and
everything will be absolutely perfect.

MINISTER   And who will play the double-bass?

CONDUCTOR   Oh, how terrible! I didn't think of that!

MINISTER   Put the double-bass in the middle. Let anyone grab it
and saw away on it who has his hands free.

CONDUCTOR   Yes, sir, Your Excellency. [*Runs out.*]

MINISTER   Oh, what a clever, quick, resourceful man am I!

[*Two* GENDARMES *enter.*]

GENDARMES   Your Excellency, the Princess's carriage has entered
the village.

MINISTER   Attention! Orchestra! Mayor! Girls! Everybody! Gendarmes! See that the fellows toss their caps as high as they can!
[*On the other side of the fence there appears a carriage with suit-*

cases on top. The MINISTER *rushes out the gate toward the carriage. The orchestra plays. The* GENDARMES *shout "Hurrah!" Caps fly high. The* PRINCESS, *the* CHAMBERLAIN, *and the* GOVERNESS *enter.*] Your Highness . . . The excitement evoked by your arrival in this humble little village is nothing compared with that in the heart of my enamored sovereign. But nevertheless . . .

PRINCESS   Enough . . . Chamberlain! Where are my handkerchiefs?

CHAMBERLAIN   Eh! Uh! Oho-ho! Just a minute, Your Highness, I'll pull myself together and ask the governess. M-m-muih. [*Growls. Calms down.*] Madam Governess, where do the handkerchiefs honor to the Princess have belonging be?

GOVERNESS   The handkerchiefs have belonging honor be in the suitcase, Plenipottyteathratrictentienary.

CHAMBERLAIN   H-order! [*Growls.*] The handkerchiefs are in the suitcase, Princess.

PRINCESS   Get them. Can't you see that I'm about to cry. Get the handkerchiefs. And bring them here. [*Suitcases are brought in.*] And have my bed prepared. It will soon be dark. [*Aside.*] And I'm terribly tired. The dust, the heat, the bumpy road. To bed, to sleep, as soon as I can! And in my dreams I'll see my dear Heinrich. I'm so fed up with these absolutely foreign monkeys. [*Goes out to the hotel.*]

[*The* CHAMBERLAIN *digs in the suitcase.*]

MINISTER   Won't the Princess have supper?

CHAMBERLAIN [*growls*]   Eh, uh, oho-ho! No! She hasn't eaten a thing for three weeks. She's so nervous over the forthcoming marriage.

GOVERNESS [*hurling herself at the* MINISTER OF TENDER FEELINGS] Take the hands the pockets out of! It's them disgusting to have in! *Entweder!*

MINISTER   What does this woman want of me?

CHAMBERLAIN [*growls*]   O-o-o-uh! [*Calms down. To the* GOVERNESS.] Pull yourself together in, *encore*. This your charge is not no. [*To the* MINISTER.] I'm sorry, you don't speak any foreign language?

MINISTER   No. Ever since His Majesty proclaimed our nation the finest in the world, we have been ordered to forget foreign languages entirely.

CHAMBERLAIN   This woman is a foreign governess, the wickedest in the world. All her life she has had to bring up bad children, and that has made her very hard. Now she flings herself on everyone she meets and starts training them.

GOVERNESS [*flinging herself at the* CHAMBERLAIN]   Yourself no scratch.
Not!

CHAMBERLAIN   You see? Uh-o-uh! She forbids me to scratch myself,
though I'm not scratching myself at all but just fixing my cuffs.
[*Growls.*]

MINISTER   What's wrong with you, Chamberlain? Do you have a
cold?

CHAMBERLAIN   No. It's simply that I haven't been out hunting for
a week. I'm more than full of blood-thirsty thoughts. *Oo-liu-liu!*°
The King knows that with no hunting I turn into a beast, and here
he has sent me to escort the Princess. Excuse me, Minister, I
must go see what the Princess is doing. [*Roars out.*] Tally-ho!
[*Calms down.*] Governess, madam, your feet, set out after. The
Princess supervision long has had not any of.

GOVERNESS   To go we plan. [*Goes. To the* MINISTER *on her way.*]
Breathe one must the nose through! Bad, bad boy are you,
higgledy-piggledy, offices three! [*Goes out with the* CHAMBERLAIN.]

MINISTER   Extraordinarily suspicious! Why should the King, her
father, send such fierce people to accompany the Princess? There's
some hidden purpose to it. But I'll find it all out! All of it! Twelve
bottles of strong wine will make this fierce watchman tell everything. Everything! Ah, how clever I am, cunning, resourceful,
imaginative! Before two hours are up the Princess's whole past will
be right here in the palm of my hand. [*Twelve young girls come
by with feather beds. Each girl has two.*] Aha! Now comes the
business of the pea. [*To the* FIRST GIRL.] You beautiful thing, here,
two words with you. [*The* GIRL *punches him in the ribs. The*
MINISTER *jumps back. He goes up to the* SECOND.] My beautiful
darling, here, two words with you. [*The same thing happens. All
twelve* GIRLS *push the* MINISTER *away and disappear into the
hotel. The* MINISTER *rubs his sides.*] What vulgar, what insensitive
girls! Now, what about the pea, heaven help us! Gendarmes!

[*The* GENDARMES *come up to the* MINISTER.]

GENDARMES   What do you wish, Your Excellency?

MINISTER   The mayor.

GENDARMES   Yes, sir, Your Excellency.

MINISTER   I'll have to bring that idiot into the business. There's
nobody else. [*The* GENDARMES *escort the* MAYOR *in.*] Gendarmes,
stand nearby and see that we're not overheard. I'll be talking to
the Mayor about secret matters of national urgency.

° A hunting halloo.

GENDARMES   Yes, sir, Your Excellency! [*They stand beside the* MAYOR *and the* MINISTER.]

MINISTER   Mayor, your girls . . .

MAYOR   Ah-hanh, I see. Certainly. You, too?

MINISTER   What?

MAYOR   Our girls . . . You're rubbing your side. Uh-hunh. Certainly.

MINISTER   What are you mumbling?

MAYOR   You made passes at the girls, they pushed you away. Certainly. I know by personal experience. I'm a bachelor myself.

MINISTER   Just a minute!

MAYOR   No. Oh, they love, indeed, they do. Only, young men. Silly girls. I love them. . . . Well, well . . . But not they. Not me . . . You, too. Not a thing I can do.

MINISTER   Stop! That isn't why I called you here. Your girls misunderstood me. I was going to entrust them with a matter of national urgency. But now you'll have to do it.

MAYOR   Anh-hanh. Well, well. Yes, certainly.

MINISTER   You'll have to get yourself into the Princess's bedroom.

MAYOR   [*laughing*]   Oh, you . . . Of course, now . . . Nice idea . . . But no . . . I'm an honest man.

MINISTER   You misunderstand me. You have to go in there just for a second, after the girls have made up the feather beds for Her Highness. And put this tiny little pea on the boards on the bottom of the bed under all the twenty-four feather beds. That's all there is to it.

MAYOR   What for?

MINISTER   None of your business! Take the pea and be off!

MAYOR   I won't. No . . . Not for anything in the world.

MINISTER   Why not?

MAYOR   There's something wrong about it. I'm an honest man. Yes, indeed. Not on your life. Here, I'm about to get sick—and you can't make me! Not on your life! Yes, indeed!

MINISTER   Oh, damn it, what an idiot! Oh, all right, I'll tell you the whole story. But remember: this is a secret of national urgency. The King has ordered me to find out if the Princess really is of noble birth. Maybe suddenly she'll turn out not to be the King's daughter!

MAYOR   She is. Takes after her father. Yes, indeed.

MINISTER   That doesn't prove a thing. You have no idea how cunning women are. Only this pea can give us a sure answer. People of truly royal birth are distinguished by exceptional sensitivity and tender skin. The Princess, if she really is a princess, will feel this pea through all twenty-four feather beds. She won't sleep all night and will complain to me about it the next day. Or if she does sleep, that will show it's a bad business. Get it? Now go!

MAYOR   Aha . . . [Takes the pea.] Well, well . . . Sort of interested myself . . . Takes after her father so—and then suddenly . . . True, her father has a beard. . . . But her little mouth . . . And the little nose . . .

MINISTER   Go on!

MAYOR   Her little eyes.

MINISTER   Get going, you hear!

MAYOR   That little forehead.

MINISTER   Don't you waste any time, you fathead!

MAYOR   I'm going, I'm going! And her figure in general—so much like her father. Ai-ai-ai! [Goes out.]

MINISTER   Thank god!

MAYOR   [coming back]   And her little cheeks.

MINISTER   I'll draw and quarter you!

MAYOR   I'm going, I'm going. [Goes out.]

MINISTER   Well, sir, I'll straighten out the question of birth! Now all I have to do is to call the chamberlain and the governess, get them drunk, and find out all the details of the Princess's daily life. [The GIRLS who had brought the feather beds in run past with a shriek. Behind them, rubbing his side, comes the CHAMBERLAIN.] So, Chamberlain, I see by the motions of your hands that you attempted to have a chat with those girls.

CHAMBERLAIN   I did have a shot at it. . . . [Growls.] They kick and butt like wild goats. Stupid things!

MINISTER   Mr. Chamberlain, when a woman is annoying, you'll find that wine is mollifying.

CHAMBERLAIN   Nothing of the sort. As soon as I've had a drink, I start longing for women.

MINISTER   Ah, no matter! Let's have a drink, Chamberlain! The wedding will be soon! Here we have wonderful wine, laughing wine. Let's sit up all night, eh?

CHAMBERLAIN   [growls]   Oh, how I'd like to sit up! Oo-liu-liu! But no, I can't! I gave my word to the King that just as soon as the Princess goes to bed I'll lie down outside her door and guard her without sleeping a wink. Me at the door, the governess by the bed—that's how we'll guard her the whole night through. We'll catch up on our sleep in the carriage. Tally-ho!

MINISTER   [aside]   Very suspicious! He has to be gotten drunk no matter what. Mr. Chamberlain . . .

[*A shout and scream upstairs, a din on the stairs. The* MAYOR *bursts in, followed by an enraged* GOVERNESS.]

MAYOR   Oi, save me, she'll devour me! Oi, save me, she'll kill me!

CHAMBERLAIN   What happened *entweder-oder, aber?*

GOVERNESS   This old hurdy-murdy into the Princess's bedroom had to be going was! And I have the biting off of his head to be, Plenipottyteathratrictentientententennary!

CHAMBERLAIN   This brazen bastard crept into the Princess's bedroom. Tally-ho!

MINISTER   Stop! I'll explain everything to you. Come here, Mayor. [*Softly.*] Did you put in the pea?

MAYOR   Oh, I did. . . . Yes . . . She pinches.

MINISTER   Who?

MAYOR   The governess. I put the pea in. . . . So . . . Take a look at the Princess. . . . Amazing how she resembles her father. . . . The little nose, the little mouth . . . Suddenly . . . such a jump . . . Her . . . The governess.

MINISTER   Be off. [*To the* CHAMBERLAIN.] I've clarified everything. The Mayor only wanted to find out if he couldn't in some little way be of further help to the Princess. The Mayor offers to make amends for what he did with twelve bottles of strong wine.

CHAMBERLAIN   *Ooh-liu-liu!*

MINISTER   Listen, Chamberlain! Cut it out, honestly, huh? Go on! You've already crossed the border! Her father won't find a thing out. Let's have a good time! And we'll call the governess. Here, right here on this table, my word of honor, honest to god, on my honor! And I'll send two of these fine, husky young gendarmes upstairs. The most reliable, faithful, choicest dogs in the kingdom. They won't let anybody pass, neither into the Princess nor out again. Ah, Chamberlain? *Oooh-liu-liu?*

CHAMBERLAIN [*to the* GOVERNESS]   They suggest on the tables *schnapps trinken.* Two gendarmes upstairs they to be sending have. Gendarmes like dogs humpty-dumpty doberman-boberman. *Una duna* guess?

GOVERNESS   The stairs here is alone?

CHAMBERLAIN   Alone.

GOVERNESS   *Cinque, baba,* yes.

CHAMBERLAIN [*to the* MINISTER]   So, fine, let's have a drink! Send up your gendarmes.

MINISTER   Gendarmes! Go upstairs, stand at the Princess's door, and keep guard. Lively now!

GENDARMES   Yes, sir, Your Excellency! [*They run up.*]

MINISTER   Mayor! Bring in the wine, the legs of bear meat, the sausages. [*Chuckles. Aside.*] Now! Now I'll bring all the ins and outs to light! How clever I am! How cunning I am! What a splendid fellow I am!

The light downstairs goes out. The second floor opens up. The Princess's room. The Princess in her nightcap lies high up on the twenty-four feather beds.

PRINCESS [*sings*]
>   As vast as the plains, as high as the trees—
>   That's my love for you.
>   Princess, I won't give you up;
>   My love for you is true.

But what's happening? Every night I used to go to sleep so nicely to this song. I always sing it—and right away I become peaceful and relaxed. Right away I'm sure that Heinrich really won't give me up to this fat, old king. And then I dream. And in my dreams I see Heinrich. But today nothing is happening at all. Something is digging into me through all these twenty-four feather beds and keeping me from sleeping. Either a feather got into the down, or there's a twig in the bedboards. I'm probably all black-and-blue. Oh, what an unhappy princess I am! I was looking out the window: there girls are walking with their friends, but here I lie, wasting away for no reason! I wrote down a little note today of what to ask Heinrich when I see him in my dream. Because otherwise I always forget. Here's the note. . . . First, did he love other girls before he met me? Second, when did he first realize that he had fallen in love with me? Third, when did he first realize that I had fallen in love with him? I thought about that the whole way here. After all, we only managed to kiss once—and then they separated us! And there was no chance to have a chat. Have to do it in dreams. But my dreams won't come. Something is rolling around under the feather beds. I'm so terribly unhappy! I'll try singing again. [*Sings.*]

>   I wander through the wide, wide world,
>   Full of fire, I.

[Two male voices join in.]

Henrietta is my love,
And I'm the apple of her eye.

PRINCESS   What's that? Maybe I'm already dreaming.

DUET

As vast as the plains, as high as the trees—
That's my love for you.
Princess, I won't give you up;
My love for you is true.

PRINCESS   Oh, how interesting! It's incomprehensible and scary and pleasant.

DUET

We'll battle for our happiness,
Then peacefully go home,
You and I together, love,
You and I alone.

PRINCESS   I'll slip down now and peek out. I'll wrap myself up in a blanket and have a peek. [*Slides down off the feather beds.*]

DUET

I gaily roam the wide, wide world,
Full of fire, I.
Henrietta is my love,
And I'm the apple of her eye.

PRINCESS   Where are my slippers? There they are! Actually outside the door. . . . [*Flings the door open. There stand the* TWO GEN-DARMES.] Who are you?

GENDARMES   We are the gendarmes of His Majesty the King.

PRINCESS   What are you doing here?

GENDARMES   We are guarding Your Highness.

PRINCESS   Who was doing the singing?

GENDARMES   The singing was done by the man who swore to wed your sweet person no matter what the cost. He has loved you forever and ever because you are so nice, so kind, so tender. He doesn't whimper or cry or waste his time. He is wandering around here everywhere to save you from your cursed bridegroom. He sang to remind you of himself, and his friend joined him in singing.

PRINCESS   But where is he? [*Without saying a word, the* GENDARMES *stride into the Princess's room.*] Why don't you answer? Where's Heinrich? Why do you look at me so sadly? Maybe you've come to cut my throat?

GENDARMES Pull our beards.
PRINCESS Your beards?
GENDARMES Yes.
PRINCESS What for?
GENDARMES Don't be afraid, pull!
PRINCESS But I don't know you!
GENDARMES Heinrich asks you to pull our beards.
PRINCESS Well, all right. [*Pulls.*]
GENDARMES Harder!

[*The* PRINCESS *pulls as hard as she can. The* GENDARMES' *beards and mustaches come off in her hands. Before her stand* HEINRICH *and* CHRISTIAN.]

PRINCESS Heinrich. [*Throws herself at him, but stops.*] But I'm not dressed. . . .
CHRISTIAN That doesn't matter, Princess; after all, you'll soon be his wife.
PRINCESS I'm not stopping because it's improper but because I don't know whether I'm pretty or not.
HEINRICH Henrietta! I would sooner die than leave you, so glorious are you. Don't worry—we're following right behind you all the time. Yesterday we made the gendarmes drunk, tied them up, hid them, and came here. Don't forget: we think only of one thing, we have only one aim—freeing you and taking you away with us. If it doesn't work the first time, we'll try again. If not the second, we'll try a third. Nothing important ever comes on the first try. To make it work you have to try today and tomorrow and the day after tomorrow. Are you prepared?
PRINCESS Yes. But please, Heinrich, tell me: did you love other girls before me?
HEINRICH I hated them all!
CHRISTIAN Poor Princess—how thin she has grown!
PRINCESS And tell me, Heinrich, please . . .
CHRISTIAN Later, poor Princess, we'll chat later. But now listen closely to us.
HEINRICH We'll try to escape with you today.
PRINCESS Thanks, Heinrich.
HEINRICH But maybe it won't work.
PRINCESS Nothing important ever comes on the first try, Heinrich darling.
HEINRICH Take this paper.
PRINCESS [*takes it*] Did you write it? [*Kisses the paper. Reads it.*]

"Damn you to hell and gone." [*Kisses the paper.*] "Shut your trap, you old bag." [*Kisses it.*] What is this, Heinrich?

HEINRICH   In case the escape doesn't work, you have to memorize that and say it to the King, your bridegroom. You yourself are very bad at cursing, so memorize this and give him what he deserves.

PRINCESS   With pleasure, Heinrich. [*Reads.*] "Get the holy hell out of here." Oh, fine! [*Kisses the paper.*]

HEINRICH   There's a pea under all your feather beds. That's what was keeping you from sleeping. Tomorrow say that you slept soundly all night long. Then the King will reject you. Understand?

PRINCESS   Not a thing, but I'll say it. How clever you are, Heinrich!

HEINRICH   If he doesn't reject you, don't despair. We'll be nearby.

PRINCESS   All right, Heinrich. I'll sleep well even on a pea, if I have to. How many feather beds do you have at home?

HEINRICH   One.

PRINCESS   I'll learn to sleep on just one. But where will you sleep, poor thing? No, of course, we'll . . .

CHRISTIAN   I beg you to keep quiet, Princess! You're so innocent that you can say absolutely terrible things!

HEINRICH   Get dressed, Princess, and let's go. Downstairs they're completely drunk. We can make our escape.

CHRISTIAN   And if we don't, the pea will help.

HEINRICH   And if it doesn't, we'll be nearby and we'll get you out, even if at the altar from under the wedding-crown. Let's go, my poor darling!

PRINCESS   One thing, my dear, sweet friends. You won't get angry if I ask you just one thing?

HEINRICH   Of course not, go ahead! I'll do anything for you.

PRINCESS   Well then, even if it holds us up a lot, please be so kind as to—kiss me.

[HEINRICH *kisses the* PRINCESS.]

The upstairs lights go out. The hotel courtyard is lit up. At table sit the Minister of Tender Feelings, the Governess, the Chamberlain. All are drunk, the Minister most of all.

MINISTER   I'm very tricky, y'know that, Chamberlain? I'm so smart! The King gives me the order: find out on the sly if the Princess had any previous adventures. . . . Y'understand! *Troo-lia-lia!* Very delicately find out, he says. Now what would another fellow have done? Lost his head, he would have! But I thought up something! I'll get you drunk, and you'll beal the . . . you'll still the . . . you'll bill the speans! Right? Clever, no?

CHAMBERLAIN   *Oooh-liu-liu!*

MINISTER   Right! So, out with it! No hiding from me anyway. No, sir! Beal the . . . beasle . . . peel the steans! What can you tell me about the Princess?

CHAMBERLAIN   We ran her down with the foxhounds! [*Falls under the table. Crawls out.*]

MINISTER   What for?

CHAMBERLAIN   Has a beautiful tail. *Ooh-liu-liu!*

MINISTER   [*falls under the table. Crawls out.*]   Tail? She has a tail?

CHAMBERLAIN   Right y'are. Tally-ho!

MINISTER   Why a tail?

CHAMBERLAIN   That's the breed. *Ooh-liu-liu!*

MINISTER   The whole breed? Her father . . . has a tail, too?

CHAMBERLAIN   Why, sure. Father, too.

MINISTER   You mean you have a king with a tail?

CHAMBERLAIN   Ah, no! We have a tailless king. But her father has one.

MINISTER   You mean the King isn't her father?

CHAMBERLAIN   Why, naturally!

MINISTER   Hurrah! [*Falls under the table. Crawls out.*] Beal the . . . peel the . . . Who's her father?

CHAMBERLAIN   The fox. Tally-ho!

MINISTER   Who?

CHAMBERLAIN   Fox. The vixen's father is a fox.

MINISTER   What vixen?

CHAMBERLAIN   The one we were talking about. . . . [*Punches the* GOVERNESS *with his elbow.*]

[*They both guffaw drunkenly.*]

GOVERNESS   If only know you could dandy-sugar-candy, how she and the swineherd was kissing herself back and forth! Take your elbows from the table *auf*! No winking-blinking!

CHAMBERLAIN   Tally-ho!

GOVERNESS   A blockhead you are!

MINISTER   What are they saying?

CHAMBERLAIN   *Oo-liu-liu!*

MINISTER   Swine! That's no commer . . . not comradely. I'll lay

you flat. [*His head falls on to the table.*] Mayor! Mayor! Some
more wine. [*Falls asleep.*]

GOVERNESS   That stupid blockhead to himself sleeps. Oh, fortunate
man! To lie so and fall asleep. But sleep I not. Sleep I not so
many nights. *Under-munder.* [*Falls asleep.*]

CHAMBERLAIN   *Oo-liu-liu.* A stag! A stag! [*Runs, falls, and goes to
sleep.*]

MAYOR [*enters*]   Here. Some more wine. Oh, yes, yes. Minister!
Asleep. Chamberlain! Asleep. Madam Governess! Asleep. I'll have
a seat. Yes, yes. They'll probably wake up. No, no. [*Dozes.*]

[*The door softly, slowly opens. Out comes* CHRISTIAN, *looks around.
Gives the sign. The* PRINCESS *and* HEINRICH *come out. They steal
toward the exit. The* MAYOR *catches sight of them, jumps up.*]

MAYOR   Where you going? . . . That is. Ah . . . The Gendarmes . . .
Shaved . . . Strange . . . Back!

HEINRICH   I'll kill you!

MAYOR   I'll scream. . . . I'm bold.

CHRISTIAN   Take this money and let us go.

MAYOR   Oh, no! I'm honest. I'll whistle this instant!

PRINCESS   Let me say something. Mayor, have pity on me, please.
Though I am a princess, I'm also a girl! [*The* MAYOR *sobs.*] If you
betray me, they'll take me by force to the altar to marry an old
man I don't know. [*The* MAYOR *sobs.*] Now, is that good? Your
King is whimsical. And I'm weak and frail. [*The* MAYOR *weeps.*]
Would I endure in that captivity? I would die in an instant!

MAYOR [*bellows at the top of his voice*]   Oi, run off as fast as you
can! Oi, or you'll die! [*Wails.*] Run! Oi!

[ALL, *except the* MINISTER, *jump up. The* GOVERNESS *grabs the* PRIN-
CESS, *carries her off upstairs. The* CHAMBERLAIN *whistles, halloos
(the* oo-liu-liu *of before). The* GUARD *runs in.* HEINRICH *and* CHRISTIAN
push their way through to the exit. ALL *run after them. Horse hoof-
beats are heard. Singing:*]

> As vast as the plains, as high as the trees—
> That's my love for you.
> Princess, I won't give you up;
> My love for you is true.

CHAMBERLAIN [*enters*]   Got away. It's easier to run down a hundred
stags than to lead one king's daughter safely to her bridegroom.
[*Looks at the* MINISTER.] And this one is oversleeping himself:

sleep on, sleep on, get your strength back. You'll have another scamper yet with our soft, gentle lady. *Oo-liu-liu!*

CURTAIN

ACT II

A reception room separated from the King's bedchamber by an arched doorway with a velvet curtain. The reception room is crowded. Right next to the curtain stands the Valet, pulling the bell-rope. The bell itself hangs in the bedchamber. Beside the Valet, Tailors hurriedly finish sewing the King's outfit. Next to the Tailors is the Chef, whipping the cream for the King's chocolate. Farther off stand the Bootblacks, cleaning the King's footwear. The bell rings. There is a knock on the door.

BOOTBLACKS   Someone is knocking on the door of the King's reception room, Master Chef.

CHEF   Someone is knocking on the reception room door, Master Tailors.

TAILORS   Someone is knocking on the door, Master Valet.

VALET   Knocking? Have them come in.

[*All the while the knocking increases.*]

TAILORS [*to the* CHEF]   Let them come in.

CHEF [*to the* BOOTBLACKS]   Let them in.

BOOTBLACKS   Come in.

[HEINRICH *and* CHRISTIAN *enter, dressed as weavers. They have gray wigs, gray beards. They look around. Then they bow to the* VALET.]

CHRISTIAN *and* HEINRICH   Hello, Master Bell-ringer. [*Silence.* HEINRICH *and* CHRISTIAN *exchange glances. They bow to the* TAILORS.] Hello, Master Tailors. [*Silence.*] Hello, Master Chef. [*Silence.*] Hello, Master Bootblacks.

BOOTBLACKS   Hello, weavers.

CHRISTIAN   They answered. Isn't that wonderful! So, tell us, what
about these other gentlemen—are they deaf or dumb?

BOOTBLACKS   Neither one nor the other, weavers. But in accordance
with the etiquette of the Court you should have turned to me
first. When I find out what you want, I'll let them know about
you in the line of ascent. Well, sirs? What do you want?

HEINRICH   We're the most amazing weavers in the world. Your king
is the greatest dandy and man of fashion in the world. We wish
to serve His Majesty.

BOOTBLACKS   Aha. Master Chef, some amazing weavers want to be
of service to our most benign sovereign.

CHEF   Aha. Master Tailors, some weavers are here.

TAILORS   Aha. Master Valet, some weavers.

VALET   Aha. Hello, weavers.

HEINRICH *and* CHRISTIAN   Hello, Master Valet.

VALET   You want to be of service? Very good! I'll inform the Prime
Minister personally about you, and he'll tell the King. For weavers
we arrange an ultra-expeditious audience. His Majesty is getting
married. He needs weavers very much. Therefore he will receive
you with the utmost rapidity.

HEINRICH   Rapidity! It took us two hours just to get to you. What
a little system!

[*The* VALET *and* ALL *the others shudder. They look around.*]

VALET [*quietly*]   Master weavers! You are venerable, aged men. Out
of respect for your gray hairs, let me warn you: not a word about
our national, ancient traditions made sacred by Our Creator himself. Our state is the finest in this world! If you continue to doubt
this, I must, despite your age . . . [*Whispers something into* CHRIS-
TIAN'S *ear.*]

CHRISTIAN   Impossible.

VALET   A fact. So that you'll have no children, who might tend to
be critical. You're Aryans?

HEINRICH   For ever so long.

VALET   That's nice to know. Sit down. Though I've been ringing
for an hour now, the King still won't wake up.

CHEF [*trembles*]   I'll try to h-he-help y-y-you this minute. [*Runs
out.*]

CHRISTIAN   Tell me, Master Valet: why, despite the heat, does the
Chef tremble as if he had a fever?

VALET   The Royal Master Chef never leaves his stoves and is so
accustomed to heat that last year, for example, in the July sun

he froze his nose. [*A dismal howl is heard.*] What is that? [*The* CHEF *runs in, followed by little* COOKS *carrying a big trough. The howling comes from the trough.*] What is it?

CHEF [*trembling*]   It's a stuck pig,° Master Valet. We'll put it i-in the King's b-b-bed-ch-chamber, and the stuck pig wi-will ho-howl like a st-stuck pig and wa-wake up th-the K-King.

VALET   Out of the question.

CHEF   But why?

VALET   Out of the question. A stuck pig is, nevertheless, forgive me . . . rather . . . red. And you know how the King reacts to that. . . . Take it away! [*The* COOKS *run out with the trough.*] There, that's better, Master Chef. Hey! Call up a platoon of soldiers; have them fire off volleys under the bedchamber windows. That might help.

CHRISTIAN   Does His Majesty always sleep so soundly?

VALET   Five years or so ago he would wake up very quickly. I would cough—and the King would fly out of bed.

HEINRICH   Really!

VALET   Word of honor! In those days he had many worries. He was always attacking his neighbors and fighting them.

CHRISTIAN   But now?

VALET   But now he has no worries at all. His neighbors have captured all the lands they possibly can. And so the King sleeps and dreams of revenge.

[*The thunder of drums is heard. A platoon of* SOLDIERS *enters, led by a* SERGEANT.]

SERGEANT [*commanding*]   'Ten-tion! [*The* SOLDIERS *stand still.*] [*Commands.*] Upon entering the royal reception room give a sigh of de-vo-tion! [*The* SOLDIERS *all together give a loud, groaning sigh.*] Thinking of his power and might, tremble with awe and ven-er-a-tion! [*Their arms spread wide, the* SOLDIERS *tremble.*] Hey, you, there, spaghetti-legs, what kind of trembling is that? Tremble precisely, the whole forefront! Fingers! Your fingers! So! I don't see any trembling in the belly! All right. 'Ten-tion! Listen to my order! Thinking of the good fortune of being one of the King's soldiers, start dancing from an excess of joyous e-mo-tion! [*The* SOLDIERS *dance in time to the drum, all together as one man, without breaking ranks.*] 'Ten-tion! On tiptoes now! On tiptoes—

°In the Russian, a *beluga*, a white sturgeon, famous for its caviar. "To howl like a sturgeon" is an idiom meaning to howl violently, furiously.

'arch! To the right! A little more ri-i-i-ght! On the portrait of His
Majesty's grandfather, dress right! On his nose. On the grandfather's
nose. Forward, 'arch! [*They disappear.*]

CHRISTIAN   Did the King really suffer defeat with such disciplined
troops?

VALET [*throwing up his hands*]   Who would have believed it.

[*The* PRIME MINISTER *enters, a fussy man with a great gray beard.*]

PRIME MINISTER   Greetings, subordinate officials!

ALL [*together*]   Greetings, Mister Prime Minister.

PRIME MINISTER   Well, so? Everything in order, Valet? Huh? Tell
the truth. Speak the truth boldly.

VALET   Absolutely, Your Excellency.

PRIME MINISTER   But the King is asleep! Huh? Answer plainly.
Frankly.

VALET   He is, Your Excellency.

[*A volley offstage.*]

PRIME MINISTER   Aha! Speak bluntly: they're shooting. Means His
Majesty will soon arise. Tailors! How are things going? Spill the
truth! Between the eyes!

FIRST TAILOR   We're putting in the last stitches, Mister Minister.

PRIME MINISTER   Show me. [*Looks.*] Count them up. You know our
requirements? The last stitch is put in just before His Majesty
dresses. Every day the King puts on a new robe still fresh from
the needle. Let a minute pass after the last stitch and he won't,
to put it bluntly, don his robe. You know that?

FIRST TAILOR   We do, exactly so.

PRIME MINISTER   The needles are gold?

FIRST TAILOR   Gold, exactly so.

PRIME MINISTER   Takes his robe directly from the gold needle.
Directly and openly. Chef! You have, to put it bluntly, whipped
the cream? Huh? Speak up, without fooling and quibbling! You've
whipped the cream for the King's chocolate?

CHEF   Ye-yes, sir, Your Excellency.

PRIME MINISTER   Show me. Un-huh. Although . . . Valet! Who's
that? Be bold. No fooling. Speak up.

VALET   These are weavers who have come to offer their services,
Your Excellency.

PRIME MINISTER   Weavers? Show me. Aha! Greetings, weavers.

HEINRICH *and* CHRISTIAN   Good day to you, Your Excellency.

PRIME MINISTER   The King, to put it plainly, without any secret purpose, needs weavers. His bride arrives today. Hey! Chef! What about Her Highness's breakfast? It ready? Huh?

CHEF   Eg-eg-exactly so, ready.

PRIME MINISTER   What kind? Huh? Show me!

CHEF   Hey! Bring in the pastries prepared for Her Highness!

PRIME MINISTER   They're getting them, but meanwhile I'll have a look to see if the King hasn't, to say it without any nonsense, opened his eyes. [*Goes out into the bedchamber.*]

CHEF   Princess Henrietta didn't eat a thing for three whole weeks.

HEINRICH   Poor girl! [*Quickly writes something on a scrap of paper.*]

CHEF   But now she eats all day long.

HEINRICH   To her health. [*The* COOKS *bring in a platter of pastries.*] Ah! What pastries! I have been in many courts, but I've never seen anything like it before! What aroma. How nicely browned. How soft and light!

CHEF [*flattered, smiling*]   Y-yes. They are so soft and light that they will get dented just from an intense look.

HEINRICH   You're a genius.

CHEF   H-have one.

HEINRICH   I don't dare.

CHEF   No, go ahead! Y-you are a connoisseur. That's so rare.

HEINRICH [*takes one, pretending to bite into it. He quickly hides a note in the pastry*]   Ah! I'm overcome! There's no one your equal in the world.

CHEF   But my skill, alas, will perish with me.

HEINRICH [*pretending to chew*]   Why so?

CHEF   My book *Here's How to Cook, Ladies and Gentlemen* perished.

HEINRICH   What! When?

CHEF [*in a whisper*]   When it became fashionable to burn books in the public squares. In the first three days they burned all the really dangerous books. But the fashion didn't pass. Then they began burning all the other books indiscriminately. Now there are no books at all. They burn straw.

HEINRICH [*in a whistling whisper*]   But you know, that's awful! Isn't it?

CHEF [*looking around, in a whistling whisper*]   You're the only one I can tell. It is. Awful!

[*During this brief dialogue,* HEINRICH *has managed to put the pastry with the note back on the very top.*]

VALET   Quiet! I believe the King sneezed.
                              [ALL *listen intently.*]

HEINRICH [*to* CHRISTIAN, *softly*]   I put a note into a pastry, Christian.
CHRISTIAN   Fine, Heinrich. Don't get upset.
HEINRICH   I'm afraid the note will get greasy.
CHRISTIAN   Heinrich, take it easy! We'll write another.

[*The* PRIME MINISTER *crawls out from behind the curtain.*]

PRIME MINISTER   The Sovereign has opened one eye. Be ready! Call
    the chamberlains! Where are the ladies-in-waiting? Hey, trumpeters!
    [*Enter* TRUMPETERS, CHAMBERLAINS, COURTIERS. *They quickly fan
    out on both sides of the curtain to the bedchamber. The* VALET,
    not taking his eyes off the PRIME MINISTER, *holds the tassel of the
    curtain.*] [*In a desperate whisper.*] Everything ready? Tell the truth.
VALET   Exactly so!
PRIME MINISTER [*desperately*]   Let 'er go, right at my head!

[*The* VALET *pulls the cords. The curtain parts. Beyond it nothing
can be seen except a huge pile of feather beds disappearing above
the archway.*]

CHRISTIAN   Where's the King?
CHEF   He sleeps on one hundred and forty-eight feather beds—that's
    how noble he is. You can't see him. He's right under the ceiling.
PRIME MINISTER [*peeping*]   Quiet. Get ready! He's turning over. He
    has scratched his eyebrow. He's frowning. He has sat up. Trumpets!

[*The* TRUMPETERS *sound off.* ALL *shout three times:* "Hurrah for the
King! Hurrah for the King! Hurrah for the King!" *Dead silence. After
a pause, there comes from up near the ceiling a whimsical voice:*
"Ah! Ah! Oh, what is this? Oh, what for? Why did you wake me
up? I was dreaming of a nymph. What swinishness!"]

VALET   I make bold to remind Your Majesty that today marks the
    arrival of the Princess, Your Majesty's fiancée.
KING [*from up above, capriciously*]   Ah, what is this, mockery is what
    it is. Where's my dagger? I'll slit your throat this minute, you bad
    man, and that's that. Oh, where is it? Oh, how many times have I
    told you—put my dagger right under my pillow.
VALET   But it's already half past ten, Your Majesty.
KING   What? And you didn't wake me up! This is what you get for
    that, you ass! [*The dagger flies down. It sticks into the floor right
    at the* VALET's *feet. A pause.*] Well! Why aren't you bellowing?
    Didn't I wound you?
VALET   Not at all, Your Majesty.
KING   Well, maybe I killed you?

VALET   Not at all, Your Majesty.

KING   Didn't kill you, either? What swinishness! I'm unlucky! I've lost all accuracy. Oh, what is this, just what is this! Step back! You see I'm getting up!

PRIME MINISTER   Be ready! The Sovereign has risen to his full height on his bed! He is taking a step forward! He is opening his umbrella. Trumpets!

[*The* TRUMPETERS *sound off. The* KING *appears from under the arch. He comes down under an open umbrella, as if under a parachute. The* COURTIERS *shout* "Hurrah!" *The* KING, *having reached the floor, throws down the umbrella which the* VALET *immediately picks up. The* KING *is in a luxurious dressing-gown with a crown tied to his head by a ribbon. The ribbon is tied under his chin in a big bow. The* KING *is about fifty, full-fleshed and healthy. He looks at nobody, although the reception room is full of* COURTIERS. *He behaves as if he were alone in the room.*]

KING [*to the* VALET]   What is this! What is all this! Why don't you say anything! Sees his Sovereign is out of sorts and can't think of a thing to do. Pick up the dagger. [*For a while reflectively studies the dagger returned him by the* VALET, *then puts it in his dressing-gown pocket.*] Lazy! Aren't even worthy of death from a noble hand. I tipped you yesterday with a gold coin?

VALET   Exactly so, Your Majesty!

KING   Give it back. I'm displeased with you. [*Takes the money from the* VALET.] Even disgusted . . . [*Paces back and forth, touching with the skirts of his gown the* COURTIERS, *who are frozen in reverence.*] Dreamed of a lovely, noble little nymph, of exceptionally fine breed and pure blood. She and I at first crushed all our neighbors and then afterwards we were happy. I wake up— and there in front of me is this repulsive lackey! What was it I said to the nymph? Sorceress! Enchantress! A man in love with you can't help but love you! [*With conviction.*] Well said. [*Capriciously.*] But what is all this? What is this? Well? What did I wake up for? Hey, you! What for?

VALET   In order to don a new robe, fresh from the needle, Your Majesty.

KING   Blockhead! I can't get dressed when I'm out of sorts. First cheer me up. Call my Fool; quickly, my Fool!

VALET   His Majesty's Fool!

[*The* FOOL *steps forward from among the* COURTIERS, *who are stand-*

ing stockstill. He is a stolid man in a pince-nez. Jumping and leap-
ing, he draws near the KING.]

KING [*with official brazenness and cunning. Loudly*]   Hello, Fool!
FOOL [*in the same way*]   Hello, Your Majesty!
KING [*sinking into an armchair*]   Cheer me up. Be quick about it.
   [*Whimsically and plaintively.*] It's time for me to dress, but I keep
   being angry, plain out of sorts. Well! Start in!
FOOL [*seriously*]   Now this, Your Majesty, is a very funny story. A
   certain merchant . . .
KING [*captiously*]   What's his name?
FOOL   Petersen. A certain merchant, by the name of Petersen,
   started out of his shop but tripped—and fell flat on his face on
   the pavement.
KING   Ha-ha-ha!
FOOL   And just at that moment along came a painter with a bucket
   of paint, tripped over the merchant, and spilled his paint all over
   an old woman who was walking by.
KING   Really? Ha-ha-ha!
FOOL   And the old woman got frightened and stepped right on her
   dog's tail.
KING   Ha-ha-ha! Fie on you, my god! Ha-ha-ha! [*Wiping away tears.*]
   Right on its tail?
FOOL   On its tail, Your Majesty. And the dog bit a fat man.
KING   Oho-ho-ho! Ha-ha-ha! Oi, stop!
FOOL   And the fat man . . .
KING   Stop, stop! I can't stand it, I'll burst. Go back, I've cheered
   up. We'll start dressing. [*Unties the bow under his chin.*] Take
   my night crown. Give me the morning one. So! Call the Prime
   Minister.
VALET   His Excellency the Prime Minister to His Majesty!

[*The* PRIME MINISTER *runs up to the* KING.]

KING [*dashingly*]   Hello, Prime Minister!
PRIME MINISTER [*in the same way*]   Hello, Your Majesty!
KING   What do you say to that, old man? Ha-ha-ha! What a Fool
   I have! Grabbed the old woman by the tail! Ha-ha-ha! What I
   like about him is that it's pure humor. Without any hints or digs
   or sly remarks. Merchant bit the fat man! Ha-ha-ha! Well, what's
   new, old man? Huh?
PRIME MINISTER   Your Majesty! You know that I'm an honest old
   man, a forthright old man. I tell the truth straightforwardly right

in one's face, even if it's unpleasant. I was standing here the whole time, watching how you, to speak frankly, woke up, listening to how you, to put it bluntly, laughed, and so forth. Permit me to tell you straightforwardly, Your Majesty . . .

KING   Out with it, out with it. You know I never get angry at you.

PRIME MINISTER   Allow me to tell you straightforwardly, bluntly, from an old man's point of view: you are a great man, Sire!

KING [*very, very pleased*]   Oh, come now, why say that?

PRIME MINISTER   Yes, Your Majesty, yes. I can't restrain myself. I will say again—forgive me my unbridled willfulness—you are a giant! A luminary!

KING   Ah, what a man you are! Ah, ah!

PRIME MINISTER   You, Your Majesty, ordered the Court Scholar to compile, pardon me, the Princess's genealogy. To find out, to put it bluntly, one thing and another about her ancestors. Forgive me, Your Majesty, for being straightforward—that was a marvelous idea.

KING   Oh, go on with you! Oh, heavens!

PRIME MINISTER   The Court Scholar, to put it plainly without frills or furbelows, is here. Shall I call him? Oh, King! [*Shakes his finger at him.*] Oh, you clever man!

KING   Come here, righteous old man. [*Deeply moved.*] Let me kiss you. And never fear to speak the truth right to my face. I'm not like other kings. I love the truth, even when it's unpleasant. The Court Scholar is here? All right! Good enough! Have him come in. I will dress and drink my chocolate, and he can talk. Give the order for the robing with chocolate, honest old man.

PRIME MINISTER   Yes, Your Majesty! [*With a flourish.*] Lackeys!

[*To the sound of trumpets, the* LACKEYS *bring in a screen. The* KING *conceals himself behind it, so that only his head is visible.*]

Tailors!

[*A still more majestic fanfare. The* TAILORS, *taking the last stitch as they go, go up and stop by the screen.*]

Chef!

[*To the trumpeting, the* CHEF *marches up to the screen. He hands the cup of chocolate to the* VALET. *He moves away backwards and disappears behind the* COURTIERS.]

Scholar!

[*The* COURT SCHOLAR, *carrying an enormous book, takes a position in front of the screen.*]

'Ten-tion!

[*He looks around. Everyone is motionless. He gives the next order.*]

Ready. Begin!

[*The trumpet fanfare changes into light, rhythmic music, as if a music box were playing. The* TAILORS, *standing stock still in front of the screen, now vanish behind it. The* VALET *feeds the* KING *his chocolate with a spoon.*]

KING [*after several swallows, shouts dashingly*]   Hello, there, Scholar!
SCHOLAR   Hello, Your Majesty.
KING   Speak up! No, stop, wait! Prime Minister! Let the courtiers hear this, too.
PRIME MINISTER   Ladies and gentlemen of the court! His Majesty has remarked your presence.
COURTIERS   Hurrah for the King! Hurrah for the King! Hurrah for the King!
KING   And the girls are here. The ladies-in-waiting. Koo-koo! [*Ducks behind the screen.*]
FIRST LADY-IN-WAITING [*an elderly, energetic woman, speaks in a moderate, low voice*]   Koo-koo, Your Majesty.
KING [*creeping out*]   Ha-ha-ha! [*With a flourish.*] Hello, naughty girl.
FIRST LADY   Hello, Your Majesty.
KING [*playfully*]   What did you dream of, you playful thing?
FIRST LADY   You, Your Majesty.
KING   Me? Good girl!
FIRST LADY   I want to do my best, Your Majesty.
KING   And you, girls, what did you dream of?
OTHER LADIES-IN-WAITING   You, Your Majesty.
KING   Good girls!
OTHER LADIES   We want to do our best, Your Majesty.
KING   Splendid. First Lady-in-Waiting! You were successful in militarizing the girls. They respond today very dashingly. Know that you have my gracious approval. What rank are you?
FIRST LADY   Colonel, Your Majesty.
KING   I promote you to general.
FIRST LADY   My humble gratitude, Your Majesty.

KING   You deserve it. You've been my leading beauty for thirty years now. Every night you've dreamed of me, only of me. You're my chicky, General!

FIRST LADY   I want to do my best, Your Majesty.

KING [*softening*]   Oh, you sweet sugar-plums, Don't go far away, dearies. Or the professor will dry me up. So, Scholar of the Court, let fly!

SCHOLAR   Your Majesty. With the assistance of Adjunct Professor Brockhaus and Assistant Professor Efron,° I have compiled an absolutely accurate genealogical table of your most royal guest.

KING [*to the* LADIES-IN-WAITING]   Koo-koo! Hee-hee-hee!

SCHOLAR   First, her coat of arms. A coat of arms, Your Majesty, is an hereditary armorial symbolic representation, yes, representation, composed of figures and colors based on well-known rules, yes, rules.

KING   I myself very well know what a coat of arms is, Professor.

SCHOLAR   From time immemorial there have come into usage symbolic signs, yes, signs, which are inscribed on rings.

KING   Tiu-tiu!

SCHOLAR   And drawn on weapons, standards, and other such, yes, and other such.

KING   Chick-chick! Chickies!

SCHOLAR   These signs came about as a result of . . .

KING   That's enough about signs, get down to business. . . . Koo-koo!

SCHOLAR   . . . Yes, as a result of a desire to indicate separation of oneself from the masses, yes, separation. To lend oneself a clear mark of distinction, noticeable even in the heat of battle. That's it. Battle.

[*The* KING *comes from behind the screen. He is brilliantly dressed.*]

KING   To business, Professor!

SCHOLAR   Coats of arms . . .

KING   To business, you've been told! Cut it short!

SCHOLAR   Ever since the time of the Crusades . . .

KING [*waves his dagger at him*]   I'll kill you like a dog! Make it short!

°A reference to the famous Brockhaus encyclopedia, first edition published by F. A. Brockhaus in 1810–1811, continued by his family, and translated into Russian, among other languages, by S. K. Efron and others. Its short articles in popular form were aimed at the general reader, not the specialist. Biographies of living men were included.

SCHOLAR   In that case, Your Majesty, I'll start blazoning.°

KING   Huh? What'll you start?

SCHOLAR   Blazoning!

KING   I forbid it! And what kind of another dirty trick is that! What does the word mean?

SCHOLAR   But blazoning, Your Majesty, means describing a coat of arms.

KING   Then say that!

SCHOLAR   I'm blazoning. The Princess's coat of arms. On a gold field strewn with crimson hearts, three crowned azure partridges, with a leopard couchant.

KING   What, what? Couchant?°

SCHOLAR   Indeed, Your Majesty . . . Around, a border of flowers of the kingdom.

KING   Oh, very well . . . It's not to my liking. But let it be! Tell me the family tree, but keep it brief.

SCHOLAR   Yes, Your Majesty! When Adam . . .

KING   How awful! The Princess is a Jewess?

SCHOLAR   What do you mean, Your Majesty!

KING   Well, after all, Adam was a Jew.

SCHOLAR   That's a moot question, Your Majesty. I have evidence that he was a Karaite.°°

KING   Well, there you are! For me the chief thing is that the Princess is pure-blooded. That's very fashionable now, and I'm a man of fashion. Am I not a man of fashion, chickies?

LADIES-IN-WAITING   Exactly so, Your Majesty.

SCHOLAR   Yes, indeed, Your Majesty. You, Your Majesty, have always kept up with the very latest ideas. Indeed, with the very latest.

KING   Isn't that so? Just think of what my trousers alone cost! Go on, Professor.

SCHOLAR   Adam . . .

KING   Let's leave that delicate question and skip to later times.

SCHOLAR   Pharaoh Isameti . . .

KING   We can skip him, too. Very ugly name. Next . . .

SCHOLAR   Then permit me, Your Majesty, to proceed directly to Her Highness's dynasty. The founder of the dynasty was Georg I, for

°The word "blazoning" puns on the Russian word meaning to tempt, to seduce, to deceive. The word translated "couchant" (lit., "burdened") puns on the word meaning pregnant.
°°An heretical Jewish sect, founded in Baghdad in the eighth century A.D., once widespread but now small, most of its followers living in southern Russia.

his deeds otherwise known as The Great. Yes, otherwise known as.

KING   Very good.

SCHOLAR   He was followed by his son, Georg II, for his deeds otherwise known as The Ordinary. Yes, The Ordinary.

KING   I'm in a hurry. Simply list her ancestors. I'll understand precisely what they received their nicknames for. Otherwise, I'll slit
your throat.

SCHOLAR   Yes, Your Majesty. I proceed: Wilhelm I The Gay, Heinrich I The Short, Georg III The Dissolute, Georg IV The Pretty,
Heinrich II The Hell With Him.

KING   What did he get that nickname for?

SCHOLAR   For his deeds, Your Majesty. Then comes Philip I The
Abnormal, Georg V The Funny Boy, Georg VI The, Negative,
Georg VII The Barefoot, Georg VIII The Anemic, Georg IX The
Blunt, Georg X The Spiderlegs, Georg XI The Bold, Georg XII
The Antipathetic, Georg XIII The Impudent, Georg XIV The In-
teresting, and finally, the presently reigning father of the Princess,
Georg XV for his deeds otherwise known as The Bearded. Yes,
otherwise known as.

KING   A very rich and varied collection of ancestors.

SCHOLAR   Yes, Your Majesty. The Princess has eighteen ancestors,
not counting the escutcheons of the maternal side. . . . Yes, has.

KING   Completely adequate . . . Off with you! [*Looks at his watch.*]
Oh, how late! Call the Court Poet, hurry!

PRIME MINISTER   The Poet to the Sovereign! Make it snappy!

[*The* COURT POET *dashes up to the* KING.]

KING   Hello, Court Poet.

POET   Hello, Your Majesty.

KING   You have the welcoming speech ready?

POET   Yes, Your Majesty. My inspiration . . .

KING   And the poem for the Princess's arrival?

POET   My muse helped me find five hundred and eight couplets of
the most magnificent rhymes, Your Majesty.

KING   What, are you just going to read off the rhymes? What about
the verses, where are they?

POET   Your Majesty! My muse had barely managed to complete the
lines on your parting from the right-wing lady-in-waiting. . . .

KING   Your muse is forever lagging behind events. All the two of you
know how to ask for is a summer cottage or a little house or a cow.
Damned if I know what else! What, for example, does a poet want

a cow for? But as for writing some verses, you were too late, didn't manage . . . You're all like that!

POET   However, my devotion to Your Majesty . . .

KING   I don't need devotion, but some verses!

POET   But the speech is ready, Your Majesty.

KING   The speech . . . You're all past-masters at that! Well, let's have the speech at least.

POET   It's not actually a speech, but a conversation. Your Majesty speaks, and the Princess replies. A copy of the responses was sent special delivery by courier to meet the Princess on her way. Will you permit me to recite it?

KING   You may.

POET   Your Majesty says, "Princess! I am happy that you have risen on my throne like the Sun. The light of your beauty illuminates Everything all around." To which the Princess replies, "The Sun is you, Your Majesty. The brilliance of your deeds casts all your rivals into shadow." To that you say, "I'm happy that you appreciate my merit." And the Princess replies, "Your virtues are the pledge of our future happiness." You respond, "You have understood me so well that I can only say that you are as wise as you are beautiful." Then the Princess says, "I am happy that Your Majesty is pleased with me." And you say, "I sense that we love each other, Princess, let me kiss you."

KING   Very good!

POET   The Princess says, "I am so confused . . . but . . ." At this point the cannon thunder, the troops shout "Hurrah!"—and you kiss the Princess.

KING   I kiss her? Ha-ha! That's all right! On the mouth?

POET   Exactly so, Your Majesty.

KING   That's clever. Off with you. Ha-ha! Old man, that's nice! Yes, indeed! Well, well! Eh! [*Dashingly putting his arm around the waist of the senior* LADY-IN-WAITING.] Who else is waiting to see me? Huh? Speak up, you candid old man.

PRIME MINISTER   Your Majesty, I won't conceal the fact that some weavers are still waiting to see you.

KING   Ah! Why haven't they been let in? Hurry up, chase them in here to me on the double!

PRIME MINISTER   Weavers to the King—at a gallop!

[HEINRICH *and* CHRISTIAN *with a flourish fly hoppingly into the middle of the stage.*]

KING   What old men— Means they're experienced. How lively—must be hard-working. Hello, weavers.

HEINRICH *and* CHRISTIAN   Good day to you, Your Majesty.

KING   What have you got to say? Huh? Well! Why don't you speak up? [CHRISTIAN *heaves a big sigh.*] What did you say? [HEINRICH *heaves a big sigh.*] What?

CHRISTIAN   The poor king! Oh-uh!

KING   What are you trying to frighten me for, you fools? What's up? Why am I a poor king?

CHRISTIAN   Such a great king—and dressed like that!

KING   How am I dressed? Huh?

HEINRICH   Normally, Your Majesty.

CHRISTIAN   Like everybody.

HEINRICH   Like all the kings around.

CHRISTIAN   Oh, Your Majesty, oh!

KING   Ah, what is this! What are they saying?! It's not possible! Open up my wardrobe. Give me cloak number four thousand nine from the lace suit. Look at that, you fools. Pure faille. Edged with pleated guipure. Alençon lace on top, and Valenciennes on the bottom. That goes with my lace holiday suit. And you say—like everybody else! Give me my boots! Look—even my boots are trimmed with Brabant lace. Have you ever seen anything like it?

HEINRICH   Have we ever!

CHRISTIAN   Many times!

KING   Well, now, damn it all! Then give me my dinner outfit. No, not that one, you ass! Number eight thousand four hundred ninety-eight. Hey, you, look at this! What's this?

HEINRICH   Trousers.

KING   Out of what?

CHRISTIAN   Why bother asking? It's *gras-de-Naples.*

KING   Oh, you unscrupulous . . . What, you think *gras-de-Naples* is nothing? And the camisole? Pure *gros-de-Tour.* And the sleeves *grosgrain.* And the collar—*peau de soie.* And the cloak is turquoise with lengthwise stripes of rep. Look and admire that! Why are you turning away?

HEINRICH   We've seen it.

KING   And stockings of *drap-de-soie?*

CHRISTIAN   That, too.

KING   But feel them, you fool.

HEINRICH   But why . . . I know it.

KING   You do? Bring me my trousers for the wedding ball! Now, what's this?

CHRISTIAN   Covert cloth.

KING   Right, but what kind? Where in the world is there anything
else like it? And the camisole is cheviot with a collar of Boston!
And the cape? Tricot. You ever seen that, you fool?

HEINRICH   Actually every fool has seen that, Your Majesty.

CHRISTIAN   But we can make such cloth . . . oho! . . . which only
a wise man will ever see. We'll make you an unheard-of wedding
outfit, Your Majesty.

KING   Indeed! They all say that! You have any references?

CHRISTIAN   We worked for the Turkish sultan for a year; his pleasure
was such that it couldn't be put in writing. And so he didn't write
anything for us.

KING   Just think, the Turkish sultan!

CHRISTIAN   The Great Mogol of India thanked us personally.

KING   Just think, the Indian Mogol! Don't you know that our nation
is the greatest in the world? All the rest are no good, but we're
great fellows. Haven't heard, hunh?

CHRISTIAN   Besides, our cloth possesses one unheard-of miraculous
quality.

KING   I can imagine. . . . What?

CHRISTIAN   I already told you, Your Majesty. Only a wise man will
ever see it. Our cloth is invisible to people who are unsuited for
their jobs or are utter fools.

KING [*beginning to be interested*]   Well, sir, well, now. What about
it?

CHRISTIAN   Our cloth is invisible to people who are unfit for their
jobs or stupid.

KING   Ha-ha-ha! Oho-ho-ho! Oi, you're killing me! Fie, damn it all!
So that Prime Minister there—you mean, if he's unfit for his job
he won't see that cloth?

CHRISTIAN   No, he won't, Your Majesty. That's the miraculous property of the cloth.

KING   Aha-ha-ha! [*Becomes limp from laughter.*] Old man, you hear
that? Huh, Minister? I'm talking to you!

PRIME MINISTER   Your Majesty, I don't believe in miracles.

KING [*waving his dagger around*]   What? Don't believe in miracles?
Right beside the throne itself a man who doesn't believe in mira-
cles? Why, you materialist! Why, I'll send you to the dungeon!
You brazen boor!

PRIME MINISTER   Your Majesty! Permit me to reproach you a little
from an old man's point of view. You didn't let me finish. I was
going to say: I don't believe in miracles, says the madman in his

heart of hearts. It's the madman who doesn't believe, but only by a miracle do we stand firm!

KING   Ah, so! Well, then all right. Wait a minute, weavers. What a remarkable cloth! Means that with it I'll see which of my people is in the wrong place?

CHRISTIAN   Exactly so, Your Majesty.

KING   And I'll instantly know who is stupid and who is wise?

CHRISTIAN   In a flash, Your Majesty.

KING   Silk?

CHRISTIAN   Pure, Your Majesty.

KING   Wait a minute. I'll have a talk with you after I receive the Princess. [*The trumpets sound off.*] What's going on there? Huh? Find out, old man!

PRIME MINISTER   Your Majesty's Minister of Tender Feelings has arrived.

KING   Aha, aha, aha! Well, sir, well, now. Hurry up, Minister of Tender Feelings! Come on, now, hurry up! [*The* MINISTER OF TENDER FEELINGS *enters.*] Good news? I can see by your face it's good. Hello, Minister of Tender Feelings.

MINISTER OF TENDER FEELINGS   Hello, Your Majesty.

KING   Well, so, my dear man. I'm ready to listen, my angel.

MINISTER OF TENDER FEELINGS   Your Majesty. Alas! In terms of morality the Princess is absolutely irreproachable.

KING   Heh-he! Then why "alas"?

MINISTER OF TENDER FEELINGS   The pure-bloodedness, alas, Your Majesty. The Princess didn't feel the pea under the twenty-four feather beds. Moreover, the whole rest of the way she slept on just one feather bed.

KING   What are you smiling for? Ass! That means there'll be no wedding! And I had so settled on it! Oh, what is this! Oh, what a dirty trick! Come here, I'll slit your throat!

MINISTER OF TENDER FEELINGS   But, Your Majesty, I didn't think I had the right to conceal this unpleasant truth from you.

KING   I'll show you an unpleasant truth this minute! [*Chases him with the dagger.*]

MINISTER OF TENDER FEELINGS [*screams*]   Oi! Ah! I'll never do it again! Have mercy on me! [*Runs out of the room.*]

KING   Get out! Everybody get out! You've upset me! Insulted me! I'll stab you all! Put you in prison! Sterilize you! Out! [ALL *run out of the reception room except the* PRIME MINISTER.] [*Running up to the* PRIME MINISTER.] Chase her away! Immediately chase the

Princess away! Maybe she's a Semite? Maybe a Hamite? Away!
Out!

PRIME MINISTER   Your Majesty! Listen to an old man. I talk simply,
bluntly, like a bear. Chasing her away because she supposedly isn't
pure-blooded—well, her father will be insulted.

KING [tapping his foot]   So, let him!

PRIME MINISTER   War will break out.

KING   I sneeze at it!

PRIME MINISTER   But it would be better for you to have a little meeting with the Princess and for you to tell her gently, delicately: I
don't like your looks, you could say. I'll put it bluntly, plain and
direct: You, Your Majesty, you know, are an expert in these matters.
It's hard to satisfy you. Well, and then we'll gently, secretly see the
Princess on her way. I see it! I see it! Ah, King, ah, you clever fellow! He sees that I'm right! He agrees!

KING   I agree, old man. Go get everything ready for the reception,
then I'll see her off. Let her be received in the Court!

PRIME MINISTER   Oh, King! Oh, you genius! [Goes out.]

KING [whimsically]   Oh this, oh this is awful! Again I'm upset. Fool!
Fool, come here, hurry up! Speak up, Fool. Cheer me up! Be funny!

[The FOOL runs in, hopping.]

FOOL   A certain merchant . . .

KING [captiously]   What's his name?

FOOL   Ludwigsen. A certain merchant was crossing a little bridge and
plop! fell into the water.

KING   Ha-ha-ha!

FOOL   A rowboat was passing under the bridge. His heel landed on
the oarsman's head.

KING   Ha-ha-ha! On his head! Ho-ho-ho!

FOOL   The oarsman also plopped into the water, and at this moment
there was an old woman walking along the bank. He caught her by
the dress—and she went into the water, too.

KING   Ha-ha-ha! That's killing! Oho-ho-ho! Ha-ha-ha! Ha-ha-ha!
[Wipes tears away without taking his triumphant glance off the
FOOL.] So?

FOOL   And she . . .

CURTAIN

The royal courtyard paved with variously colored planks and slabs. At the back wall, the throne. On the right, a fence for the public.

MINISTER OF TENDER FEELINGS [*comes in limping slightly, shouts*]   Oh! Over here, Master Chamberlain! Oh!

CHAMBERLAIN   Why are you moaning? Did you get wounded? Ah! *Oo-liu-liu!*

MINISTER   Ah! No, not wounded! Killed! Over here! Bring the *porte-chaise* with the bride over here! Oh!

CHAMBERLAIN   But what happened? Ooauwoo!

MINISTER   You'll see! [*Runs out.*]

[*The sedan chair with the* PRINCESS *is brought in. The* GOVERNESS *and the* CHAMBERLAIN *walk alongside the chair.*]

CHAMBERLAIN [*to the* PORTERS]   Put the chair down and make your-selves scarce. Don't creep up to the window, you rascals! Tally-ho!

GOVERNESS [*to the* CHAMBERLAIN]   Be told to them: hands to taken be *von* pockets out. No nose don't pick. Straight so stand!

CHAMBERLAIN   Ah, me no bringing up can do. Eyes out keep, lest Princess yours and mine a note overhands to humpty-dumpty! [*To the* PORTERS.] What are you listening for? Makes no difference, you don't understand foreign languages anyway. Out with you! [*The* PORTERS *run off.*] [*To the* GOVERNESS.] Well, *una* load *de* shoulders that is off by itself has gotten *ein, zwei, drei.* Now *diese* Princess to the King we give one hand to the other. And *una, dua,* guess.

GOVERNESS [*gaily*]   *Cinque, baba,* yes. *Und* glad is me.

CHAMBERLAIN [*to the* PRINCESS]   Your Highness. Get ready. I will go now and announce our arrival to the King. Your Highness! You asleep?

PRINCESS   No, I was thinking.

CHAMBERLAIN   Oh! Well, all right. [*To the* GOVERNESS.] The self posi-tion *von* the gate by, labby-tabby. And everything out of be look-ing. Myself to the King I'm a-winding.

GOVERNESS   *Und!* [*Stands at the entrance to the courtyard.*]

PRINCESS   Here everything is foreign, everything is stone, not a single blade of grass. The walls look down like wolves on a lamb. I would be scared, but the note from wonderful, curly-headed, my kind, gentle, own, handsome Heinrich made me so happy that I'm even smiling. [*Kisses the note.*] Ah, how wonderfully it smells of nuts.

Ah, how beautifully oily it has become. [*Reads.*] "We're here. I have white hair and a white beard. Scold the King. Tell him he's badly dressed. Heinrich." I don't understand a thing. Oh, how clever he is! But where is he? If only I could see him for a second . . .

[*Singing comes from behind the wall. Two male voices sing softly:*]

> We'll battle for our happiness,
> Then peacefully go home,
> You and I together, love,
> You and I alone.

PRINCESS   Oh, that's his voice! That means he'll come right away. That's how it was last time—he sang and then appeared! [*The* PRINCE MINISTER *comes out and stops in his tracks, seemingly overcome by the* PRINCESS's *beauty.*] There he is! With white hair and a white beard.

PRIME MINISTER   Allow me, Your Highness, allow me in a blunt, fatherly way from an old man's point of view to tell you, I'm beside myself from your beauty.

PRINCESS [*runs up to him*]   Well!

PRIME MINISTER [*puzzled*]   Indeed, Your Highness.

PRINCESS   Why don't you say pull my beard?

PRIME MINISTER [*in horror*]   Pull what, Your Highness?

PRINCESS [*laughs*]   Oh, you! You won't fool me now! I recognized you right away!

PRIME MINISTER   My god!

PRINCESS   Now I've learned how to pull properly! [*Pulls his beard as hard as she can.*]

PRIME MINISTER [*shrieking*]   Your Highness! [*The* PRINCESS *pulls his hair and rips off his wig. He is bald.*] Help!

[*The* GOVERNESS *runs in to him.*]

GOVERNESS   What's he with her doing, strange man old man! *Lia! Pas de trois!*

PRIME MINISTER   Of His Majesty is me the Prime Minister.

GOVERNESS   You, Princess, what for him *bitte-dritte?*

PRINCESS   Let him go to hell and gone, for all I care!

GOVERNESS   Drops be drinking, *wass is das.*

PRINCESS   But I beat the hell out of them, the bastard.

PRIME MINISTER [*laughs gaily. Aside*]   Indeed, she's absolutely mad! That's just fine! We'll very easily send her back. I'll go tell the King. But, on the other hand, no, he dislikes unpleasant reports. Let him see for himself. [*To the* PRINCESS.] Your Highness, allow me to tell you straightforwardly, from an old man's point of view: you're such a naughty girl a man's heart is delighted. The ladies-in-waiting will love you, honest to god. I'll call them, may I? They'll help you clean up from your trip, show you one thing and another, and meanwhile we'll get things ready here for your reception. Girls! [*The* LADIES-IN-WAITING *file in.*] Princess, let me present our ladies-in-waiting to you. They're very pleased to meet you.

PRINCESS   Me, too. I'm so lonely here, and almost all of you are as young as I am. Are you really glad to see me?

FIRST LADY   The report, Your Highness.

PRINCESS   What?

FIRST LADY   Your Highness! While I was on duty nothing exceptional occurred. Four ladies-in-waiting accounted for. One in the police station. One on duty detail. Two in hysterics on the occasion of the impending marriage. [*Salutes.*]

PRINCESS   What are you, a soldier?

FIRST LADY   Not in the least; I'm a general. Proceed into the palace, Princess. Girls! My command! For-ward ha-arch! [*They go.*]

PRINCESS   That's awful!

[*They disappear in the doorway.*]

PRIME MINISTER   Hey, you there! Bring in the soldiers. I'll go get the crowd. [*Goes out.*]

[*The* SOLDIERS *enter, led by an* OFFICER.]

OFFICER   Having a premonition of a meeting with the King, weaken from excita-a-tion! [*The* SOLDIERS *sink to a squatting position.*] In squatting position, ha-arch! [*The* SOLDIERS *move on in squatting position.*] Le-eft! Ri-ight! To the wa-all! 'Ten-tion!

[*The* CROWD *comes in. The* PRIME MINISTER *leads it behind the fence.*]

PRIME MINISTER [*to the* CROWD]   Though I know that you're the most loyal and trusted citizens, I still want to remind you: in His Majesty's palace one opens one's mouth only to shout "Hurrah!" or to sing a hymn. Understand?

CROWD   We do.

PRIME MINISTER   Badly, you do. You're already in the royal palace. How could you, instead of shouting "Hurrah!," say something else? Huh?

CROWD [*shattered*]   Hurrah!

PRIME MINISTER   For he's the King! Get that: the King—and suddenly so close to you. He's wise, he's special! Not like other people. And such a miracle of nature suddenly two paces from you. Amazing! Huh?

CROWD [*with goodwill*]   Hurrah!

PRIME MINISTER   Stand silently until the King appears. Sing a hymn and shout "Hurrah!" until the King says "At ease." After that, be quiet. Only when the Royal Guard shouts at a signal from His Excellency, then you shout, too. Understand?

CROWD [*soberly*]   Hurrah.

[*A shout draws near:* "Make way for the King! Make way for the King! Make way for the King!" *The* KING *enters with his* RETINUE.]

OFFICER [*giving the command*]   At the sight of the King faint away from excitement and anima-a-tion! Plop!

[*The* SOLDIERS *fall down.*]

PRIME MINISTER [*to the crowd*]   Sing the hymn!

CROWD   That's how the King, And so the King, Fie there, Hi there, Oh what a King! Hur-rah! That's how the King, And so the King, Fie there, Hi there, Oh what a King! Hur-rah!

KING   At ease!

[*The* CROWD *falls silent.*]

OFFICER   Co-ome to!

[*The* SOLDIERS *get up.*]

KING   But where is she? Oh, what is this! How annoying! I'd like to have lunch right away, but here this . . . half-breed . . . Where is she? Have to send her on her way quickly.

PRIME MINISTER   She's coming, Your Majesty.

[*The* PRINCESS *and the* LADIES-IN-WAITING *come out.*]

OFFICER [*giving the command*]   At the sight of the young and beautiful Princess jump up and down in buoyant expecta-tion!

[*The* SOLDIERS *jump up and down.*]

[*From the moment the* PRINCESS *appears, the* KING *begins behaving in a puzzling way. His face shows perplexity. He speaks dully, as if hypnotized. He stares at the* PRINCESS *with his head bent forward like a bull. The* PRINCESS *goes up on to the dais.*]

OFFICER [*giving the command*]   Pa-rade rest!

[*The* SOLDIERS *stop.*]

KING [*as if sleepwalking, in a throaty tenor*]   Hello, Princess.
PRINCESS   Damn you to hell and gone.

[*For a while the* KING *looks at the* PRINCESS *as if trying to grasp the meaning of what she said. Then, with a queer smile, swings around in a salute and clears his throat.*]

OFFICER [*giving the command*]   Be weak and stunned by such attention!
KING [*still in the same voice*]   Princess. I am happy that you have risen on my throne like the sun. The light of your beauty illuminates everything all around.
PRINCESS   Shut your trap, you old bag.
KING [*in the same way*]   I'm happy that you appreciate my merit.
PRINCESS   Ass.
KING [*in the same way*]   You have understood me so well, Princess, that I can only say that you are as wise as you are beautiful.
PRINCESS   You mangy idiot. You stupid sheep.
KING   I sense that we love each other, Princess, let me kiss you. [*Takes a step forward.*]
PRINCESS   Get away from me, you son of a bitch!

[*A cannonade. A triumphant "Hurrah!" The* PRINCESS *descends from the dais. With a queer walk, not bending his knees, the* KING *moves downstage on to the apron. The* LADIES-IN-WAITING *surround him. The* PRIME MINISTER *supports him by the elbow.*]

FIRST LADY   Your Majesty! Will you let me pinch the hussy?
PRIME MINISTER   Your Majesty, I'll call a doctor.
KING [*with difficulty*]   No, not a doctor . . . No . . . [*Shouts.*] The weavers!
PRIME MINISTER   They are here, Your Majesty.
KING [*shouting*]   Immediately make me a wedding outfit!
FIRST LADY   But, Your Majesty, you heard how she violated discipline!
KING   No, I didn't! I only saw her! I'm in love! She's miraculous! I'm going to get married! Right now! How dare you look surprised! I don't give a damn about her parentage! I'll change all the laws—she's pretty! No! Take this down! I bestow upon her this instant the most noble, the most pure-blooded parentage! [*Bellows.*] I'm going to get married even if the whole world is against me!

CURTAIN

A corridor in the palace. A door leads into the Weavers' room.
The Princess stands pressed against the wall. She is very sad.
Outside the wall a drum is rolling.

PRINCESS   It's very difficult and wearisome, living in somebody else's
country. Everything here is . . . oh, what's the word . . . mili . . .
militarized. . . . Everything is done to the drum. The trees in the
garden are lined up in platoons. The birds fly in battalions. And
besides that, there are these awful, centuries-old, sacred traditions
which make it completely impossible to live. At dinner you get
served chops, and then orange jelly, and then soup. It's been done
like that since the ninth century. They powder the flowers in the
garden, and they shave the cats, leaving only sideburns and a little
brush on the end of the tail. And you can't change it or go against
it at all, or else the whole state will perish. I'd be very patient if
Heinrich were with me. But Heinrich has gone, Heinrich is lost!
How can I ever find him with the court ladies following me everywhere in ranks? My life is my own only when they are taken away
for instruction. . . . It's been very hard pulling every beard. You find
a bearded man in the hall and you give his beard a yank—but the
beard stays on as if it were stitched to him, and the man shrieks—
no pleasure at all. They say the new weavers have beards, and right
now the ladies are out marching around on the square, getting ready
for the wedding parade. The weavers work here. Shall I go in, pull
their beards? Oh, it's so scary! Suddenly maybe Heinrich won't be
here, either! Maybe they suddenly caught him and following the
eighth-century traditions drummed him into the square and cut off
his head! No, I have a feeling, I have a feeling I'm going to have
to slit that king's throat, and that's so repulsive! I'll go see the
weavers. I'll put gloves on. I have blisters on my fingers from all
these beards. [*Takes a step toward the door, but the* LADIES-IN-
WAITING *enter the hall in formation.*]
FIRST LADY   Do you wish the report, Your Highness?
PRINCESS   A-bout fa-ace! [*The* LADIES *turn around.*] Ha-arch!

[*The* LADIES *go off. They disappear. The* PRINCESS *takes a step toward
the door. The* LADIES *come back.*]

FIRST LADY   The wedding gown . . .
PRINCESS   A-bout fa-ace! Ha-arch!

[*The* LADIES *take several steps, then return.*]

FIRST LADY   . . . is ready, Your Highness.
PRINCESS   A-bout fa-ace! Ha-arch!

[*The* LADIES *turn around, start out. They are met by the* KING *and the* PRIME MINISTER.]

FIRST LADY   'Ten-tion!
KING   Ah-ah, my sweeties. A-a-ah! There she is. And just exactly as I saw her in my dream, only much angrier. Princess! Sweetie. A man in love with you can't help but love you.
PRINCESS   Get the hell out, scram! [*Runs out, accompanied by the* LADIES-IN-WAITING.]
KING [*laughs loudly*]   Her nerves have completely gone to pieces. I understand her so well. I, too, am completely consumed with impatience. No matter. The wedding is tomorrow. Right now I'll go in and have a look at that wonderful cloth. [*Goes toward the door and stops.*]
PRIME MINISTER   Your Majesty, you were going, as you always do, correctly. This way, this way.
KING   Just you wait a minute . . .
PRIME MINISTER   The weavers, you know, pardon my bluntness, are working right in here.
KING   I know, I know. [*Goes downstage on to the apron.*] Indeed . . . The cloth is something special. . . . Of course, I have no reason to feel uneasy. First of all, I'm wise. Secondly, I'm absolutely not suited for any other position except that of king. Even as king, I'm always finding something missing, I'm always getting angry, but in any other position I would be simply terrifying. . . . All the same . . . It might be better if somebody else went in to the weavers first. Now, there's the Prime Minister. The old man is honest, wise, but still stupider than I am. If he sees the cloth, then I will have seen it all along. Minister! Come here!
PRIME MINISTER   Here I am, Your Majesty.
KING   I just remembered that I still have to run over to the treasure-house to pick out some diamonds for the bride. Go in and have a look at that cloth and then report to me.
PRIME MINISTER   Your Majesty, pardon my bluntness . . .
KING   I won't. Go on! Look lively! [*Runs out.*]
PRIME MINISTER   Ye-es. It doesn't amount to anything. . . . However . . . [*Shouts.*] Minister of Tender Feelings!

[*The* MINISTER OF TENDER FEELINGS *comes in.*]

MINISTER OF TENDER FEELINGS   Hello.

PRIME MINISTER   Hello. Oh yes—they're waiting for me in the office. Go in to the weavers and report to me what they have and how they are doing. [*Aside.*] If this fool sees the cloth, then I will have seen it all along.

MINISTER OF TENDER FEELINGS   But, Mister Prime Minister, I must go down immediately to the barracks of the King's Ladies-in-Waiting and persuade them not to cry during the wedding tomorrow.

PRIME MINISTER   You'll have time. Go ahead in to the weavers. Look lively. [*Runs out.*]

MINISTER OF TENDER FEELINGS   Ye-es. I, naturally . . . However . . . [*Shouts.*] Court Poet! [*The* COURT POET *enters.*] Go in to the weavers and report to me what they have and how they are doing. [*Aside.*] If this fool sees the cloth, then I will have seen it all along.

COURT POET   But, Your Excellency, I'm just finishing the verses about the Princess's departure from her own kingdom and her coming to our native land.

MINISTER OF TENDER FEELINGS   Who is interested in that now? The Princess arrived two weeks ago. Go on in. Look lively! [*Runs out.*]

COURT POET   Naturally, I'm no fool. . . . But . . . Oh, here goes! If worst comes to worst, I'll lie. It wouldn't be the first time! [*Knocks on the door.*]

CURTAIN

The Weavers' room. Two large hand looms are set against the wall. Two large frames stand in the middle of the room. The frames are empty. A big table. On the table are scissors, a pincushion with gold pins, a folding yardstick.

CHRISTIAN   Heinrich! Heinrich, cheer up! We have the finest silk, which we were given for weaving; it's there in the bag. Out of it I'll weave a wonderful dress for your bride. And in this purse there's gold. We'll ride home on the finest horses. Cheer up, Heinrich!

HEINRICH   I'm very cheerful. I'm silent, because I'm thinking.

CHRISTIAN   About what?

HEINRICH   How Henrietta and I will stroll along the river beside our house in the evening.

[*A knock on the door.* CHRISTIAN *grabs the scissors, bends over the table, and pretends to be cutting.* HEINRICH *draws on the table with a piece of chalk.*]

CHRISTIAN   Come in.

[*The* COURT POET *enters.*]

COURT POET   Hello, Court Weavers.

CHRISTIAN [*without stopping his work*]   Hello, Court Poet.

COURT POET   Now, you see, Weavers, the thing is I've been sent on a very important mission. I must look at and make a description of your cloth.

CHRISTIAN   Please do, Mister Poet. Heinrich, what do you think, should we put the roses with the leaves up or the petals up?

HEINRICH [*frowning*]   Yes. I think so, yes. With the petals, I think. The silk shimmers more beautifully on the petals. The King will take a breath, and the petals will quiver as if they were real.

COURT POET   I'm waiting, Weavers!

CHRISTIAN   For what, Mister Poet?

COURT POET   What do you mean, for what? I'm waiting for you to show me the cloth which you have made for the King's suit. [HEINRICH *and* CHRISTIAN *drop their work. They stare at the* COURT POET *in great astonishment.*] [*Frightened.*] Oh, never mind, never mind! You hear? Why keep staring? If I've made a mistake, point it out to me, but there's no point trying to bewilder me! My work is intense and high-strung! I must be spared things!

CHRISTIAN   But we are extremely amazed, Mister Poet!

COURT POET   At what? Speak right up, at what?

CHRISTIAN   Why, all the cloths are before you. Here, on these two frames the silks are stretched for drying. Here, they are in piles on the table. What color, what patterns!

COURT POET [*clears his throat*]   Of course, they're there. There, lying there. What a heap. [*Recovering himself.*] But I was giving you directions about showing me the silk: showing me and explaining which is for the camisole, which for the cape, and which for the caftan.

CHRISTIAN   Why, surely, Mister Poet. On this frame there are three kinds of silk. [*The* POET *writes in a notebook.*] One, the one with the roses, is for the King's camisole. It will be very lovely. The King will take a breath, and the petals will quiver as if they were real. On this middle one are the devices of the royal coat of arms. That's for the cape. On this one are little forget-me-nots—for the King's trousers. The pure white silk on this frame will be for the King's underclothes and his stockings. This satin is for covering the King's shoes. On the table there are scraps of all kinds.

COURT POET   Now tell me, I'm very interested, what you, in your plain language, call the color of this first piece? The one with the roses.

CHRISTIAN   In our plain language the background of this piece is called green. What is it in yours?

COURT POET   Green.

HEINRICH   What a gay color—isn't it, Mister Poet?

COURT POET   Indeed. Ha-ha-ha! Very gay! Yes. Thanks, Weavers. You know, the whole palace is talking about nothing but your amazing cloth. Each is just trembling with the desire to make sure of the stupidity of the next man. The Minister of Tender Feelings will be here in a minute. Good-bye, Weavers.

CHRISTIAN *and* HEINRICH   Good-bye, Court Poet.

[*The* POET *goes out.*]

HEINRICH   Well, now things are going all right, Christian.

CHRISTIAN   Now I'll make the Minister of Tender Feelings hop a bit, Heinrich.

HEINRICH   Hop how, Christian?

CHRISTIAN   Like a ball, Heinrich.

HEINRICH   You think he'll do what you say, Christian?

CHRISTIAN   I'm simply convinced of it, Heinrich.

[*A knock on the door. The* MINISTER OF TENDER FEELINGS *enters. In his hands he has the pages from the* POET's *notebook. He goes self-confidently up to the first frame.*]

MINISTER OF TENDER FEELINGS   What splendid roses!

CHRISTIAN [*shrieks wildly*]   Aaah!

MINISTER [*with a hop*]   What's the matter?

CHRISTIAN   Pardon me, Mister Minister, but don't you see? [*Points under his feet.*]

MINISTER   What don't I see? What the hell am I supposed to see?

CHRISTIAN   You're standing on the silk from which we were about to cut out the King's camisole.

MINISTER   Ah, I see it, I see! [*Steps aside.*]

HEINRICH   Aaah! You're trampling on the King's cape!

MINISTER   Oh, damned absent-mindedness! [*Takes a big jump to the right.*]

CHRISTIAN   Aah! The King's underclothes!

[*The* MINISTER *takes a big jump to the left.*]

HEINRICH   Aaah! The King's stockings!

[*The* MINISTER *jumps and hops out the door. He pokes his head into the room.*]

MINISTER [*through the door*]   Ah, what magnificent work! We ministers are obliged by our position to hold our heads high, and therefore, what's down below on the floor I, being unaccustomed to looking down, see badly. But what's in the frame, and what's on the table—the roses, the coats of arms, the forget-me-nots—it's beautiful, beautiful! Keep on, Master Weavers, keep on. The Prime Minister will be here in a minute. [*Goes out, closing the door.*]

CHRISTIAN   Who was right, Heinrich?

HEINRICH   You were, Christian.

CHRISTIAN   And I'll call the Prime Minister a fool right to his face, Heinrich.

HEINRICH   Right to his face, Christian?

CHRISTIAN   Right to his face, Heinrich.

[*The* PRIME MINISTER *opens the door, pokes his head in.* CHRISTIAN, *pretending not to notice him, goes behind the frame.*]

PRIME MINISTER   Hey, Weavers! You ought to pick things up from the floor. Such fine, expensive cloth—and lying about in the dust. Ai, ai, ai! The King will be here in a minute.

HEINRICH   Very well, Your Excellency. [*Pretends that he picks up the cloth and folds it and lays it on the tables.*]

[*The* PRIME MINISTER *enters. He cautiously stands by the door.* CHRISTIAN, *having gone behind the frame, takes a bottle out of his pocket. He drinks.*]

PRIME MINISTER   Hey there, you insolent scoundrel, how dare you drink vodka on the job?

CHRISTIAN   Who's the fool bellowing away there?

PRIME MINISTER   Huh?! You blind or something? It's me, the Prime Minister!

CHRISTIAN   Forgive me, Your Excellency, because of the cloth I can't see you and I didn't recognize your voice. But how you saw me—that I don't understand!

PRIME MINISTER   Why, I . . . by smell. I dislike that cursed liquor. I can smell it a mile away.

[CHRISTIAN *comes from behind the frame.*]

CHRISTIAN   But this isn't vodka—it's water, Your Excellency.

PRIME MINISTER   What are you sticking your nasty bottle under my nose for? Stand right there! The King is coming! [*Goes out.*]

[*From the wings, the sound of singing: the* KING *is approaching and singing gaily.*]

KING [*in the wings*]   Now I'll go and have a look, now I'll go and have a look, troo-lia-lia! Troo-lia-lia! [*Gaily enters the room. Behind him, the* COURTIERS.] Troo-lia-lia! Troo-lia-lia! [*In a lowered voice.*] Troo-lia-lia! [*A pause. With a vague smile makes an extraordinarily elaborate sweep with his hand.*] Well! Well, how are things going? Huh?

COURTIERS   It's wonderful, marvelous, what cloth!

PRIME MINISTER   The cloth is elegant and noble, Your Majesty.

COURTIERS   Indeed it is! So suitable! Elegant and noble!

KING [*to the* PRIME MINISTER]   And what do you say, honest old man? Huh?

[*The* KING *is crushed, but keeps up his spirits. He talks to the* PRIME MINISTER *but keeps his eye on the table and the frames, obviously hoping to see at last the marvelous cloth. On his face the same frozen smile.*]

PRIME MINISTER   Your Majesty, this time I'll tell you such pure, straightforward truth as the world has never seen. Maybe you'll be surprised, Your Majesty, maybe I'll astound you, but I'll say it.

KING   That's the way.

PRIME MINISTER   Forgive me, now, but at times a man wants to be really straightforward. No cloth, Your Majesty, will you ever find anywhere like this. It's both luxurious and colorful.

COURTIERS   Oh, so true! Luxurious and colorful! Very rightly said.

KING   Yes, the weavers are great fellows. I see you have that . . . everything pretty much ready? . . .

CHRISTIAN   Yes, Your Majesty! I hope Your Majesty won't object to the color of these roses?

KING   No, I won't. Indeed, I won't.

CHRISTIAN   We decided that anybody can see plenty of red roses on bushes.

KING   See on bushes. Indeed. Lovely, lovely.

CHRISTIAN   And therefore on the silk we made them slav . . . [*coughs*] slav . . . [*coughs.*]

COURTIERS   Lavender, how clever! How original—lavender! Luxurious and noble.

CHRISTIAN   Silver, ladies and gentlemen of the Court.

[*A pause.*]

MINISTER OF TENDER FEELINGS   Bravo, bravo! [*Applauds; the* COURTIERS *join in.*]

KING   I was about to thank you for making them silver; that's my favorite color. Literally, I was just about to. You have my royal gratitude.

CHRISTIAN   And, Your Majesty, how do you find the cut of this camisole—not too bold?

KING   No, not too. No. That's enough talking about it, let's try them on. I still have a lot of things to do.

CHRISTIAN   I would like to ask the Minister of Tender Feelings to hold the King's camisole.

MINISTER OF TENDER FEELINGS   I don't know if I'm worthy of that.

KING   You are. Indeed. Well, sir. [*Trying to keep up his pluck.*] Hand him that lovely camisole. . . . Undress me, Prime Minister. [*Undresses.*]

CHRISTIAN   Aaah!

MINISTER OF TENDER FEELINGS [*with a hop, looking underfoot*]   What is it?

CHRISTIAN   How are you holding the camisole, Mister Minister?

MINISTER OF TENDER FEELINGS   Like a sacred object . . . What about it?

CHRISTIAN   But you're holding it upside down.

MINISTER OF TENDER FEELINGS   I got carried away by the pattern. [*Turns the nonexistent camisole around in his hands.*]

CHRISTIAN   Would the Prime Minister be kind enough to hold the King's trousers?

PRIME MINISTER   I've just come from the office, my friend, my hands are covered with ink. [*To one of the* COURTIERS.] Take them, Baron!

FIRST COURTIER   I forgot my glasses, Your Excellency. Now, the marquis here . . .

SECOND COURTIER   I'm too excited, my hands are shaking. Now, the count here . . .

THIRD COURTIER   In our family it's a bad sign to be holding the King's pants. . . .

KING   What's all this about? Dress me and be quick about it. I'm in a hurry.

CHRISTIAN   Very well, Your Majesty. Heinrich, come here. Your foot,

Your Majesty. Left! Right! I'm afraid the gentlemen of the Court would dress you much more smartly. We are embarrassed in the presence of such a great king. There, the trousers are on. Mister Minister of Tender Feelings, the camisole. I'm sorry, but you're holding it backwards. Aah! You dropped it! Please, we better do it ourselves. Heinrich, the cape. That's everything. The charm of this cloth is its lightness. You don't feel it at all on your shoulders. The underclothes will be ready by morning.

KING   It's tight in the shoulders. [*Turns around in front of the mirror.*] The cape is a little too long. But, in general, the suit is fine for me.

PRIME MINISTER   Your Majesty, pardon my bluntness. You are, in general, a handsome man, and in this suit—doubly so.

KING   Really? Well, take it off. [*The* WEAVERS *undress the* KING *and put his suit back on.*] Thanks, Weavers. Great fellows. [*Goes toward the door.*]

COURTIERS   Great fellows, the weavers! Bravo! Luxurious and noble! Elegant and colorful! [*They slap the* WEAVERS *on the back.*] Well, now we won't let you go. You must clothe all of us!

KING [*stopping in the door*]   Ask whatever you like. I'm satisfied.

CHRISTIAN   Let us accompany you, Your Majesty, in the wedding procession. That would be our best reward.

KING   I so decree. [*Goes out with the* COURTIERS.]

HEINRICH *and* CHRISTIAN *(sing)*

> We're stronger than the lords and earls,
> We're bolder than the pushy churls.
> Afraid to lose your places means
> Your consciences are far from clean.
> We're not afraid of anything.
>
> The reason why we wove was real;
> Our cloths have greater strength than steel.
> They will astound—and drive to jigs—
> Both full-grown swine and suckling pigs.
> We're not afraid of anything.
>
> If we sink our enemies,
> We'll praise ourselves for our good deeds.
> But if they are beyond our scope,
> We'll end up swinging from a rope.
> We're not afraid of anything.

The curtain is lowered for several seconds. It rises. The same
room in the morning. Crowd noises can be heard outside the
window. The King is being dressed behind a screen. The Prime
Minister stands downstage by the proscenium.

PRIME MINISTER   Why did I ever become Prime Minister? Why?
Weren't there enough other positions? I have a feeling today's business will end badly. Fools will see the King naked. That's awful!
Awful! Our whole national system, all our traditions depend on and
are supported by steadfast fools. What will happen if they start
giving way at the sight of the nude sovereign? The foundations will
shake, the walls will crack, smoke will rise over the state! No, the
King must not be let out naked. Elegance is the great buttress of
the throne! I had a friend, a colonel in the guards. He retired, came
to see me without his uniform. And suddenly I realized that he
wasn't a colonel, but a fool. It was awful! Gone with his uniform
were his prestige, his enchanting qualities. No! I'll go tell the Sovereign frankly: You mustn't go out! No! You mustn't!

KING   Honest old man!

PRIME MINISTER [*runs*]   Speaking bluntly, here I am.

KING   How do these underclothes look?

PRIME MINISTER   Speaking straight to your face, they're beautiful.

KING   Thanks. That's all!

PRIME MINISTER [*again by the proscenium*]   No! I can't! Can't say a
thing, my tongue won't do it! It's lost the habit after thirty years
in the service. Should I tell him? Or shouldn't I? What will happen!
What will happen!!

CURTAIN

A square. In the foreground, a dais covered with rugs. On both
sides leading from the platform, roads laid with carpeting.
The left road leads to the gates of the royal castle. The right
disappears into the wings. A fence, decorated with luxurious
cloths, separates the crowd from the road and the dais. The
crowd sings, whistles, makes noise. When the noise abates,
various conversations become audible.

FIRST LADY   Oh, I'm so excited about the King's new clothes! Yesterday I had heart-failure twice from excitement.

SECOND LADY   And I was so excited that my husband fainted.

BEGGAR   Help! Guards!

VOICES   What's that? What happened?

BEGGAR   Somebody stole my purse!

VOICE   Oh, but probably there were just some coppers in it.

BEGGAR   Coppers! You insolent scum! The most experienced, skill-
ful, oldest beggar have coppers? There was ten thousand talers!
Ah! Here it is, my purse, in the lining. Thank god! . . . Alms, for
love of the Lord.

SHAVED GENTLEMAN   What if suddenly the King, her Father, is late?

BEARDED GENTLEMAN   Didn't you hear the cannonade? He has already arrived. He and the Princess will come to the square from
the harbor. The King, her Father, came by sea. Riding in a carriage makes him sick.

SHAVED GENTLEMAN   But doesn't he get seasick?

BEARDED GENTLEMAN   At sea it's not so embarrassing.

BAKER WITH WIFE   Please, gentlemen, please let us through! You can
stare but we have business!

VOICES   Everybody has the same business!

BAKER   No, not everybody! For fifteen years my wife and I have been
arguing. She says I'm a fool, and I say she is. At last, today the
King's clothes will solve our quarrel. Let us through!

VOICES   We won't! We're all here with our wives, everybody has
been arguing, we're all here on business!

MAN WITH A CHILD ON HIS SHOULDERS   Make way for the child, let
the child through! He's six years old, and he can read, write, and
knows the multiplication tables by heart. For that I promised to
show the King to him. Boy, how much is seven times eight?

BOY   Fifty-six.

MAN   You hear that? Let the child through, make way for my clever
son! And how much is six times eight?

BOY   Forty-eight.

MAN   You hear that, ladies and gentlemen? And he's only six years
old. Make way for the wise boy, let my son through!

ABSENT-MINDED MAN   I forgot my glasses at home and now I won't
see the King. Damned myopia!

PICKPOCKET   I can very easily cure you of that!

ABSENT-MINDED MAN   Really! How?

PICKPOCKET   By massage. Right now, right here.

ABSENT-MINDED MAN   Oh, please do. My wife told me to look carefully and describe everything to her in detail, and here I've forgotten my glasses.

PICKPOCKET   Open your mouth, close your eyes, and loudly count to
   twenty.

[*The* ABSENT-MINDED MAN *counts aloud without closing his mouth.
The* PICKPOCKET *steals his watch, his wallet, his purse, and disappears
in the crowd.*]

ABSENT-MINDED MAN [*having finished the count*]   Where is he? He
   ran off! And I see worse than ever. I don't see my watch, my wallet, or my change-purse!
MAN   Make way for my boy! Let my intelligent son through! How
   much is six times six?
BOY   Thirty-six.
MAN   You hear that? Clear the way for my son! Make way for the
   child prodigy!

[*A roll of drums is heard. Movement in the* CROWD. *They climb up
columns, pedestals, on to each other's shoulders.*]

VOICES   He's coming! He's coming!
   There he is!
   How handsome!
   And handsomely dressed!
   You crushed my watch!
   You're sitting on my neck!
   You can ride in your own carriage if you feel there's not enough
      room here!
   Has his helmet on, too!
   And his glasses!

[SOLDIERS *come in.*]

GENERAL [*commanding*]   Move the crowd awaiting the King back
   from the fe-ence!
SOLDIERS [*all together*]   Beat it. Scram. Beat it. Scram. Beat it.
   Scram. Beat it. Scram. [*Push the* CROWD *back.*]
GENERAL   Turn your ba-acks on the crowd!

[*The* SOLDIERS *turn their backs on the crowd, face toward the dais.
The trumpets thunder.* HERALDS *march down the road.*]

HERALDS   Hats off, hats off, hats off before His Majesty!

[*They go into the palace. From the wings on the right comes the elegantly dressed* KING HER FATHER *with the* PRINCESS *in her wedding
gown. They go to the dais. The* CROWD *quiets down.*]

PRINCESS   Father, for once in your life, believe me. On my word of
  honor: the groom is an idiot!
KING HER FATHER   A king can't be an idiot, daughter. Kings are always wise.
PRINCESS   But he's fat!
KING HER FATHER   Daughter, a king can't be fat. It's called "stately."
PRINCESS   I think he's deaf. I swear at him but he pays no attention
  and gives a coarse laugh.
KING HER FATHER   A king can't give a coarse laugh. He smiles graciously. Why do you keep pestering me? Why are you looking at
  me with sorrowful eyes? I can't do a thing! Look there! See, I've
  brought you the pot. After all, the King won't be with you all
  day every day. You can listen to the music, to the little bells. When
  nobody is near, you can even listen to its song. A Princess can't
  marry a swineherd! She can't!
PRINCESS   He's not a swineherd, but Heinrich!
KING HER FATHER   Makes no difference! Don't be a silly fool; don't
  undermine respect for the King's authority. Otherwise, neighboring
  kings will be smiling graciously on *you*.
PRINCESS   You're a tyrant!
KING HER FATHER   Not in the least. There—look. There's the Minister
  of Tender Feelings running. Cheer up, daughter. Look how ridiculous he is!
MINISTER OF TENDER FEELINGS   Your Majesty and Your Highness! My
  Sovereign will be out presently. At the moment he deigns, dagger
  in hand, to chase the second chamberlain, who laughed derisively
  at the sight of our most gracious Sovereign's new clothes. As soon
  as the insolent scoundrel is punished, our Sovereign will appear.
  [*A fanfare of trumpets.*] The chamberlain has been punished!

[HERALDS *come out.*]

HERALDS   Hats off, hats off, hats off before His Majesty!

[*From the palace come* TRUMPETERS, *followed by the* LADIES-IN-
WAITING *in formation, behind them the* COURTIERS *in embroidered
uniforms; behind them, the* PRIME MINISTER.]

PRIME MINISTER   The King is coming! The King is coming! The King
  is coming! [*Turns and looks back. No king.*] As you were! [*Runs
  into the palace. Comes back. To the* KING HER FATHER.] Now! Our
  sovereign was detained, to put it bluntly, in front of the mirror.
  [*Shouts.*] The King is coming! The King is coming! The King is
  coming! [*Turns and looks back. No king. Runs into the palace.*

Comes back. To the KING HER FATHER.] They're bringing him, they're bringing him! [*Loudly.*] The King is coming! The King is coming! The King is coming!

[*The* KING *is brought in in the sedan chair. Smiling graciously, the* KING *peers out the window. The chair stops. The* CROWD *cries* "Hurrah!" *The* SOLDIERS *fall flat. The doors of the chair open. The* KING *jumps out. He is completely naked. Shouts of greeting burst forth all at once.*]

PRINCESS   Aah! [*Turns away.*]

GENERAL   Co-ome to! [*The* SOLDIERS *get up, glance at the* KING, *and again fall flat on their faces in horror.*] Co-ome to! [*With difficulty, the* SOLDIERS *rise.*] Look a-way!

[*The* SOLDIERS *turn their heads away. The* CROWD *is silent. The* KING *slowly, smiling self-confidently, without taking his eyes off the* PRINCESS, *moves toward the dais. He approaches the* PRINCESS.]

KING [*gallantly*]   Even the most elegant clothing cannot conceal the flame burning in my heart.

PRINCESS   Papa, now do you see that he's an idiot?

KING   Greetings, Cousin.

KING HER FATHER   Greetings, Cousin. [*In a whisper.*] What are you doing, Cousin? Why do you appear before your subjects like this?

KING [*in a whisper*]   What? You, too? Ha-ha-ha!

KING HER FATHER   What do you mean, me, too?

KING   Either you don't have the right job or you're a fool. Whoever doesn't see this cloth either doesn't have the right job or is a fool.

KING HER FATHER   The fool is the one who sees it, you shameless man!

KING   Who is shameless?

KING HER FATHER   Not so loud! Or the mob will hear us. Don't speak so loudly—and smile. You're shameless!

KING [*constrainedly smiling. Quietly*]   Me?

KING HER FATHER   Yes!

KING [*for a while says nothing, filled with indignation. Then asks in a low voice*]   Why?

KING HER FATHER [*hisses maliciously, smiling all the while*]   Because you appeared in the square, filled with people, without your trousers!

KING [*slaps his leg*]   And what's this?

KING HER FATHER   A leg!

KING   A leg?

KING HER FATHER   Yes!

KING   No.

KING HER FATHER   A bare leg!

KING   Why lie so? I give you my honest royal word that I'm dressed as pretty as a picture!

KING HER FATHER   You're naked, naked, naked!

KING   Well, what is this! Well, what a dirty trick! Well, what for! Courtiers! Am I dressed?

COURTIERS   Elegantly and colorfully! Luxuriously and nobly!

KING   Got that? Prime Minister! Am I dressed?

PRIME MINISTER   [*in his usual voice*]   Pardon my bluntness, Your Majesty. [*Ferociously.*] You're naked, you old fool! Y'understand? Naked, naked, naked!

[*The* KING *lets out a strange wail, something like a hiccup. It is a wail full of extreme amazement.*]

Look at the people! Go ahead, look at the people! They're thinking to themselves. Thinking to themselves, you miserable clown! The traditions are cracking! Smoke is rising over the state!

[*The* KING *gives the same howl again.*]

Shut up, you tub of nothing! General! Come here!

[*The* GENERAL *trots over to the dais.*]

Can the troops be counted on? They'll stand by the King in case something happens? You hear how silent the people are?

GENERAL   The weather let us down, Mister Prime Minister!

KING   Huh?

GENERAL   The weather, Your Majesty. It was overcast this morning, and many in the crowd brought their umbrellas just in case . . .

KING   Umbrellas?

GENERAL   Yes, Your Majesty. They're armed with umbrellas. If the crowd were unarmed, it would be one thing, but here they have umbrellas.

KING   Umbrellas?

GENERAL   If we're speaking completely frankly, I can't swear for the soldiers, either. They'll retreat! [*In a whisper.*] They're demoralized! [*The* KING *lets out the same howl again.*] I'm surprised myself, Your Majesty. There are no books, no pamphlets, no agitators, the discipline is superb, but each day they get more and more demoralized. I tried giving the command: Cease demoral-i-za-tion! But it won't work!

MINISTER OF TENDER FEELINGS   Oh, I don't know, can't allow this;

I'm dissatisfied, too; I'll just go over there, where the people are.

PRIME MINISTER   Shut up!

MINISTER OF TENDER FEELINGS   We must establish a Provisional Committee for the Security of the Courtiers.

PRIME MINISTER   Shut up! There's no time to lose! We must stun the crowd by our bold insolence! We have to go on with the wedding as if nothing at all had happened!

PRINCESS   I . . .

PRIME MINISTER [with a bow]   Shut up!

KING HER FATHER   He's right! On with it, go on!

MINISTER OF TENDER FEELINGS   My Ladies-in-Waiting are militarized. They'll stand by our committee.

PRIME MINISTER   Your ladies are a lot of nonsense! Take the Princess's hand, King. [Waves to the HERALDS.]

HERALDS   Silence! Silence! Silence!

[A pause.]

BOY   But Papa, he has no clothes on!

[Silence, and then an explosion of shouting.]

MINISTER OF TENDER FEELINGS [runs into the palace, shouting as he goes]   My mother was a blacksmith, my father was a washerwoman! Down with autocracy!

BOY   He's naked, and he's fat!

SHOUTS   Y'hear what the boy says? And he can't have the wrong job! He's not a public servant!
He's smart, he knows the multiplication tables!
The King is naked!
Has a wart on his belly, and he collects taxes!
Has a belly like a watermelon, and he says—obey!
He has a pimple! See, there, he has a pimple!
Serves him right, the sterilizer!

KING   Be quiet! I did it on purpose. Yes. I did it all on purpose. This is my command: From now on everybody gets married naked. So! [A sharp whistle.] You mangy fools! [A sharp whistle. The KING dashes into the palace. The PRIME MINISTER, followed by all the COURTIERS, dash after him. The KING HER FATHER and the PRINCESS remain on the dais.]

KING HER FATHER   Let's fly! You see the look in the eyes of those people on the other side of the fence? They saw the king naked. They're undressing me, too, with their eyes. They'll fling themselves on me in a minute!

HEINRICH *and* CHRISTIAN [*jumping onto the dais, shout*] Oo-hoo-
hoo!
KING HER FATHER Ah, it's started! [*Gathering his robe up, runs off
along the road on the right.*]
PRINCESS Heinrich!
HEINRICH Henrietta!
CHRISTIAN [*to the* CROWD] Dear friends! You came to enjoy a festive
day, but the groom ran off. Yet still the festival took place. Isn't
this a real holiday? At last the young girl has been united with her
darling Heinrich! They were going to marry her to an old man,
but the power of love overcame all obstacles. We salute your just
anger at those grim scenes. Now you in turn salute us, salute love,
friendship, laughter, and joy!

PRINCESS   Darling Heinrich, fierce in fight,
                    Heinrich is my own.
                    Left—right, left—right
                    Now he'll take me home.

CROWD   Let the earth exult today,
                    We chased the King away!
                    Let the earth exult today,
                    We chased the King away!

                         [*They dance.*]

HEINRICH   Any man of common sense
                    Will hurtle straight and fast
                    Left—right, left—right
                    To happiness at last!

ALL   Let the earth exult today,
                    We've chased the King away!
                    Let the earth exult today,
                    We've chased the King away!

                         CURTAIN

IT'S Been AGeS!

BY VERA PANOVA

CHARACTERS

Bakchenin
Shemetova
Nyusha ⎱ *Shemetova's daughters*
Alyona ⎰
Grandmother
Grandfather
Kolosyonok
Linevsky
Lyusya, *a waitress*
Ivan Gavrilovich, *newsdealer*
Slavik, *Lyusya's husband*
The Airport Manager
Tamara, *an airport secretary*
An Old Woman in Glasses
Linevsky's Boss
Arefyev
Officers
Men and Women Passengers

1

The stage is the main building of an airport, shown in cross-section. We see part of the lower level and part of the upper—the exit to loading ramps, a stairway, the waiting room, a newsstand, a corner of the restaurant, closed office doors with and without nameplates. Timetables are on the walls.

A snowstorm swirls outside the huge windows. A real blizzard.

The terminal is full of people. They crowd from the information booth to the post office, stand in line at the telephone booth, sit on benches and in armchairs, collect in anxious little groups. From time to time pilots and elegant, slim-waisted stewardesses walk through the groups of passengers with indifferent self-confidence.

It is not yet dusk but the lights are on. Otherwise it would be dark in the terminal.

VOICE ON THE P.A. SYSTEM   Your attention please! Flight sixty-two, an IL-18 to Tashkent, is delayed. Announcement will be made of the departure time.

OLD WOMAN IN GLASSES   What did I tell you: another one is delayed.

LYUSYA *[runs downstairs, ducks into* TAMARA's *office]*   Tamarònka, dearònka, let me use your phone!

TAMARA   What next.

LYUSYA   Angel, just a minute, to call home, Slavik—

TAMARA   You have two kopeks? Use the pay phone.

LYUSYA   The line's a mile long.

[The phone on the desk rings.]

TAMARA   The airport. Yes, unchanged. I can't say; ask Information. I can't say. Well, either you understand or you don't! *[Slams the receiver down; it immediately rings again.]* The airport.

LYUSYA   Oh Lord! *[Runs to the pay phone.]*

P.A. VOICE   Your attention please! Flight three-two-three-six, an

IL-18 to Sverdlovsk–Perm–Moscow, is delayed. Announcement will be made of the departure time.

OLD WOMAN   What did I tell you!

LYUSYA   Oh, people, please let me in first! Won't you, please! It's terribly important! Please!

VOICES IN THE LINE   As if it weren't important for us! You think we'd be standing here if it weren't important?

LYUSYA   I work here. You know what that means? I've left work to call.

VOICES IN THE LINE   Everybody works some place, girl. If you work here you must have an office phone.

LYUSYA   Oh Lord! [*Gets at the end of the line.*]

LINEVSKY [*in the phone booth*]   It's me. Well? Called again? What did he say?

WOMAN IN THE LINE   If only I had known, I could have stayed home rather than wait around here who knows how long.

MAN IN THE LINE   But, you know, that would be taking a chance. There you are home and suddenly the plane up and takes off.

WOMAN   But nothing is taking off at all now.

LINEVSKY [*into the receiver*]   You tell him I don't want to hear a thing about it! Tell him none of this stuff. Let him fire me; let there be a scandal, whatever he likes! No, they're not going yet. No word. Yes, sure, I'm sitting here; what else can I do? You tell him, hear, to go right ahead. If it weren't for him, I would have been in Odessa this morning.

[*A motor sounds louder and louder.*]

VOICES IN THE LINE   Another one in. They're only landing.

[*The silhouette of a plane, moving to the ramp, passes through the storm.*]

P.A. VOICE   Attention please! Announcing the arrival of flight four hundred seventy-five, four-seven-five, TU-104, Moscow to Novosibirsk.

VOICES IN THE LINE   Moscow-Novosibirsk. Moscow-Novosibirsk. Well . . . [*The* AIRPORT MANAGER *comes in.*] The Manager! The Manager! Hey, there! Manager! Mister! Mister Manager! [*They rush toward him.*]

MAN [*to the* MANAGER]   What's the latest report?

MANAGER [*smiling cheerfully*]   None so far.

WOMAN   Will it soon be over?

MANAGER   It just started.

WOMAN   It's more than two hours already! If not three!

MANAGER   Strictly speaking, snow began to fall at midnight. The forecast was unfavorable. But the weather bureau didn't anticipate such a storm.

WOMAN   They never anticipate anything! Or else they predict the opposite of what happens.

MANAGER   [*completely self-possessed*]   Why do you say "the opposite," my friends? Snowfall, let me repeat, was anticipated. Only the amount was not anticipated. And you're not too uncomfortable here, are you, really? At any rate, we'll do all we can to make you comfortable.

WOMAN   It's not your comfort we need; we have to fly.

MAN   Exactly. We all have things to do.

BAKCHENIN   [*coming up, solidly*]   I, for example, have to make a report at a ministry meeting tomorrow morning.

MANAGER   You'll fly, my friends, all of you will.

VOICES   But when, when?

MANAGER   As soon as possible.

WOMAN   What if it lasts for days and days?

MANAGER   [*leaving*]   A natural calamity, my friends. A blizzard unlike any the world has ever seen. In both hemispheres. [*Goes out.*]

VOICES   What did he say? It's like this everywhere, he says. In both hemispheres.

LINEVSKY   [*running up*]   When does eight-oh-four leave? For Odessa? Did he say?

[LYUSYA, *taking advantage of the scattered line, has slipped into the phone booth.*]

LYUSYA   Please, Slavik. Unh-huh, wake him up, please. Slavik? Slavik, can you hear me? Slavik, I woke you up, I'm sorry, because . . . Sure, you see . . . Slavik, it's about Vitalik. The weather report says they don't know when it will be over, maybe not for some time. I'm on till eight, but I just don't know when I'll get home—they say the buses can hardly get through. . . . When you pick Vitalik up, don't forget there's a bottle between the window and the storm window; that's freshest; put the bottle in warm water, well, you know, and give it to him.

P.A. VOICE   Your attention please! Will Kolosyonok, the passenger who lost his ticket and travel papers, please report to the main desk? I repeat: Will Kolosyonok, the passenger who lost his ticket and travel papers, please report to the main desk?

MAN   Some fellow called Kolosyonok lost his travel papers.

WOMAN   This is enough to make you lose your mind, not just your travel papers.

[*The line returns and forms as before.*]

LYUSYA   Try it on your tongue—can you hear me?—to see if it's warm enough. [*Shouts into the receiver, covering it with her hand.*] Can you hear me clearly? Don't give it to him cold. Or hot, either. That's right. That's right. In the closet on the middle shelf. And on the line in the hall. Slavik, how do you feel? Did you get enough sleep? No? Well, go back to bed. Thank god you finished your shift. The weather is awful, just terrible. All right, Slavik, there are a lot of people waiting. A lot of people! All right. So long. [*Leaves the booth.*]

WOMAN   Look at that, if you please! She squeezed in ahead, anyway!

[*Passengers from the recently arrived Moscow-Novosibirsk flight come in, shaking off snow. The* SHEMETOV FAMILY *is among them: a youngish-looking mother, two daughters—twenty-four and eighteen— a grandmother, and a grandfather. Their general and very attractive characteristic is calm, the absence of worry, a benevolent gentleness. They seem to breathe tranquility. Only* ALYONA, *the younger daughter, is an exception, but even she, despite the garishness of her semi-boyish clothing and the independence of her behavior, lacks coarse loudness, and her escapades, thanks to her innate charm, are treated sympathetically.*]

ALYONA   Oho! Lots of people . . .

GRANDMOTHER   It would be nice to sit down.

NYUSHA   Maybe there's more room upstairs. I'll take a look.

ALYONA   Just a minute, Granny. Nyusha and I will scoot upstairs.

GRANDMOTHER   We'll all go up. There's a draft from the door here.

[*They go to the upper level.* GRANDFATHER *stops on the landing at the newsstand.*]

GRANDFATHER   All the Moscow papers, please, and the local one, too.

IVAN G. [*giving him the papers*]   Twenty-two kopeks, Academician.

GRANDFATHER   You think I am?

IVAN G.   At least a Corresponding Member. No mistake about that.

GRANDFATHER [*doffing his cap*]   The best of everything to you.

IVAN G.   And to you.

[*The* FAMILY *has moved into the upper waiting room.*]

SHEMETOVA   Take your coats off, girls, it's hot. [*They take their coats off.*] I wonder how long it can go on.

GRANDMOTHER   [*sitting down in one of the two empty chairs by the entrance*] Not a thing you can do about it. We'll just have to be patient. Where are the meat pies?

SHEMETOVA   Nyusha, where are the meat pies?

NYUSHA   With the suitcases.

GRANDMOTHER   You checked them?

NYUSHA   We checked everything.

ALYONA   We're barren people on the barren earth.

GRANDMOTHER   Sit down, Olya; why are you standing?

SHEMETOVA   Let Grandpa join you. There's one free over there.

[*She goes to sit in a chair, just vacated, beside* BAKCHENIN, *who is reading a paper; takes a book out of her handbag. Downstairs,* LINEVSKY *dashes into the phone booth.*]

LINEVSKY   I can't wait! It's crucial!

VOICES IN THE LINE   Outrageous! What in heaven's name does he think he's doing? You just were on the phone! He was on three times! I've been standing here twenty-five minutes!

LINEVSKY   It's a matter of life and death!

VOICES IN THE LINE   Maybe it is for all of us; how do you know?

LINEVSKY   I mean literally! [*With trembling fingers drops a coin into the phone.*] It's me. It's me. Me! Well? Did he call? You told him? Louder. I can't hear you! Louder!

GRANDFATHER   [*having sat down beside* GRANDMOTHER *and opened his paper*] If my ladies had only heeded my advice, we would be on our way right now.

GRANDMOTHER   On our way some forty-eight hours.

GRANDFATHER   But my emancipated ladies as usual wouldn't listen.

GRANDMOTHER   Things are undoubtedly the same with the trains. Undoubtedly there are huge drifts. It's a lot better to be sitting here in civilized warmth than tooting away in the middle of a snow-covered field.

ALYONA   Grandpa, imagine how depressing that is, tooting away in the middle of a snow-covered field.

GRANDFATHER   But from a train you can see the countryside and not just so much cloudy cotton.

GRANDMOTHER   I can't stand talk of trains when I know there are IL's and TU's. When I'm shaking to death on a train and somebody is flying six hundred miles an hour overhead, I feel like a Scythian.

ALYONA   You see, Grandpa. How could you let Granny feel like a Scythian?

GRANDMOTHER   Go away! . . . [*To* GRANDFATHER.] By train, we would have had to leave on Sunday to get there in time. But it wasn't until dinner yesterday that you said you were free and could go. Be at least minimally fair, my dear.

ALYONA   Let's go, Nyusha. Let's buy some books, see who's here.

P.A. VOICE   Your attention please! Will Kolosyonok, the passenger who lost his ticket and travel papers, please report to the main desk? I repeat: Will Kolosyonok, the passenger who lost his ticket and travel papers, please report to the main desk?

[KOLOSYONOK, *who has been drinking beer in the restaurant, feels his pockets and rushes out.*]

GRANDFATHER   Kolosyonok. A Belorussian name.

GRANDMOTHER   In our days there was no such service. Now you lose your travel papers, and right away they hand them back to you.

GRANDFATHER   [*deep in his paper*]   It certainly is convenient.

ALYONA   [*walking with* NYUSHA]   Not a single soul you would want to take with you to another planet. [*They stop at the newsstand.*] Do you have any poetry?

IVAN G.   Of course, of course, all the poetry you want. Who are you looking for?

ALYONA   [*surfeited*]   I don't really know . . .

IVAN G.   There's a new one, just came out—Elistratov. Ariadne Sabinina. Salomatov. We don't have the most popular ones; they never send us those.

[*A delightedly excited* KOLOSYONOK *appears.*]

ALYONA   Who cares about them, about the popular ones? I'm sick of them. I'll take Ariadne and Elistratov and Salomatov.

KOLOSYONOK   Let me have something to read. Can you imagine it: I lost my travel papers and didn't even know it! There I was, sitting in the restaurant, drinking beer. . . . Suddenly I hear an announcement. I feel in my pockets—empty! No passport, no identification card, no travel authorization! Only a boarding coupon. Just imagine if I had flown off without anything—

ALYONA   I don't think we'll be flying very soon, anyway.

IVAN G.   Are you Kolosyonok, Citizen Kolosyonok? They've been calling you on the public address system for the last hour.

KOLOSYONOK   That's what I just heard. And all the while I was sitting drinking beer! Day-dreaming! After all, nobody else knew I

was Kolosyonok. Finally it registered with me. I take a look—no
passport, no identification, no travel authorization—

ALYONA   It's a lovely name—Kolosyonok—isn't it, Nyusha?

[NYUSHA *turns away, going through books.*]

KOLOSYONOK   You think my name's all right?

ALYONA   Oh, marvelous! Suppose it were printed here on this jacket,
for example; why, it would be eighty percent of the book's success. "Have you read Kolosyonok's poetry?" It's lovely! But look—
Elistratov. How dull.

KOLOSYONOK   Alas, I don't write poetry.

ALYONA   But you like it?

KOLOSYONOK   Who doesn't nowadays?

ALYONA   And you can read it? I mean, recite?

KOLOSYONOK   Well, I've never tried. Oh, I did in school, of course.
Part of the exams. Last year I was asked to join an amateur group,
take a little part, but I—

ALYONA   I bought some poems by Ariadne Somebody. A demonic
name. Let's see what she's done. You like Innokenty Annensky?

KOLOSYONOK   Who's that?

ALYONA   A poet at the end of the nineteenth—beginning of the
twentieth century.

KOLOSYONOK   Ah!

ALYONA   He was a school superintendent, by the way.

KOLOSYONOK   Really?

ALYONA   A strange combination, isn't it? School superintendent—
and then suddenly poet. I'll recite you some of his poems, if you
like. But, first, let's read this Ariadne. Nyusha, you coming soon?

NYUSHA [*softly*]   Here, too, of all places!

ALYONA   Nyushechka, just look what a nice, sweet man he is. . . .
and we're doomed to wait and wait—

NYUSHA   If only for the grandparents' sake . . .

ALYONA   They couldn't care less. It's you who worries about every
little thing. Oh, don't start pouting. Please. Please. Wonderful
sister. [*To* KOLOSYONOK, *smiling.*] Come on!

[KOLOSYONOK *tags after her.*]

LYUSYA [*leaving the restaurant*]   Oh, Ivan Gavrilych, what's happening—

IVAN G.   A storm is a storm.

LYUSYA   I can't remember one like this before.

IVAN G.   I can remember worse. It'll snow awhile and then stop.

LYUSYA   We haven't any more eggs for omelettes. And we're running out of sausages.

IVAN G.   All the papers are gone, too. The magazines—everything. They're even starting to buy *Science and Religion*.

LYUSYA   They say the buses are hardly moving. How will I get home? And maybe the next shift won't get here?

IVAN G.   The buses will run.

LYUSYA   When, is the question. It doesn't make any difference to you, Ivan Gavrilych; nobody's waiting for you.

IVAN G.   How so? My old woman is waiting.

LYUSYA   Your wife—that's different. Here I am, on the job, but my hands are all thumbs, I'm scared to death I'll drop a tray. I set a bottle between the window and the storm sash and left the house without another thought, had no idea— If the buses stop, I'll walk home.

IVAN G.   Silly girl. Going to walk home. And what if you get stuck in a snowbank and make your baby an orphan?

LINEVSKY [*sitting down beside* GRANDFATHER]   It's terrible! [*Sways, holding his head.*]

GRANDFATHER   Excuse me, perhaps I could—

LINEVSKY [*vaguely*]   What?

GRANDFATHER   Be of some assistance?

LINEVSKY   Can you stop this damn storm? My mother gets buried in Odessa today at five. I'm flying, taking the chance of being fired from my job, because that thickheaded idiot won't stop at anything to further his ambition—in fact, you can already assume I've been fired—I'm flying, and instead of being in Odessa, here I sit; why? what for? what kind of madness is this? Ten miles from my job, my apartment, headed neither one way nor the other!

GRANDFATHER   I wouldn't like to upset you further, but if one takes an objective view of the matter, it's possible that you won't get to Odessa by five.

LINEVSKY   By five? The interment is at five. I have to be in Odessa by three-thirty to get to the cemetery—by four at the latest. My brother is waiting for me at the airport with a car. He's sitting there; I'm sitting here; and at five she'll be buried without us!

GRANDFATHER   That's why I favor the train.

LINEVSKY   I wanted to take the train. I wanted to! I wanted to! I even had my tickets! But he dawdled away, played on my nerves, wouldn't let me go until I gave him the material for the report! The material! For his report! . . . When my father died, he left six of us, right in a row, see, one after the other, like a diagram.

She brought us all up, gave us all she could. . . . I argued with him, pled with him, told him what people would say—and finally I saw that there was one plane left. The thing that's most unbearable about it is, you think there's such a hurry, such a rush for that material? You think he himself, the fat idiot, doesn't get all upset from his own stubbornness? He would wait out another five days in cold blood—a week even—but he made a blunder, and now he's all in a lather. . . . He's upset, I'm upset, the public is upset. Is that living?

GRANDFATHER   Considering the way things have developed, I fear there's no hope of being in Odessa by four; perhaps it would make sense for you to go back. To restore normal relations. To pour oil, so to speak, on the troubled waters. Grief is grief, heaven knows! But if you're going to be too late anyway? It's very hard to work, you know, when . . .

LINEVSKY   No, that's more than he bargained for! For me to come crawling to him on my hands and knees the very moment she is being buried! Impossible! I'll show him that I, too . . . me, too . . . And why are you so sure there's no hope of making it? Suppose they suddenly announce our flight? You know, they could, any minute. Any minute!

GRANDFATHER [almost apologetically]   But the storm is—

GRANDMOTHER   You're right. They could announce it any minute.

LINEVSKY   You think so, too? . . . You know what's most ironic about it? He and I studied together. We've been close ever since our student days. He was an all-right fellow, even sincere. And then suddenly something happened to him. He changed completely!

GRANDMOTHER   He can't fire you; he's just threatening to. There's no law that lets him.

LINEVSKY   You don't know the kind he is! He has laws that haven't been written.

GRANDMOTHER   Oh, nonsense. They're written for everyone. Both civil laws and moral laws—they're written for everyone.

LINEVSKY   Oh, to hell with him. He'll fire me, or he won't. If only I could get to Odessa by four.

ALYONA [talking to KOLOSYONOK, who sits on the windowsill; NYUSHA reads a magazine not far away]   We're flying to see Papa. He's a wonderful man, the embodiment of refined wit and elegant irony; I adore him! He's in Novosibirsk, in the Academicians' Section; you've probably heard of it. He's there part of the time and in Moscow part of the time, and we fly out to see him; sometimes Mama, sometimes me, sometimes my sister, mostly Mama; though,

of course, both during holidays and sometimes just any time somebody is always flying in or flying out, and we even take his favorite stuffed cabbage pie with us by air from Moscow. When I
finish the university, I'll go work in Novosibirsk, too; it'll be just
thrilling to be there with Papa.

KOLOSYONOK   Your parents won't object?

ALYONA   In our family we don't try to control each other. Each does
what he wants.

KOLOSYONOK   Are you graduating soon?

ALYONA   I love those places. The combination of old tradition and
new construction. A feeling of grandness rings in your ears! Right
now the whole barnyard of us, Grandma and Grandpa, too, are
flying out for a special reason. . . .

GRANDMOTHER [*to* LINEVSKY]   Well, our reason for traveling is not
so important. Today is our son's birthday; he works in Novosibirsk. We're in the habit of being with him on this day, and we,
and his wife, and their two daughters, already young ladies now—

GRANDFATHER   The man is upset. He's not even listening to you.

GRANDMOTHER   He can hear a voice talking to him. That's better
than ignoring him when he's so upset. [*To* LINEVSKY.] He's our
only child, unfortunately. Everything was focused on him—our
affection, our hopes . . . Now I'm ready to die peacefully, content that he's surrounded by a devoted, closely knit family. Family
is a very important thing. You see with your own eyes how life
is handed down from generation to generation. . . .

OLD MAN [*passing by, very annoyed*]   I told you so! Now the buses
have stopped!

LINEVSKY [*jumping up*]   I must call home. . . .

[*The storm howls. It grows dark.*]

ALYONA [*to* KOLOSYONOK]   We were flying above the clouds; there
was such a bright blue, blue sun there, really amazingly blue, we
had no idea what was happening down on the ground. And then
suddenly there's an announcement that we're going to land in this
completely unexpected place. We dive through the clouds, and
suddenly everything's dark, and there's a whirl of something very
gray, gray. . . .

KOLOSYONOK   But wouldn't it be more accurate to say that what
was blue was the sky, and the sun was what the sun usually is,
and the snowstorm wasn't gray but its usual white?

ALYONA   Word of honor, the sun was bright blue and the storm was
gray, I swear it! [*Points to the window; outside, darkness has*

clearly started falling.] Isn't it actually gray? But I can't call you Anatoly. That's outrageously pompous. Something Latin about it. Sort of like Capitoline.

KOLOSYONOK   Call me simply Tolya. I'd like that.

ALYONA   Tolya, Tolechka . . . Tolechka, don't you really know a single poem?

KOLOSYONOK   I honestly don't. Except for Krylov's fables. One summer day the lamb went down to the stream to drink . . . Once a swan, a crab, and a pike . . . A learned cook dashed from his kitchen to the inn. . . .

ALYONA   I'll recite some poems. You know, of course, that poetry, like music, mustn't be interrupted?

KOLOSYONOK   I won't interrupt for anything!

ALYONA   Listen: The strength of the Lord is in us,
                       I'm tortured by dreams and visions . . .
                       Worse than mortal anguish,
                       Worse than white nights' desire,
                       They have pierced my body's cover,
                       They have ground my bones to powder,
                       They have burned my eyes *sans* fire. . . .

                    [BAKCHENIN *notices* SHEMETOVA.]

BAKCHENIN   Olya?

                    [SHEMETOVA *is startled, looks at him.*]

ALYONA   By dreams in which at times I
                            Know no likenesses . . .

BAKCHENIN   Olya, that you?°

ALYONA   By dreams in which at times I
                            Begin to leave this life . . .

SHEMETOVA   Hello, Sergei Georgievich.

BAKCHENIN   My god! Olya! It's been ages! I guess I'm . . . an old geezer.

SHEMETOVA   That's putting it rather strongly. We've both gotten older.

BAKCHENIN   But you're so young-looking, so lovely. Even prettier than before. Really! You know, I've never seen you dressed so

°Bakchenin addresses Shemetova in the second person singular form, *ty,* indicating old, close friendship. Addressing him, Shemetova uses the polite or formal form *vy* and insists that he "use *vy,* also." He tries for a while, then stays with *ty.* She keeps to *vy* except in moments when past intimacy surfaces anew.

nicely. You always had on that field jacket. Now, so young-looking, all fresh—it's wonderful! You always were beautiful!

SHEMETOVA Not so—enthusiastic, please.° As for being young, my older daughter is twenty-four. I could already be a grandmother.

BAKCHENIN You say "older," meaning . . .

SHEMETOVA I have a younger daughter, also. I have two daughters. Do you have children?

BAKCHENIN Sort of. I do and I don't. I pay support for two children to my two former wives.

SHEMETOVA You divorced your first. . . . You and Nina were divorced?

BAKCHENIN No. Nina—Nina died.

SHEMETOVA Long ago?

BAKCHENIN Long ago. In general, my private life hasn't worked out well. Deaths, separations, disappointments . . . The children are growing up away from me—are actually strangers to me, no spiritual bond between us, they feel themselves closer and more kindred to other people. I lead a lonely life. . . .

SHEMETOVA Well, that could be remedied, I should think.

BAKCHENIN Well, you see, my love, it's not so simple.

SHEMETOVA None of that, please.

BAKCHENIN I'm tired, don't even want to think that some extra person will show up in the house and be talking away and demanding attention. When you're young, you have the energy, but when old age comes . . . It's better being alone. But what about you?

SHEMETOVA I have a family.

BAKCHENIN Same one?

SHEMETOVA Yes.

BAKCHENIN You didn't get divorced?

SHEMETOVA No.

BAKCHENIN And—you're happy?

SHEMETOVA Yes.

BAKCHENIN The old folks living?

SHEMETOVA They're sitting over there. There, the elderly couple by the entrance. And the girls are around somewhere.

BAKCHENIN A full quorum?

SHEMETOVA Except for my husband. We're flying to join him for his birthday.

BAKCHENIN You settled down well, my love.

SHEMETOVA No, no "love." Don't.

°"Let's use *vy*, please."

BAKCHENIN All right, but you settled down well. When I get home —late in the evening—unlock the door and open it—there's not a soul. The janitor's wife has left something to eat in the icebox, whatever she feels like, some kind of sausage maybe, and I put the kettle on and sit down by myself to have some tea. . . .

SHEMETOVA [*with a fleeting smile*] You used to love roast lamb.

BAKCHENIN You get roast lamb in a restaurant. . . . So there I sit, listening to the radio, only disembodied voices all around me, and then maybe somebody calls up on the phone.

SHEMETOVA Why, that sounds like a man's paradise! I can imagine how many men envy you.

BAKCHENIN Oh, sure, some do. I keep up appearances: you poor fellows, I say, look how I live—like a god! But let me tell you frankly, my love, living like that is no good. It's not—human. Cold . . . Those aren't your girls, are they? There, by the window?

SHEMETOVA Yes, they are.

BAKCHENIN See, I guessed. They look just like you.

SHEMETOVA What are you now, Sergei Georgievich, what kind of work do you do?

BAKCHENIN I'm a scientist, a chemist, director of the laboratory in one of our biggest chemical enterprises, and next year I'll get my doctorate. What about you?

SHEMETOVA I teach in a foreign-language institute.

ALYONA [*to* KOLOSYONOK] How do you like Annensky?

KOLOSYONOK He was a school superintendent?

ALYONA What about it?

KOLOSYONOK Now I know why at the beginning of the century students shot themselves. If the superintendents wrote poems like that . . .

ALYONA Death is a theme which has always inspired poets. Especially since man stopped believing in his own immortality.

KOLOSYONOK I thought they were more inspired by love.

ALYONA They're interrelated: love, immortality. . . . You don't know Omar Khayyam either?

KOLOSYONOK Who's that?

ALYONA A mathematician, astronomer, philosopher, and an amazing poet.

KOLOSYONOK Living?

ALYONA He died eight hundred and fifty years ago.

> We are no other than a moving row
> Of Magic Shadow-shapes that come and go

Round with the Sun-illumined Lantern held
In Midnight by the Master of the Show;

But helpless Pieces of the Game He plays
Upon this chequer-board of Nights and Days;
   Hither and thither moves, and checks, and slays,
And one by one back in the Closet lays.*

GRANDFATHER   It's so quiet. More like an aquarium than an airport.

GRANDMOTHER   No departures or arrivals. Our plane was the last.

GRANDFATHER   A strange sensation of paralysis.

GRANDMOTHER   Passivity.

GRANDFATHER   Of a stolen holiday. As if we had been plucked out of life for no reason at all.

GRANDMOTHER   Read your paper.

GRANDFATHER   Olya is talking very seriously. I don't think that's a new acquaintance.

GRANDMOTHER   I'm interested in Alyona. That acquaintance is absolutely new. [*Beckons to* NYUSHA.]

ALYONA   Then to the Lip of this poor earthen Urn
I leaned, the Secret of my Life to learn:
   And Lip to Lip it murmured—"While you live,
Drink!—For, once dead, you never shall return."

I think the Vessel, that with fugitive
Articulation answered, once did live,
   And drink; and Ah! the passive Lip I kissed.
How many Kisses might it take—and give!*

[NYUSHA *goes up to* GRANDMOTHER.]

GRANDMOTHER   Nyusha, who is that with Alyona?

NYUSHA   Kolosyonok.

GRANDMOTHER   The one who lost his papers? . . . Is she reciting poetry to him?

NYUSHA   About death. One after another. At first he protested, but now he doesn't move a muscle.

GRANDMOTHER   She shouldn't be so obvious about it. People are staring at her. I called you over because, if we're stuck here until tomorrow, it would be nice at least to drink to your father.

NYUSHA   Why not. In the restaurant. You want champagne?

GRANDMOTHER   If they have any. Find out. Just in case. Of course, you can never tell, we may take off any minute.

*The Edward FitzGerald translation.

NYUSHA   I'll find out. [*Goes out.*]

ALYONA   A Moment's Halt—a momentary Taste
          Of Being from the Well amid the Waste—
          And lo!—the phantom Caravan has reached
          The Nothing it set out from— Oh, make haste!

LYUSYA [*running out of the restaurant*]   Did you hear, Ivan Gavrilych, the buses have stopped! [*Runs down the stairs to* TAMARA.]
   Tamara, no more buses! I've got to call!

TAMARA   Use the pay phone!

LYUSYA   Why are you so mean! Why so nasty!

TAMARA   The pay phone!

LYUSYA   Why can't you be kind to people when everything's difficult? What will I do about Vitalik now?

TAMARA   Vitalik, Vitalik! Your little Vitalik is just fine! He'll cry
   a little maybe. . . . [*Cries.*] I . . . I was invited to the theater
   tonight.

LYUSYA   Tamarka! Who?

TAMARA   A lieutenant I know.

LYUSYA   Grisha?

TAMARA   No, you don't know him. It's all over with Grisha.

LYUSYA   Think how . . .

TAMARA   Now he'll use those tickets to go with somebody else. And
   he hasn't called. If only he would call, say he was sorry.

LYUSYA   He has to!

TAMARA [*blows her nose*]   That's always my luck. It's been like that
   all my life. And Grishka turned out to be a first-class rat. . . .
   Call up.

LYUSYA [*lifting the receiver*]   For some reason there's no dial tone.

TAMARA   Really?

LYUSYA   Tamara, it's out.

LINEVSKY [*in the phone booth trying to make the pay phone work*]
   Damn it! Hello! [*Breathes in the mouthpiece.*] Hello! Hello! [*Leaves
   the booth.*] It's not working. [*Passes the line.*] It's out of order.
   Not working.

LYUSYA [*having gone upstairs*]   The phone's out, too. There we are,
   Ivan Gavrilych. There you have it.

IVAN G.   Well, so what about the phone? You can't nurse him by
   phone.

LYUSYA   Still, you feel better when you know. . . . Now it's as if
   they were as far away as the moon.

IVAN G.   But you left something to eat there, just in case.

LYUSYA   And during the night?

IVAN G. Night is still a long way off. If worse comes to worst, your Slavik will cook some porridge for him.

LYUSYA You don't understand what you're saying.

IVAN G. I understand very well. Did it myself.

LYUSYA It will drive me mad, that's what.

NYUSHA [*to* LYUSYA] Excuse me. Do you have champagne?

LYUSYA Depends. Sweet?

NYUSHA Semi-dry.

LYUSYA I'll see. [*Goes into the restaurant.*]

LINEVSKY [*having come upstairs*] Not working.

IVAN G. Who isn't?

LINEVSKY [*as if sleep walking*] The phone. [*Goes into the waiting room.*]

IVAN G. Everybody is upset. That woman is worried about her baby; the baby is over in town, she's here; nothing to get so upset about, the baby'll be all right, but she's nursing, see?

NYUSHA Is it far to town?

IVAN G. Depends where in town. About ten miles to the center.

NYUSHA And here we bother her about some champagne.

IVAN G. Oh, come, that's her job.

LYUSYA [*returning*] You want one bottle of semi-dry?

NYUSHA Two. And some fruit, please.

LYUSYA A table for how many?

NYUSHA Five, please. Only not right now; a little later.

LYUSYA Let me know.

NYUSHA But could I have some sort of cocktail now?

LYUSYA We don't serve cocktails. Just fruit drinks.

NYUSHA Well, then, a fruit drink. [*Sits down at a little table.* LYUSYA *brings the fruit drink.*] Who is home with the baby?

LYUSYA Right now he's at the nursery. [*Moves off but comes back.*] Then my husband will pick him up. [*Moves off but comes back again; the subject interests her.*] We take turns picking him up, first my husband, then me. Or if we're both working, then our neighbor does; lives in the same apartment; retired; a nice old man.

NYUSHA It's hard for you.

LYUSYA I'll say! . . . Let me tell you: if it weren't for the nursery in the first place, and for people who care in the second, could we take care of Vitalik? Impossible! We got married young, we hadn't settled into anything yet, and we lived in dormitories—but luckily we got a room. We were very lucky: while I was still in the hospital, my husband got a requisition, so Vitalik and I came straight home from the hospital to our new apartment, and the crib was all set up, and a little tub, my husband had done everything. . . . If it weren't so far to work!

NYUSHA   You ought to get another job.

LYUSYA   Well, I can't do that, drop such a good job as this. My cousin got me this job; he's a test pilot. I've gotten used to the trip back and forth. It's just that today the weather is dreadful. Lord, I only hope it eases up by nighttime. I can just hear the baby screaming. And everybody says there's no point in thinking of trying to walk home.

NYUSHA   You're a lucky woman.

LYUSYA   Well, you know, in general, despite the difficulties . . .

NYUSHA   There are so many important, real things in your life. Basic things . . . A child. A tub. A crib. A good husband . . . Is he a good man?

LYUSYA   He's all right.

[*In the upstairs waiting room.* BAKCHENIN *and* SHEMETOVA.]

BAKCHENIN   Your daughter is smiling at me.

SHEMETOVA   Not at you. At the man she's talking to.

BAKCHENIN   She's looking at me.

SHEMETOVA   But smiling at him. In an hour she'll announce she's going to marry him. In two, she'll forget him entirely. But for the time being she is taken up with him completely.

BAKCHENIN   Your daughters are lovely.

SHEMETOVA   Which is more so?

BAKCHENIN   Couldn't say. Both of them. But you more. You were lovelier than they twenty years ago, and still are.

SHEMETOVA   As we know by experience, that in itself means nothing. . . .

BAKCHENIN   You can't relive the past? True enough. I don't know about you, but just the memory of it warms me inside. I get cold and feverish—and it warms me. You probably have a real home. . . .

SHEMETOVA   You know, when you have two children, and two grand-parents, and your work, and a very busy husband you have to help, there simply isn't time to be cold and to freeze. There are things to think about from one end of the day to the other.

BAKCHENIN   Now, for me . . .

SHEMETOVA   You probably have enough to think about, too, even if you are alone.

BAKCHENIN   For me it's something else. Worries, business—and right beside me, you. Standing quietly, watching out of your two eyes. In a little field jacket . . . My angel! All my life I've remembered you in a field jacket. Did you throw it out?

SHEMETOVA   I can't remember. . . .

BAKCHENIN   If I look at things clearly—there was never anyone else.

SHEMETOVA   Sergei Georgievich!

BAKCHENIN   I shouldn't? No point, is there?

SHEMETOVA   Exactly. It's pointless.

[*They talk, as they have so far, without raising their voices, without gestures.*]

BAKCHENIN   But if it's something that can't go unsaid?

SHEMETOVA   Oh, really. We're mature adults.

BAKCHENIN   What does that mean, "mature adults"? That everything has gone as far as it can for them and nothing can change? Then they're corpses. And I refuse to think that you and I, my love, have died.

SHEMETOVA   I sincerely and seriously beg you not to address me like that.

BAKCHENIN   I'm trying, I'm trying. But for me you were "my love" for twenty years—I can't undo it in an hour. And all these twenty years—or almost twenty, we haven't seen each other for about nineteen years, have we?—did you think about me and tell me your thoughts?

SHEMETOVA   At first.

BAKCHENIN   And then?

SHEMETOVA   And then you slipped away. You left.

BAKCHENIN   Completely?

SHEMETOVA   Yes.

BAKCHENIN   But you, on the contrary, drew closer to me. In the beginning, right after the war, I sort of started fussing around. . . . But now, now that the sun is sinking toward the horizon—and has been for some time—and there comes a need to turn around, to look back and take stock— Are you really indifferent to what happened?

SHEMETOVA   Nothing happened.

BAKCHENIN   Oh. So.

SHEMETOVA   Understand that: nothing happened.

BAKCHENIN   What are you saying, Olya? What are you afraid of?

SHEMETOVA   Let's stop it.

BAKCHENIN   Nothing happened? Really nothing? In a crematorium they burn the bodies—and even there a little handful of ashes remains. Don't you remember when we were first together? The last time we met?

SHEMETOVA   A wartime story. Lots of things happen to us women. Even without a war.

BAKCHENIN   Our evenings together, don't you remember? And how I ran to you from the hospital? Don't you remember how happy we were? How desperate? . . .

[*The storm whirls.*]

2

BAKCHENIN'S VOICE   Don't you really remember?

The airport has gone; the stage is bare and dark. . . . A small stove crackles. It is in the room where Shemetova lives in a small town near the front lines. Artillery fire sounds in the distance. A loudspeaker, turned down, whispers. By the stove are Shemetova, young, in a field shirt with lieutenant's shoulder loops, and Bakchenin, a young officer.

BAKCHENIN   I would never have thought it.

SHEMETOVA   Well, just imagine.

BAKCHENIN   That a woman like you—wasn't happy! But you loved him, didn't you? Earlier. In the beginning.

SHEMETOVA   Yes, of course. Yes, probably—because otherwise why would I have married him? He did everything so handsomely. . . . That's something he knows how to do, his whole family does. They know when to bring just which flowers, and how to celebrate each holiday, and when to speak and when not to, and how to receive different people. . . . In general, they know how to live. But for some reason, with them I feel as if I were in a dream . . . strange. . . .

BAKCHENIN   And I thought, and others did, too, that somewhere, waiting for you, was a very special man.

SHEMETOVA   Why did you think that?

BAKCHENIN   Well—you often get letters.

SHEMETOVA   Mostly from my husband's parents. News about my
little girl's health. True, my husband also writes regularly.
BAKCHENIN   Where did you say he is?
SHEMETOVA   He's still in Kazan. Apparently they're about to return
to Moscow.
BAKCHENIN   He's never been to the front?
SHEMETOVA   He's a scientist; he's deferred. Don't make fun of it,
please; he really is an important scientist. They won't give him
a chance to be shot at.
BAKCHENIN   But they gave you one.
SHEMETOVA   Oh, me! You know what helped me—knowing German.
So I've been on various staffs since forty-three. . . .
BAKCHENIN   And he didn't object?
SHEMETOVA   Oh, of course. But once a person has made up his or
her mind . . . In our family we don't press each other. At any
rate, there are no tempests. We even argue quietly, sensibly.
BAKCHENIN   What is your daughter like?
SHEMETOVA   She's still little. She's all right with her grandma and
grandpa.
BAKCHENIN   But you miss her?
SHEMETOVA   Oh heavens!
BAKCHENIN   Grandpa and grandma—those are—?
SHEMETOVA   My husband's parents. Mine are dead. Before the
war . . . It's amazing!
BAKCHENIN   What is?
SHEMETOVA   You go out flaunting death almost every night and you
still have the time and the desire to keep track of who gets how
many letters . . .
BAKCHENIN   You don't keep track of things like that?
SHEMETOVA   I don't flaunt death. Give me some German, and I
translate it—I have a simple job.
BAKCHENIN   Oh, Olga Vasilievna, the living think of living. As long
as we're alive, why worry about death?
SHEMETOVA   I loathe your recklessness. I loathe it! This wild des-
peration . . . This devil-may-care attitude that goes beyond all
bounds. . . .
BAKCHENIN   Time and again, let me tell you, the daredevil gets
through where the cautious man gets caught. Without even—as
you put it—having flaunted death to his heart's delight.
SHEMETOVA   You crawl into the jaws of hell, and what for: for
some old rotten mutton!
BAKCHENIN   That's unfair! I didn't expect that from you. Have you

forgotten how good the roast lamb was? Juicy and tender, not lamb at all but some heavenly creature, the bones just melted in the mouth; you praised it yourself; and now you say "old rotten mutton"—oh-oh-oh!

SHEMETOVA   To steal into enemy territory under fire just for some roast lamb . . .

BAKCHENIN   What fire? Somebody popped off his submachine gun for a while. They were all making up a story for you.

SHEMETOVA   I'm serious. That's not bravery, Seryozhka! It's stupidity, madness to risk your life like that when the end is in sight.

BAKCHENIN   What end?

SHEMETOVA   The end of the war.

BAKCHENIN   When do you think the end will come?

SHEMETOVA   Well, maybe in six months; at most, in a year.

BAKCHENIN   You and I can know for sure, eh? When it started, lots of people said: At most, a year. I thought so myself. And what's a year? A highly relative quantity. And six months, too. And a day. A minute. Time is one thing in peace but another thing in war, isn't it? A minute has one amount of time in it in Kazan, but a different amount for a scout in enemy territory. So "the end in sight" depends on who for. . . . And, generally speaking, it's non-sense. What happens happens. You can't duck what's coming. In our business, like it or not, you become a fatalist.

SHEMETOVA   That's foolish.

BAKCHENIN   Not at all foolish, and very helpful. How could a man help it: think of that. My wife saw me off in forty-one; I even got angry at her: What are you doing, crying over me as if I were a corpse already, I'm still alive, thank god! And, in fact, the whole family was weeping and wailing. . . . But here I am, in one piece so far, and you know the kinds of scrapes I have to get into, while they, civilians all, left behind in their regular place, in their regular apartment in the heart of Leningrad—in the very first year! Every last one of them! . . . Who thought up this bitter joke, I'd like to know. Why not me, the soldier, called on to give his life? Why them, people not called on? . . . not soldiers at all, peaceful civilians. . . . [*After a silence.*] By rights I shouldn't be in one piece. Otherwise . . . where's justice?

SHEMETOVA   What was her name?

BAKCHENIN   Nina.

SHEMETOVA   Were you together long?

BAKCHENIN   A year. I finished my third year at the university— got married. . . . She was always sort of unlucky. She would fall on an icy patch on the street, hurt herself, or on the street car somebody would steal her money. . . . She had a hard childhood, no affection, nothing pretty. . . . And she had lung trouble, her health generally wasn't too good. . . . She used to say that life smiled on her only after she met me.

SHEMETOVA   Any children?

BAKCHENIN   No, thank god. What would you do with a child in the siege? It's hard enough for adults.

SHEMETOVA   How did you find out?

BAKCHENIN   Some people wrote. Took my letters out of the mailbox and wrote me saying not to write again—nobody there. . . . This has to do with fatalism being stupid . . . with taking chances being foolish. . . . Ah! all these wise and sensible words! . . . [*Looks at his watch.*] So. That was a nice chat. [*Gets up.*]

SHEMETOVA   So soon?

BAKCHENIN   Orders are orders.

SHEMETOVA   Even today, too?

BAKCHENIN   All men assemble at twenty-zero-zero. And then, as the saying goes, the one to whose lot it falls . . .

SHEMETOVA   Seryozha!

[*Call signals from the loudspeaker.*]

BAKCHENIN   The orders. [*Turns the volume up. He and* SHEMETOVA *wait in silence. The radio transmits orders from the Supreme Commander-in-Chief.* BAKCHENIN *turns the volume down.*] So that's it! And you were saying? . . . [*Puts his greatcoat on.*]

SHEMETOVA   Seryozha. All the same. Please.

BAKCHENIN   Be sensible? Good-bye, Olga Vasilievna. Thanks.

SHEMETOVA   Bye.

BAKCHENIN [*at the door*]   Can I come tomorrow?

SHEMETOVA   What do you think?

BAKCHENIN   Come in this door, and sit down on that stool, by that fire, all right? . . . Good-bye.

SHEMETOVA   Seryozhka! . . . Seryozhka, I forgot to tell you I didn't get a chance to finish reading your magazine; I'll return it tomorrow. . . .

BAKCHENIN   See you tomorrow. [*Goes out.*]

[SHEMETOVA *stands in the open doorway, watching him go. A dark blue lamp burns on the street. Weapons thunder in the distance. Call signals again come over the radio, preceding new orders.*]

BAKCHENIN'S VOICE   Do you really not remember?

   . . . The stage is bare and light; from backstage comes Bak-
chenin in a hospital gown, his arms wide, holding crutches.

BAKCHENIN   Pay no attention, please.° No crutches, see? Just an
illusion! Here, look! [*Steps forward boldly, limping.*]

SHEMETOVA   [*runs to meet him*]   O-oh-oh, don't show off! Careful!

BAKCHENIN   I was afraid, see, that without them I'd get to you
much too slowly.

SHEMETOVA   What kind of little-boy nonsense is this! Who wants it!

BAKCHENIN   I do. Me. So as to be elegant beside you.

SHEMETOVA   Silly . . . Well, let me see what you look like. I haven't
seen you for a hundred years.

BAKCHENIN   The old bastard set up such regulations! Sundays only—
that's all! Even if you were dying under his nose.

SHEMETOVA   You've gotten thin.

BAKCHENIN   A man does. What a fiend! I shouted at him until we
both were hoarse.

SHEMETOVA   You madman! Shouting at a professor! A general!

BAKCHENIN   Nothing doing: "Sundays only!" And today is still only
Wednesday!

SHEMETOVA   Did you get my note?

BAKCHENIN   Yes. You're clever. You get mine?

SHEMETOVA   Well, obviously, since I'm here.

BAKCHENIN   You've set up a spa for yourself, he says, in a front-
line hospital. . . . But what's the harm of your coming to see me?
It got me back on my feet sooner. What sort of professor is he if
he doesn't understand?

SHEMETOVA   Don't get excited. Don't get excited. Never mind him.
We're together.

BAKCHENIN   Yes, but we didn't see each other for three whole days—
and for what good reason?

SHEMETOVA   You probably skipped out on your own—or did they let
you go?

BAKCHENIN   They will; just wait. No problem; the fence is nothing.
Arefyev helped; I got on his back. And then he threw me the . . .
[*Points to the crutches.*]

SHEMETOVA   Nobody saw you?

°In the previous scene they addressed each other *vy*; now they use *ty*.

BAKCHENIN   Some soldiers were passing by. Good luck, they said, hope you make out.

SHEMETOVA   Seryozhka. You'll be caught and sent to the rear. Then what will we do?

BAKCHENIN   When they catch me we'll start thinking about what we'll do.

SHEMETOVA   Then it'll be too late. No, really: don't quarrel with him too much. I couldn't stand it if they sent you back.

BAKCHENIN   They won't. I'll be out of the hospital in a few days.

SHEMETOVA   How can I live without you? These three days have been like dying. . . . [Cries.]

BAKCHENIN   Look, my god. The news from the front is good, the weather is good, I fixed up our meeting just fine, and you . . . Here, this is me, and there's you, so what are you crying about, why?

SHEMETOVA   I don't know. I'm so happy. And now they can't send you out on scouting patrols, can they, isn't that right? They can't, can't! And we won't have to say good-bye forever every night.

BAKCHENIN   My love, my darling . . . I've beaten a path now. Over all the fences, past all the professors and generals. Now wait for me in your place. You'll come back from staff headquarters, open your door—and there I'll be. [They kiss.] If I go to the rear, Olya, it will be with a discharge after the war.

SHEMETOVA   Don't talk about discharge.

BAKCHENIN   Whether we do or not, it's not far off.

SHEMETOVA   When I hear that word, a mountain rises up in front of me. A mountain of troubles. A huge peak!

BAKCHENIN   Again, there's no point in crossing your bridges before you come to them.

SHEMETOVA   If only it were possible for us to stay together and never part . . . and nobody would suffer because of it. . . .

BAKCHENIN   Who would? Why do I have to worry about that? I want to worry about us! I've never suffered? Good Lord, how much I went through. . . . And how do you know it's going to be so hard for him? Maybe it won't be at all.

SHEMETOVA   You have no idea what a child means to him. He thinks a family must exist for the sake of the child. No matter what. A child has to have a father and a mother, he says. Well, and he . . . is decent to me.

BAKCHENIN   You wrote him?

SHEMETOVA   No. That was a conversation we had before.

BAKCHENIN   He probably won't want to give the child up.

SHEMETOVA   I won't ask him to. But when I think of myself going
   to pick Nyusha up at their place! . . . And how you have to go
   to court to get divorced. The proceedings! Talking about him,
   about you . . .

BAKCHENIN   Now stop that, my angel. I don't like seeing you torture
   yourself. You think: Court! It's merely a formality. Unpleasant,
   sure. But what can you do if, to be together, we have to make
   our way through barbed wire? Only one thing matters: that you
   love me. Tonight, when you come home and open your door,
   I'd like . . .

VOICES   Hard! Hard!*

*A fire burns in the fireplace. Beside it, Shemetova, Bakchenin
in a new field jacket, Arefyev, several other officers holding
mugs.*

AREFYEV [*raising his mug*]   Now, it's hard for people!

BAKCHENIN   See, Olya, it's hard for them. We have to show them
   you feel sorry. [*Kisses* SHEMETOVA.]

OFFICERS   Hurrah!

SHEMETOVA   Idiocy! What's this "hard"? If only you wouldn't add
   fuel to the fire, Arefyev. Especially since I'm going to get divorced!

BAKCHENIN   Easy, easy. They can't wait until you do. Maybe somebody won't make it.

[*Guns go off in the distance.*]

OFFICERS   We've opened up again. Moving out. That's a salute
   booming in Moscow now in your honor. Why isn't she drinking?

SHEMETOVA   It's dreadful.

OFFICERS   What do you mean! Just a drop. It's all right. A sip.

BAKCHENIN   Drink. To us.

[SHEMETOVA *drinks.*]

OFFICERS   Hurrah!

[*Guitar music, singing.*]

BAKCHENIN   Wait. Stop. Dear friends, I want to say something. A

*Traditional shout at a wedding party, calling for the bride and groom's first "sweet"
kiss to prevent the "bitterness" of life.

little speech. May I, Olya? All right? [*Suddenly lost in thought.*]
Now, what was I going to speak about?

OFFICERS   About love! About love! Come on, we're listening. You
need prompting? Oh, go ahead: "Dear friends, comrades-in-arms!"

AREFYEV   Doesn't matter, Seryozhka. You can hardly talk because
of all you've been through. Now go ahead—be bold.

BAKCHENIN   Comrades, sure, I'll talk about love.

OFFICERS   That's it. Right.

BAKCHENIN   But first I want to remind you of the merciless dark
night, nights without love, without hope or stars, when we go off
to flout death, and death comes out to play blind man's buff
with us.

AN OFFICER   He's reciting poetry.

AREFYEV   Let him speak the way he wants. He's happy and lucky.

ANOTHER OFFICER   Why "without hope"?

A THIRD   And usually the stars are clearly visible. . . .

BAKCHENIN   Nights when we forget that there's such a thing in the
world as a woman's silence, a woman's tenderness . . . a woman's
blessed caress . . . and that we have a sacred human right to it
all! . . . But the morning comes, comes despite everything: the
sun rises. And death crawls out along its trenches. And we go
home, still in one piece, and what do we see—above the blood-
stained, trampled ground a little morning-glory has blossomed,
so fresh, so new that your heart aches, and a bee trembles over
the tiny cup, flying down for honey, and there in the little cup
the honey is waiting for it! I don't know about you, but for me
that always seems a miracle, always. I stop, like an idiot, watching the flower and the bee, and I cry. Dear friends, I drink to the
flower, to the bee, to the miracle of life, to Olya's eyes. . . .

[SHEMETOVA *takes his hand and kisses him.*]

OFFICERS   Hard!

[*Guitar music.*]

SHEMETOVA'S VOICE   And do you remember this?

Shemetova and Bakchenin are sitting on a garden bench.

SHEMETOVA   So.

BAKCHENIN   So.

SHEMETOVA   It's hard to believe that we'll travel together, arrive together, go down the streets together, enter your house together! I'm so tired of all these different apartments, of being alone, you with Arefyev, seeing each other only in snatches, as if we were secret lovers. . . . Now your home is mine, too. My home is waiting for me in Leningrad. My own real home.

BAKCHENIN I'm a little worried about permission to register. So far we're not officially registered.

SHEMETOVA Oh, Lord. Let's go to the police station and explain things.

BAKCHENIN Maybe they won't listen.

SHEMETOVA Well, if they won't, then we'll worry about what to do next. See, you've already re-educated me. I don't want to go through all kinds of nonsense without having to. Think of it—permission to register.

BAKCHENIN It's not such nonsense as it seems. This isn't the army where everything comes your way on recommendation. We'll try dunning the men in charge.

SHEMETOVA I'll work out something about a job, fill in the papers, clean up the room—it probably looks like a nightmare.

BAKCHENIN I should imagine. First of all, all the windows were blown out, and getting glass is a problem.

SHEMETOVA How do you know they were?

BAKCHENIN They were blown out every place in Leningrad.

SHEMETOVA Doesn't matter; we'll get glass. And I'll go get Nyusha. To end everything there—in one blow. The fewer the confrontations, the fewer the terrible conversations.

BAKCHENIN You haven't written him?

SHEMETOVA No. Doing it by mail isn't right, I think. Sort of backhanded. I have to go there anyway. It's better to tell him. Face to face . . . And besides, they had such trouble returning to Moscow, my father-in-law was sick, my mother-in-law wore herself out, so that on top of it all a letter from me . . .

BAKCHENIN That's very sensible.

SHEMETOVA Understand it, darling, in the spirit I mean it.

BAKCHENIN I do.

SHEMETOVA You're honestly not angry?

BAKCHENIN Honestly not.

SHEMETOVA You know, I think I can get some in Moscow. Windowpanes. Without them, Nyusha can't come, naturally.

BAKCHENIN I'd say we oughtn't to, either. Without the windowpanes.

SHEMETOVA Oh, we can somehow. . . .

AREFYEV [*coming over*]   Hey, you happy two! Building castles in the air?

SHEMETOVA [*smiling*]   We are; we're happily building our castle in the air.

AREFYEV   Good for you, honestly. But I have to keep sounding the trumpets of war. Seems they're sending me to Germany.

BAKCHENIN   Well, that's interesting.

AREFYEV · Maybe it will be. But I'd really like to get home, to my own place. To my family. Somehow put back together everything the war broke up.

BAKCHENIN   That's the right thing to do.

AREFYEV   For some reason, lately I've been full of purely civilian wishes. Real longing. Like going out on my porch early in the morning, calling my boy over, cutting some firewood with him. . . .

SHEMETOVA   Oh, my darlings, my gentle ones. I'm so ashamed, so scared of being self-centered . . .

AREFYEV   But? You were going to say "but."

SHEMETOVA   The war didn't upset anything for me. It gave me everything I have in the world. That can happen! It gave me Seryozhka. Oh, that's dreadful; what am I saying? Think of what that means!

AREFYEV   Why "dreadful"? It's not your fault at all, all that that means. Or that that is how things worked out. You came to him as reward and consolation . . . and be happy! Those are my orders to you.

SHEMETOVA   And when your time in Germany is up, you'll come drop in on us, won't you?

AREFYEV   Sure.

SHEMETOVA   No, really! We'll always be glad to see you, won't we, Seryozhka? There'll be lots to remember together, won't there, right?

AREFYEV   You know, Olya, you've started talking like him. [*Imitates her.*] "Come drop in on us, won't you? Be lots to remember, right?" Just like Seryozhka, absolutely!

SHEMETOVA   Well, what's so strange about that? Somebody once told me that after a husband and wife have lived together a long time they even begin to look like each other.

AREFYEV [*sings softly*]   "The cossack set out for the fight-o, Farewell, my sweet little bride-o! Farewell, my bride with eyes of brown: I'm off to fight in a far-away land." . . .

SHEMETOVA   Oh! Don't. Not a sad song. Please, please. There have been only sad songs all through the war. Now it's time to be gay!

To laugh! No more "farewell," only "hello, there," remember, you hear?!

SHEMETOVA'S VOICE This is something you surely remember. You couldn't have forgotten this.

Bakchenin is waiting for Shemetova in her apartment. He is in an unusual state of morose tension. Shemetova comes in.

SHEMETOVA Seryozhenka! It's all done. No matter how you look at it. A lady civilian. Now to put some dry rations together for the road. Have you been waiting long? [*Notices his condition.*] What happened? [BAKCHENIN *helps her take off her shoulder belt.*] Something wrong?

BAKCHENIN I don't know what to call it.

SHEMETOVA What "it"? What's going on? They won't let you go? What? What?

BAKCHENIN Olya . . .

SHEMETOVA Something awful!

BAKCHENIN I don't know, Olya.

SHEMETOVA What?

BAKCHENIN I don't have a right to say—something awful.

SHEMETOVA Well, then, what?

BAKCHENIN Who could bring himself to say it? Probably it's a sin, isn't it, to tell a living man—get back in your grave?

SHEMETOVA What man? [*Sits down.*] Quickly!

BAKCHENIN I got a letter.

SHEMETOVA From Nina!

BAKCHENIN She's in Sverdlovsk. In the hospital the last two years or more. After a bombing raid. They rehabilitated her. Gave her an artificial arm. [SHEMETOVA *sits motionlessly.*] Two years of one operation after another. . . . Even before that her health wasn't good. Something they found in the lungs. I told you. . . . Now she's an invalid. The rest perished. Every one of them. One after another. From hunger. That's why they wrote me, I guess, that she, too . . . But she was carried out unconscious, badly mutilated. . . . Out on the street the bomb caught . . . [*Knock on the door.*] Yes!

AREFYEV [*entering*] Good evening. Well, Olya, are congratulations in order? *Auf Wiedersehen? Zu Hause, nach* Leningrad? All the very best . . . What's wrong with you two? Something happen?

Have an argument? Don't tell me you've already had an argument?

BAKCHENIN   Arefyev, go take a walk. We . . .

AREFYEV   Not on your life, if as soon as I leave you'll start arguing. No, sir, I didn't give you my blessing for that. Seryozhka,
did you get your mail? There was a registered letter for you.
From Sverdlovsk. I was going to bring it but she said, "Let him
come in and sign for it himself." Go get it.

BAKCHENIN   I did, I did.

AREFYEV   All right, old friends. I'll come back when you've made
up. Only, don't you insult Olya on me. Look how lovely she is,
sitting there. Stand up for yourself, Olya. Give it right back to
him! You're a strong woman; don't give in.

BAKCHENIN   Listen, go on, get out!!

[AREFYEV *goes out. Silence. It is broken by* SHEMETOVA's *shriek.*
SHEMETOVA *sobs, her head down in her hands.*]

SHEMETOVA'S VOICE   So I went back to Moscow. Back to the house
I had already said good-bye to forever in my mind.

*Shemetova with a suitcase, her greatcoat over her arm, wear-
ing a tunic without shoulder loops, rings the doorbell. It is
late at night.*

GRANDMOTHER   [*from behind the door*]   Who's there?

SHEMETOVA   Me, let me in, please.

GRANDMOTHER   [*looking past the doorchain*]   Who do you want?

SHEMETOVA   Grandma, it's me.

GRANDMOTHER   Olya! [*Quickly unfastens the chain.*] Olya, my child!
[*Seizes her, kisses her.*] My darling! I didn't recognize you in the
uniform. . . . Why, why didn't you send a telegram! We didn't
even meet you. . . . For good? Or on leave?

SHEMETOVA   Let me see Nyusha.

GRANDMOTHER   Right away, right away. Let me hang this up. [*Takes
the coat.*] Nyusha's asleep; she's better, thank god. On the mend,
now. Last week, to tell the truth, she gave us quite a scare. It's
all right—Mitya managed to get some penicillin. Now everything,
everything is all right; don't worry.

SHEMETOVA   What was it?

GRANDMOTHER   Ah, my angel, such a storm cloud passed. She caught
double pneumonia. That fool of a nurse took her out without a
scarf after she had had grippe. I had gone to get things for the

house, and she, just think of it, took her out without a scarf, and such a frail child, who catches everything! The woman didn't even button her little coat properly!

SHEMETOVA   You didn't write that she's frail.

GRANDMOTHER   Why would we have, Olya? When you couldn't come or couldn't help. It's simply stupid to make a person worry for no reason. Although, if Mitya hadn't gotten the penicillin, I would have telegraphed. There's a limit to hiding things. Now I can tell you that all these years she's been sick with almost everything. Not a day goes by without doctors or medicines.

SHEMETOVA   Where is she?

GRANDMOTHER   You probably want to wash up first. [SHEMETOVA *washes her hands.* GRANDMOTHER *brings a clean towel.*] When I wrote that Grandpa was sick, it wasn't Grandpa at all, but Nyusha. Scarlet fever. Because of that scarlet fever we spent an extra two months in Kazan. Grandpa was the hero of the day. But Nyusha takes after Mitya exactly. When he was little he was always sick, but once he grew up, it passed, as you know. Right now he's on a field trip. He'll be back in a few days. He phoned yesterday to ask about Nyusha, and whether we had had any word from you. . . . Well, let's go. I've taken her into my room. Grandpa is in yours for the time being; everything is upside-down. He stayed up with me over her for several nights. I don't know how I would have done it without him. You can't trust strangers in such moments. [*They stand at the head of Nyusha's bed.*] Has she grown?

SHEMETOVA   She's so long . . . my bones . . .

GRANDMOTHER   She's skinny, but that doesn't matter. I can't stand fat children. You don't have those—those shoulder loops, so you're home for good, thank god. I'll evacuate Grandpa from your room this minute, you want me to? I'll draw a hot bath for you. You can wash, go to bed like a princess. All your things are in the closet, neat and tidy; I set them out myself. They're waiting for you. Only, of course, they're all out of style now. Though still most people, you know, simply dress as best they can. . . .

SHEMETOVA   Maybe I could simply sleep here somewhere, near her?

GRANDMOTHER   Wherever you like, my darling. The important thing is that you're home for good. Lord, how we have waited for this! Hitler is crushed and defeated, and we're all well and in one piece, and Nyusha got better by the time you came home, and everything's fine. You must have a bite to eat. I'll put the kettle on and start heating the water for your bath.

SHEMETOVA I'll do it myself, don't bother, for heaven's sake.

GRANDMOTHER I don't know whether or not Mitya wrote you that he has such a good position now, he's so highly regarded. He was offered a directorship. He turned it down, of course; why should he get involved in all that bureaucratic red tape? [SHEMETOVA *is silent.* GRANDMOTHER *goes out, returns.*] Olechka.

SHEMETOVA Yes?

GRANDMOTHER There are things which can and must be kept secret. Absolutely must! You understand me? It's nonsense, my dear, the idea that each has to tell the other everything, pour out all of his or her secrets, so that harmony will reign. That's not harmony but middle-class licentiousness and slovenliness. A person must behave circumspectly in society. If he has self-respect and respects others . . . if he wants to strengthen life and not make it rickety and shaky . . . Olya, are you paying attention?

SHEMETOVA Yes . . .

GRANDMOTHER Do you understand?

SHEMETOVA Yes.

SHEMETOVA'S VOICE That conversation after I left, your conversation with Arefyev, don't you want to remind me of it? Oh, yes, I'm not supposed to know about it. . . .

Bakchenin is ready to leave: his suitcase is packed, he is going through old letters. Arefyev watches him.

BAKCHENIN That's the end. Strange . . .

AREFYEV What's strange?

BAKCHENIN For one thing, I'm twenty-seven. I just realized it the other day. Not much left, is there?

AREFYEV Depends what for.

BAKCHENIN I can still make up for whatever I've lost, if I want to. Once, it seemed to me I had been living for a hundred years and fighting for ninety-nine of them. [*Sings.*] "All the things I've thought of will come true in time . . ." That's it.

AREFYEV What did you think of?

BAKCHENIN I thought of life. Living! That was the question: to go for the fifth year, or the fourth?

AREFYEV Did you finish the fourth?

BAKCHENIN Oh, what do I remember? Everything has gone right through this sieve. . . . The fourth, the fourth, Sergei Georgievich! Only: pull in your belt, student, pull it in tighter.

AREFYEV   Listen, Seryozhka . . .

BAKCHENIN   To tell the truth, I hadn't a prayer. Absolutely none!
Figured it out—that was it! Somebody else would get through, sure,
but, Comrade Bakchenin, that's the end of you.

AREFYEV   You really thought you hadn't a prayer?

BAKCHENIN   Not one.

AREFYEV   How did you fight, then? Feeling they were going to get
you? . . . Nobody would ever have guessed it, looking at you. . . .
For a long time?

BAKCHENIN   From the very beginning. From the first time I heard
a mine's caterwauling.

AREFYEV   What are you talking about!

BAKCHENIN   Vile, hateful sound! A man wants to shout at it—go on,
you bastard, burst!

AREFYEV   Not because you were scared?

BAKCHENIN   Come off it! Go try to tell somebody that Bakchenin's
a coward! Go ahead! Without believing for a second that I would
stay in one place, I jumped right into the pot, right on to the
devil's horns, didn't I, admit it!

AREFYEV   Well, sure, whether or not you had to, your nerves landed
you on the horns of the devil.

BAKCHENIN   Of course, civilized man possesses heightened respon-
siveness; everyone knows that.

AREFYEV   Listen, civilized man, why did you lie to Olya?

BAKCHENIN   What do you mean!

AREFYEV   Come on, tell me, out with it: why?

BAKCHENIN   What did you do: read the letter?

AREFYEV   That's not good!

BAKCHENIN   But reading other people's letters is?

AREFYEV   Don't try to get out of it this time. And, secondly, the
letter was from a man, not a woman. And thirdly, I had a feeling, just a feeling, that you were lying, and I wanted to check
up. And fourthly, answer my question: why didn't you tell her
straight? So she would keep thinking of you as an honest man?
And not a scoundrel? How you can do it I don't understand—get
confirmation that your wife has died, has been dead for four years,
and then lie, without blinking an eye, that she's alive, spin some
fairy tale about a bomb, an operation, god knows what all you
made up. Just that itself is blasphemy: raising the dead from the
grave so that she, see, takes part in your amorous intrigues. . . .
Defiling her spirit . . .

BAKCHENIN   Spirit . . . what, don't tell me you believe in god?

AREFYEV   This has nothing to do with god, but with people. With respect for the living and the dead. I'm thinking soberly, without emotional overtones. Once you had done it, once you could treat her like that—I'm talking about the living now—what kind of life companion could you be for her, what kind of radiance could you two ever have together? And from that point of view it's not a bad thing that you broke up now and not later, but the way you did it makes me indignant. Your lying makes me indignant!

BAKCHENIN   Believe me, lying was better. Believe that.

AREFYEV   It's never better to lie!

BAKCHENIN   Maybe it isn't. . . . But then consider character. Pride. Determination. You can make a mess by telling the truth. Just because I respect her—yes, respect her and want to spare her—I lied to her; yes, I did. For myself, and for her, too, not just for myself—I created a way out.

AREFYEV   I understand that you don't love her, and that now she's in your way.

BAKCHENIN   Stop it. Words don't fit here; words are all wrong. Don't love her? It will be my most sacred memory forever and ever.

AREFYEV   Then what are you doing, I ask you! Run after her, catch her, beg her forgiveness! She'll forgive you; she'll see the mess you've made. Seryozhka, a person like that has fallen in love with you, you ass, fallen really in love, and you're flicking it off—it means nothing to you?

BAKCHENIN   Really in love . . . Love isn't that real—let me tell you—is easier. Real love is such a . . .

AREFYEV   Burden?

BAKCHENIN   Responsibility.

AREFYEV   A man accepts responsibility as a duty. Accepts it for himself and for the woman.

BAKCHENIN   Don't you start lecturing me in clichés. Old hackneyed truths aren't for me in my position. I need to start with a clean slate. I have to be free in order to make myself work, to make myself sit over books in the public library, to switch over from this life to the one I want, and we aren't machines to be switched by pressing a button! I have to have the right of living on a scholarship—half-starving because the arms that once held me up are gone. But studying and working—that's doing neither one nor the other. . . . At home—just the bare walls, and lugging this greatcoat another three years or so and wrapping myself up in it; but she would come with the little girl, you can just picture it—

two pairs of eyes staring at you—husband! step-father! and you haven't got a thing for the child. . . . The girl is used to living comfortably; they're all scholars and scientists; and Olya is used to it, though she pretends, see, that she doesn't care about panes in the windows, can make do without windowpanes. . . . And her relation to our relationship. She had stopped sorting out what's mine, what's hers. Where have you been; where are you going; what did you read; what are you thinking? . . . Having nothing you can call your own; everything out on the table, like change from your pocket. . . . It's slavery!

AREFYEV You're contradicting yourself. One minute it's responsibility; the next, it's slavery.

BAKCHENIN They're links in the same chain.

AREFYEV Take a good, close look at it. As she has.

BAKCHENIN I am. Either it's her, and everything with her and from her. The service of love. Or—I'll become something worthwhile. But I can't serve two masters.

AREFYEV You don't love her. At least, you love yourself more.

BAKCHENIN I love my life more, my life that has been preserved by some miracle. Is that a crime? [*Shuts the suitcase.*] Well, that's it. So, embrace and good-bye?

AREFYEV [*kisses him*] I'm sorry for you. More than for her. Much more. Maybe you'll run after her anyway? Ask her to forgive you?

BAKCHENIN You should be able to realize that people don't confess such things. Ah, Lord, I'm leaving—and there's so much water over the dam already, my god. . . . Well, once more. Good-bye, friend. Think well of me.

AREFYEV Good-bye, Seryozhka.

3

The Airport Manager, surrounded by passengers, crosses in front of the curtain.

MANAGER [*having become worried but continuing to comport himself valiantly*] I understand it all, comrades. But I'm not god, am I? I can't change the weather with a wave of my hand.

244   Vera Panova

A PASSENGER Some twenty-five years now I've been flying regularly, heaven knows how many times right into a snowstorm, and
nothing ever happened.
MANAGER You flew into a storm—you're absolutely right—when it was
not accompanied by electrical discharges. It's a question of your
lives, comrades. We've put the heat up for you, I believe. The
restaurant awaits your pleasure, although the next shift hasn't
come and the personnel, as they're called, have gone home. And
you have easy chairs. And our staff has given up their personal
quarters to the senior comrades among you. Have a bite to eat,
comrades, if I may offer you my advice, and take a nap. Morning brings counsel.

[*They pass.*]

*The setting of the first act. Bakchenin and Shemetova are
on the landing by the window. Evening. The passengers have
quieted down. The bookstore is shut. Outside, a searchlight
cuts into the storm.*

SHEMETOVA So that's how it was.
BAKCHENIN Arefyev couldn't stand it, he sold out? A humanist,
profound conscience . . . And you wrote him "thanks"?
SHEMETOVA For his having delivered the final blow?
BAKCHENIN That's what I was saying! He imagines he did a noble
deed.
SHEMETOVA He meant to be honest. . . . Of course, it was hard
after I left. So stifling, so bitter—but there was pride in yielding
my happiness to an unfortunate woman. And I didn't feel I was
alone, and I didn't feel you were a stranger—there was a ring of
light around our sacrifice; I could hear your voice from far away.
. . . And then that letter came from Arefyev. It turned out that
I had made no sacrifice at all; you, even less. Nobody had made
the least sacrifice. I had been sacrificed; just me.
BAKCHENIN What can I say?
SHEMETOVA Nothing to say now. Only, you made one little mistake then. You were afraid I would be a burden to you. Whatever I was, or am, believe me, I've never been a burden to anybody. That's one thing I can handle well—not being a burden.
BAKCHENIN Are you very unhappy?
SHEMETOVA Get that out of your head. Ever since I silenced the
outside voices, everything has been lovely for me. The people

around me are tactful, attentive. Our life is based on mutual respect. May god grant other women a chance to live as I do.

BAKCHENIN   Let me say this: you, too, were rash and didn't behave very correctly. If you set any store by me at all, you should have put up a struggle. Knocked sense into my fool's head.

SHEMETOVA   Struggle? Against an armless, helpless woman risen from the grave?

[ALYONA *and* KOLOSYONOK *are dancing behind the column, trying not to make noise.* KOLOSYONOK *has one arm around her; in the other hand he holds a transistor radio, barely audible.*]

ALYONA   You dance well. Lots of practice?

KOLOSYONOK   Un-hunh.

ALYONA   In cultural centers?

KOLOSYONOK   Mostly.

ALYONA   I'm glad you dance well. [KOLOSYONOK *tries as hard as he can.*] What's your job? I guess it's not dusty and dirty if you spend most of your time in cultural centers.

KOLOSYONOK   Dusty and dirty is just what it is. I'm a civil engineer.

ALYONA   You build houses?

KOLOSYONOK   Bridges.

ALYONA   I never imagined bridge builders being like this.

KOLOSYONOK   But like what?

ALYONA   Stern and mighty.

KOLOSYONOK   I work out with dumbbells every morning. And on the job I'm pretty stern.

ALYONA   No, no no, you shouldn't have any sternness! In fact, I'm glad you're such an unstern bridge builder. What's the music? I don't know it.

KOLOSYONOK   Something from overseas.

ALYONA   They say there's a blizzard in both hemispheres. Think of a snowstorm over the ocean. Huge, gigantic, endless waves with snow swirling over them, and this music, and everything whirling . . . and you and I whirling like the snow. . . .

[*By the window.* BAKCHENIN *and* SHEMETOVA.]

BAKCHENIN   Both of them were strangers. When I married, I thought: No matter she's a stranger now; later she'll become really close. Neither did! Whoever has tasted sweets, so they say, never wants things sour. I had known something which nothing could take away. Whether or not I deserved it, it had been given to me once. That's the point. And nobody could take your place.

That's vengeance on me, I guess. I keep telling myself there are other fields where I'm capable and needed; the world is bigger than love affairs or family problems! But old age looms in front of me and says: You're just a barren flower, you'll droop and die, and nobody will shed a tear. . . .

SHEMETOVA Sometimes, when the accustomed pattern of things is suddenly broken . . . like today's emergency landing . . . as if you were going along and suddenly: Stop! and you look up . . . and it's terrifying—why has this happened to me? But it's only for a moment; no more. You, too, know how it is: you fall asleep, see something terrible, and you make yourself wake up.

BAKCHENIN My darling! How true everything you say is. About the terrifying dreams, too. And about being stopped, when you look back and think—why me? why did my mind cloud over? was that really me? So: I would betray these precious hands, these eyes? You're so close to me, my own flesh and blood, so terribly much my own!

SHEMETOVA But what you did!

[ALYONA *and* KOLOSYONOK *dance.*]

ALYONA Shall I tell you what I don't like about you?

KOLOSYONOK Do, if it isn't too humiliating.

ALYONA That you have no feeling for poetry. Did I offend you?

KOLOSYONOK How can proper criticism be offensive? But maybe each person has his own ways? You have tons of poetry, so to speak, and I have this little portable transistor. Admit it, it's gayer than your poetry.

ALYONA A transistor is nothing. Anybody can have one. Though I liked the way you got it out of your suitcase at the right time— just when I wanted to dance.

KOLOSYONOK I do lots of things at the right time.

ALYONA Do you have anything else entertaining in your suitcase?

KOLOSYONOK Now it's time to get serious. After all, we're not saying good-bye forever. I'll be coming into Moscow.

ALYONA As we go to Novosibirsk! More and more often! Every week!

KOLOSYONOK Every week would be difficult.

ALYONA Well, every month.

KOLOSYONOK That wouldn't work either.

ALYONA I'll meet you at the airport and wave a bunch of flowers! By the flowers you'll see from the distance that I'm there waiting!

KOLOSYONOK I have something I want to tell you. [*Nervously.*] This is the first time in my life that I've run into someone like this. Do you believe in love at first sight?

ALYONA   Of course.

KOLOSYONOK   And do you consider me a man who could make someone happy?

ALYONA   What kind of happiness can you offer?

KOLOSYONOK   Well, for example, I could memorize all the poems of what's-his-name, the one who died eight hundred years ago.

ALYONA   Stop joking. How dull and stupid, anyway. For me nothing is greater than art; remember that. My greatest regret is that I wasn't born with any talent. When I try to write, it comes out awful. But still I adore art and will adore it all my life. Remember that!

KOLOSYONOK   I agree. You'll adore it, and I'll adore you. I'll try not to be dull.

ALYONA   Dullness is bad.

KOLOSYONOK   Much worse.

ALYONA   I'll tell you what kind of happiness we must have. I can't stand humdrum things.

KOLOSYONOK   In what sense?

ALYONA   The most obvious. Depressing things. I love the way we're living here: we eat what comes, dance where we feel like it. . . .

KOLOSYONOK   Certainly an acceptable condition. We'll dance where it comes and eat what we feel like. Can I shave in the morning?

ALYONA   Shave—yes.

NYUSHA [*passing by*]   Alyona, we're going into the restaurant to toast Papa. [*To* KOLOSYONOK.] I warn you that absolutely nothing will come of this.

ALYONA [*dancing*]   Nyushechka-dushechka, don't spoil the best evening of my life.

NYUSHA [*to* KOLOSYONOK]   Don't be fooled. It's only excitement from love of life.

ALYONA   Nyushechka, all the same my name will be Kolosyonok.

NYUSHA [*to* KOLOSYONOK]   Keep it in mind.

KOLOSYONOK   I'm very grateful, but, excuse me, it's presumptuous of me, possibly, even improper, even mad on my part, but perhaps you're wrong?

NYUSHA   Coming, Alyona?

ALYONA   Yes, yes, in a minute. [NYUSHA *goes out.*] Tolechka, you understand I can't invite you to our little family party. It's still too soon, I think.

KOLOSYONOK   I understand.

ALYONA   I'll just drink one toast.
KOLOSYONOK   I'll wait by the door.
ALYONA   Just one toast and I'll be right back.

[GRANDMOTHER, GRANDFATHER, NYUSHA, *and* LINEVSKY *have gathered around a table in the restaurant.*]

NYUSHA [*to* LYUSYA]   Another glass.

[*They turn toward the door.* ALYONA *runs in.*]

LYUSYA   Open it?
NYUSHA   Just a minute. [SHEMETOVA *comes in and sits down.*] Now you can.

[LYUSYA *uncorks the bottle. The cork pops.*]

GRANDFATHER   So—to Mitya.
ALYONA   To Papa!

[*They drink standing.*]

OLD WOMAN IN GLASSES [*going by, politely*]   Many happy returns of the day.

[*They bow to her in thanks.*]

ALYONA   Champagne is a marvelous thing. "And Lip to Lip it murmured—'while you live, drink!' " Any more?
GRANDMOTHER   What is he doing right now?
GRANDFATHER   Drinking and eating.
NYUSHA   To us.
ALYONA   The whole town is there, like last year, and drinking to us, because we aren't there, and it's much worse for them without us.
GRANDMOTHER   Nothing of the sort. He's still on the phone, calling the airport, and they keep telling him the same thing: delayed. . . .
ALYONA [*to* SHEMETOVA]   Ma!
SHEMETOVA   Yes?
ALYONA   See the man over there?
SHEMETOVA   I certainly have seen him.
ALYONA   Ma, do you like him?
SHEMETOVA   You mean: you do.
ALYONA   I think I'll marry him.
SHEMETOVA   Go ahead; nobody is stopping you. We long ago gave up trying to arrange things for you.

ALYONA   He builds bridges.

SHEMETOVA   That all?

ALYONA   His name is Kolosyonok.

SHEMETOVA   That all?

ALYONA   He is, in general, wonderful.

SHEMETOVA   My little silly . . .

GRANDMOTHER   They keep telling him "delayed," and he doesn't know what to think.

NYUSHA   Papa always knows what to think.

GRANDFATHER   Absolutely right.

ALYONA   There's a special thing about champagne. When it's poured, you think it will spill over, but when the foam has settled, it turns out that there's practically nothing, only a little on the bottom. . . .

NYUSHA   Don't hurry. He'll wait.

GRANDMOTHER   Fill the glasses. I want to drink a toast. [GRANDFATHER *fills the glasses.*] To all our lovely children, the ornaments of our old age. [*Starts to clink glasses with* LINEVSKY.]

LINEVSKY   [*puts his glass down*] Don't mind my not drinking. I sincerely, sincerely would like to join in your festivities, but I can't. I think I have to go. Here I am . . .

GRANDMOTHER   What, on foot?

LINEVSKY   Actually, it's not so far . . .

LYUSYA   What are you thinking of! You'll never make it.

LINEVSKY   I will somehow.

GRANDMOTHER   You'll get caught in the snow.

LINEVSKY   No, I won't. At least, I'll make it to work in the morning. You're right [*to* GRANDFATHER], when relations are strained, how can a man work? Impossible . . .

ALYONA   Grandma, why is the man crying?

GRANDMOTHER   He was too late for his mother's funeral.

[ALYONA *falls silent.*]

GRANDFATHER   When I said that to you, the buses were still running.

LINEVSKY   Oh, the devil is not so black. . . . If only he hasn't fired me. Probably has, though. Probably has. It would be unlike him not to. He's just like that. One way or the other, I can't sit here any longer without knowing. It's vitally important, you understand?

GRANDFATHER   On the one hand, no doubt about it . . .

LINEVSKY   And my wife all upset. Sure. Thanks for your help; I'm off. The best of luck to you in everything. Get there safely. You know, you suddenly run across people . . . Studied together, we did, on close terms ever since the institute. . . . [*Buttons his coat, puts his ear flaps down, pulls on his gloves, turns his collar up.*] Once more. To all of you. From the bottom of my heart. [*Goes out.*]

LYUSYA   Madman! We shouldn't let him.

SHEMETOVA   How will you stop him? Tie him up?

LYUSYA   Not let him, that's all. He's psycho.

GRANDMOTHER   He's a perfectly rational man. We appealed to his reason. He preferred to go. It was his free choice.

LYUSYA   But what if he gets something frozen?

GRANDMOTHER   What if our urging has even more fatal consequences for him? In matters of grave importance a man is wholly responsible for himself.

ALYONA   Bravo, Granny!

LYUSYA   [*who has grasped the point and relaxed*]   Sure, he'll only stick his nose out, see what it's like outside, and come back.

> *But Linevsky goes down the stairs, over to the exit, without stopping or hesitating. Only for a second does he pause at the door, then immediately opens it with a determined yank. The whirling, glittering snow rushes at him as if warning of what lies ahead—and Linevsky vanishes in the blizzard.*
>
> *The storm whirls—and now we are carried into its midst. The airport terminal, all lit up like a huge lantern, fades into the distance and disappears in the wild, white haze. Linevsky stubbornly stumbles on through this haze, spinning with it, defending himself against it with his upturned collar and hands in heavy gloves, while, also spinning and fighting against it, there comes toward him another man, also with upturned collar and lowered ear flaps, just as out of breath and obstinate—Linevsky's Boss. They meet.*

BOSS   Linevsky! It's you!° Linevsky!

LINEVSKY   I don't want to see you; I don't want to talk to you!

BOSS   You going home? [*Takes him by the elbow.*]

LINEVSKY   No, to a dance! Let go of me, you hear! I don't want to, I refuse!

BOSS   Look, now, how can a man talk to you, how? You're inhuman!

°They use *ty* to each other.

I fight my way through to you in weather like this god knows where, and even now you can't help but make me feel it!

LINEVSKY   Feel what, what?

BOSS   That you don't give a damn for me.

LINEVSKY   And you—what about you?

BOSS   You've made me feel that from the first day, the very first day, every step of the way. It has become the basis of your life.

LINEVSKY   And the basis of yours? What's the basis of yours?

BOSS   Linevsky . . .

LINEVSKY   Reminding me every minute, day and night, that I'm under you!

BOSS   Linevsky . . .

LINEVSKY   So that I may never all of a sudden somehow have a good opinion of myself—that's the basis of yours!

BOSS   Linevsky, what else can I do, given your attitude to me?

LINEVSKY   And to think that that man and I once studied for exams together!

BOSS   Linevsky, you know it could have been the other way around, couldn't it—I in your place, you in mine? Of course it could! Supposing you were my boss? Fine! Then would you tolerate this sort of attitude? Would you overlook all my little grins? Who is amused by them?! These little jokes, little snide remarks in front of every honest person? These constant disruptions of the way things are done—for what purpose? To undermine my authority!

LINEVSKY   How can you talk to me now about the way things are done? How can you get your tongue to say a word?

BOSS   Because you drive me to it. You think I wouldn't let you go to Odessa? I would have, even before you were finished asking—if you hadn't made a face. What did the face say? That there it is, the irony of fate, that you, Linevsky, such as you are, have to ask me, such as I am, permission for doing the most natural, most universally venerated things!

LINEVSKY   I . . .

BOSS   Linevsky, in all good faith, cross your heart, did you make a face or not?

LINEVSKY   If I did, it was a reflex.

BOSS   So much the worse, so much the more insulting, don't you see?—and you an intelligent man. It shows that your disrespect of me has gotten into your blood.

[*They stand in the storm.*]

LINEVSKY   She went to her grave without me.

BOSS   I know.

LINEVSKY   Thanks to you.

BOSS [*desperately*]   I know!

LINEVSKY   You think you strengthened your authority by doing that and increased my respect for you?

BOSS   In your bitterness . . . you're not saying the right thing . . . the appropriate thing. When I found out you hadn't flown, were sitting at the airport . . . Well, here I am before you, in all these snowdrifts! I sat down to supper—couldn't eat! I went to bed—couldn't sleep! [*Wipes his eyes.*] As if it had been my own mother . . .

[*Somewhere far away a child's cry is heard.*]

LINEVSKY   Have you fired me?

BOSS   What difference does that make? The order can be canceled in a second.

LINEVSKY   Aha, but there is an order!

BOSS [*blows his nose*]   Especially because the union committee has already filed a protest. It's not the formalities that interest me.

LINEVSKY   Aha, don't interest you! Ha-ha-ha-ha, formalities don't interest you!

BOSS   I want to finish saying what I had to say. Because of you, people think I'm a crocodile. Because of you, I really am becoming a crocodile; you're forcing me to.

LINEVSKY   Ha-ha-ha-ha, you hear that? I'm forcing him to become a crocodile!

BOSS   Linevsky, I beg you, as one man to another, adopt a new attitude toward me. At least in front of others. Linevsky? Can't you possibly make a concession?

LINEVSKY   I don't understand what you want from me. [*Walks away.*]

BOSS [*goes after him*]   When we're alone, if you have to, let go. But only when we're alone, tête-à-tête, eh, Linevsky? All right, never mind, when others are around, too. Go ahead. Criticize me at meetings, the hell with you. But let's have done with those little grins forever. Is it so hard? Those damned grins . . . eh, Linevsky?

They disappear in the storm. In the vacant airport restaurant
Nyusha, Lyusya, and Tamara sit with a bottle of champagne.

TAMARA   The most important thing is: be a man. Call up, say a
couple of words at least. Let her hear your voice. So she knows
she's not all alone. . . .

LYUSYA   But maybe he suddenly did, and the phone was out.

TAMARA   A real man would have thought of calling before. Not
waited until the phone was out. Maybe your feelings don't run
very deep. Maybe you're going to go to the theater with somebody else. But no matter what, you can show some sensitivity,
can't you?

LYUSYA   When I was marrying Slavik, everybody said, "Oh, look
at who Lyusya picked; with all the friends she has, and her cousin
a test pilot, she could have found a husband who would go much
farther." And I studied it and studied it—what were their intentions, those men who would go so far? No matter who I met,
his intentions were absolutely not solid at all or else he was married. But Slavik had serious intentions right from the start.

TAMARA   I sat here all evening putting things away and doing my
nails.

LYUSYA   You can just leave the house to him and not worry, and
everything will be as it's supposed to. Because he loves real home
life. You can surround him all around with bathing beauties,
world-famous movie stars and everything—he won't even notice.
Means nothing to him. All he cares about is having his Lyuska
with him.

NYUSHA   A divinely fortunate woman. Take a sip.

LYUSYA   Oh, honey, I couldn't possibly.

NYUSHA   [*to* TAMARA]   Let's drink to her happiness.

TAMARA   [*clinks reluctantly*]   Why drink to it: she's boasting about
it from dawn to dark.

LYUSYA   Tamaronka, I don't at all, word of honor, it just comes out
by itself; I even feel embarrassed.

NYUSHA   To you and your husband.

LYUSYA   Oh! Can't not drink to that, can I; it would be a sin,
really. [*Clinks glasses.*] I thank you sincerely for the both of us.
[*Drinks from the glass.*] And there they are, back home there,

my two boys, my angels, and here we are, having a time, and my little Vitalik, poor sweetie . . .

TAMARA   That's enough. She can't get used to the idea. In the nursery in the morning they give him enough till he bursts. Big tragedy!

LYUSYA [crying]   I'm used to it.

TAMARA   So there's no point in going into hysterics all over again.

LYUSYA   But a person can have a sore heart?

TAMARA   No reason for you to.

NYUSHA   It's all right if that's the reason. To have a child, to be really attached to it, to give up everything for it, to tremble for it—how good!

LYUSYA   You don't?

NYUSHA   No.

TAMARA   You're not married?

NYUSHA   Separated.

TAMARA   Turned out to be a skunk?

NYUSHA   He couldn't get used to our family. And I couldn't get used to him.

LYUSYA   I like your family a lot. You're all so nice, so polite.

NYUSHA   It's hard for an outsider. On the one hand, he thinks he can do everything; on the other, if he does do something, says something not just right, something that doesn't fit, he starts feeling himself—well, on the far side of the river. You can't even explain why it is. Nobody will reprimand him; nobody will pout. He himself feels it. To get along with us you have to be very much like us—or really thick-skinned.

LYUSYA   Now for a person like me it's better to say it right out, if something's not right. Keeping things in is bad for your health, too. It's better to have an argument. You argue and then you make up . . . [Cuts herself off.] Shhh! [Listens.]

TAMARA   What are you doing?

LYUSYA   No, can't be. I was imagining.

TAMARA [to NYUSHA]   Give me a cigarette. . . . I'm for it: being married and divorced. But I have absolutely no luck. . . .

LYUSYA   Shhh! [Now they all hear a child's distant crying.] That's Vitalik! . . . [Gets up trembling.]

TAMARA   She's gone nuts. Where would Vitalik come from? Lots of bawlers and squallers besides Vitalik.

[Downstairs the door opens. SLAVIK enters with a huge bundle in his arms. Both SLAVIK and the bundle are covered with snow. Cry-

*ing comes from inside the bundle. People sleeping on the benches
raise their heads.* SLAVIK *shakes the snow off the bundle first, then off
himself, exposing a blanket in which a well-padded child is wrapped
and his own policeman's uniform.*]

SLAVIK [*to the* PASSENGERS]   Can you tell me where I'll find Citizen
Syomina? Syomina. She works here . . .

PASSENGERS   Who's he looking for? Somebody called Syomina.

SLAVIK   She works in the restaurant.

PASSENGERS   We're passengers. Go ask one of the people who work
here.

SLAVIK   . . . as a waitress. [*The baby, which had almost quieted
down, cries again. A sleepy* IVAN GAVRILOVICH *comes out.*] Citizen,
you work here?

IVAN G. [*peering closely*]   So?

SLAVIK   Know the staff here?

IVAN G.   So. Go on.

SLAVIK   Can you tell me where I'll find Citizen Syomina?

IVAN G.   Lyusya, somebody wants you!

SLAVIK   She hasn't gone home?

IVAN G.   Wasn't supposed to. Run upstairs, to the restaurant. Up
those stairs. My-o-my! The mountain didn't come to Mohammed,
so Mohammed made his way to the mountain. Well done!

[*Pounding in his boots,* SLAVIK *heads for the stairs.* LYUSYA *runs to
meet him, beside herself.*]

LYUSYA   I'm going to faint!

SLAVIK   Here. I brought him.

LYUSYA [*takes the child*]   My love, my angel, little one, just a minute, my darling, my puppy, just a minute. . . . [*The child moans
and cries out greedily inside the bundle.*] Come, Slavik, come on;
I'll show you where it's warm. Only, god help us, I hope he hasn't
caught cold, not caught cold.

SLAVIK [*following her upstairs*]   He won't. I wrapped him up in
everything there was.

LYUSYA [*goes into the restaurant*]   Meet everybody, Slavik. Hang
your coat up there on the rack. This is my husband Slavik. Sit
down, Slavik. Give him something to drink to warm up. Vitalik
and I will be right back. If only he hasn't caught cold!

SLAVIK   Hurry up. He's hungry.

LYUSYA   Right away, right away. [*Takes the baby out.*]

[NYUSHA *and* TAMARA *watch her go. The child quiets down.*]

NYUSHA   Drink.

SLAVIK   Thank you.

NYUSHA   Frozen?

SLAVIK   We're used to it. It's not that cold out.

NYUSHA   I thought only mothers would do mad things for their children.

SLAVIK   Nothing mad about it. Sometimes you stand duty in weather worse than this.

NYUSHA   But still—ten miles.

SLAVIK   Well, we didn't do it all on foot. Did most of it by car. In an ambulance. I know the boys in the garage. I tell them what's happening. Right, they say, let's go. Cars were getting around some. Didn't have more than four miles to do on foot. [*He holds his glass in his big, red hand and sips from it.*] He was howling and howling. What are you going to do? Fellow next door and I did this and that. Sang to him and rocked him—nothing doing, wanted his mother. The law of nature. Outside on the street he was quiet at first, then started in crying again. Now he'll go to sleep.

[*Silence. A cradle song is heard. The blizzard abates. Night is coming to an end. Everyone is asleep, some leaning back in the armchairs, some with their heads propped in their hands.* ALYONA *and* KOLOSYONOK *sleep against each other in the window embrasure. Only* BAKCHENIN *and* SHEMETOVA *are still talking.*]

BAKCHENIN   And you can't forget?

SHEMETOVA   Why? I can. I must.

BAKCHENIN   Or forgive?

SHEMETOVA   No.

BAKCHENIN   But if . . .

SHEMETOVA   No.

BAKCHENIN   Believe me, Olya, to the end of my days . . .

[*A loud* VOICE *over the public address system wakens everyone.*]

P.A. VOICE   Attention please! Flight sixty-two, an IL-18 to Tashkent, is now boarding. Passengers are requested to proceed to the loading platform.

[*Delighted animation in the waiting room. Some head for the exit, others, for the windows.*]

A WOMAN   At last!

OLD WOMAN IN GLASSES   The Lord be praised!

[ALYONA *has awakened, smiles at* KOLOSYONOK.]

ALYONA   Good morning.
KOLOSYONOK   Good morning.
ALYONA   Any bright new prospects?
KOLOSYONOK   Seems we're going to fly.
ALYONA   I had a lovely dream about something. . . .

[BAKCHENIN *and* SHEMETOVA.]

BAKCHENIN   May I write you once in a while? Olya! May I?

[NYUSHA *comes up.*]

SHEMETOVA   That's what I wanted to do before saying good-bye—
have you meet my daughters. Nyusha! [*Introduces her.*] This is the
older one, Anna Dmitrievna Shemetova. Sergei Georgievich
Bakchenin.
BAKCHENIN   The same Nyusha? The one who was so little?
SHEMETOVA   The same one who was so little. [*To* NYUSHA.] Send
Alyona over a minute.
P.A. VOICE   Attention please! Flight eighty-four, an IL-18 to Odessa,
is now boarding. Passengers are requested to proceed to the load-
ing platform.

[ALYONA *goes over to* SHEMETOVA.]

SHEMETOVA   And this is Elena Dmitrievna Shemetova. Alenka, this
is a friend of mine from the war. There, look at her. If she didn't
have an urge always to be playing some idiotic role, she'd be all
right. [ALYONA *shakes* BAKCHENIN's *hand.*] Wish her to become
sensible, Sergei Georgievich. Wish her, wish her good luck, happiness, all the best. . . . Do that. Maybe there'll never be another
chance.
BAKCHENIN   May I kiss you, Lenochka?
ALYONA [*slightly surprised*]   If you like. . . . [BAKCHENIN *kisses her.*]
Ma?
SHEMETOVA   Go on now.
ALYONA [*having returned to* KOLOSYONOK]   These delightful old
people. There's no way of knowing how to take their little tricks.
Why in the world did he want to kiss me? One of Mother's friends;
first time we've ever laid eyes on each other. . . .
KOLOSYONOK [*jealous*]   His wish was only too human.

ALYONA   Strictly nineteenth century. Called me Lenochka. Grandpa and Grandma are a lot more modern, even if they are so
old. . . .

P.A. VOICE   Your attention, please! Flight four hundred seventy-five,
four seven five, a TU-104 to Novosibirsk from Moscow, is now
boarding. Passengers are requested to proceed to the loading
platform.

SHEMETOVA   That's ours.

BAKCHENIN   Wait. Olya, my love!

SHEMETOVA   Good-bye, Sergei Georgievich.

BAKCHENIN   Now, in a minute . . . In a minute my plane will be
announced. . . . And we'll fly together. . . .

SHEMETOVA   There's no reason for you and me to fly together.

BAKCHENIN   But she . . . ?

SHEMETOVA   She's Elena Dmitrievna Shemetova. Good-bye. Good
luck to you. [*Goes out.*]

ALYONA [*to* KOLOSYONOK]   So. Back above the clouds. Into the blue
sunlight.

NYUSHA [*comes up*]   Alyona, that's it. Be quick.

KOLOSYONOK   I'll see you off!

ALYONA   Tolechka, you heard her: "That's it." Now she'll take
Grandma's arm, I'll take Grandpa's, and we'll set off as a
sedate family group. You wave to me through that little window.
Well . . . [*Holds her hand out.*]

KOLOSYONOK   But your address! Where will I write?

ALYONA   Oh, my address! Write down: Moscow . . . You know what?
Don't.

KOLOSYONOK   What do you mean, "Don't"?

ALYONA   Well, what can we write each other? It would be better
to meet some place some time by accident—maybe ten years,
twenty years from now—be delighted to see each other, say, "It's
been ages!"—you know, that would be so much more interesting.

NYUSHA [*to* KOLOSYONOK, *with friendliness*]   Don't say you weren't
warned how this love-affair would end.

ALYONA   And then—how we'll remember our love! How we recited
poetry to each other . . . and fables, and how something in the
storm smiled down on us. . . . Oh, that's very untalented on your
part—getting cross! You make me fly off with a heavy heart.
Smile, please, so I can fly off gaily. [KOLOSYONOK *smiles.*] And
give me your hand. [KOLOSYONOK *does.*] So long!

NYUSHA   Alyona, we're late.

GRANDMOTHER   Girls, you coming?

ALYONA On our way, Grandma!

KOLOSYONOK [*to* NYUSHA] Good-bye.

NYUSHA Have a good trip. [*Goes out, letting* ALYONA *go first.*]

ALYONA [*returns, secretively*] "And lo!—the phantom Caravan has reached the Nothing it set out from— Oh, make haste!" [*Goes out.*]

[*We see all the members of the* SHEMETOV *family file downstairs and disappear through the door on to the platform.*

KOLOSYONOK *waves through the window.*

BAKCHENIN *goes up to another window, looks out. Through the ash-gray morning the red dawn pecks its way from the East. The silhouette of a TU-104 rockets into the air. The roar of its engines drowns all sound.* BAKCHENIN *lights a cigarette, throws on his coat, grabs his briefcase, and slowly leaves the waiting room.*]

CURTAIN

a warsaw melody

meLODY

BY LEONID ZORIN

A LYRICAL DRAMA IN TWO PARTS

CHARACTERS

Victor
Helya

PART I

Before the lights come up and the action begins, we hear Victor's voice, slightly altered for having been taped: "December forty-six in Moscow was mild, with fluffy snow. The air was fresh; it crunched on your teeth. Every evening the streets were noisy; people, it seemed, just couldn't stay home. At least, I couldn't. And there were lots like me."
Lights. The main auditorium of the Conservatory. High up somewhere, next to the railing, sits Helya. Victor comes in, sits beside her.

HELYA [*a slight, soft accent gives her speech a casual air*]   Young man, that seat is taken.

VICTOR   Taken—how so? Who dared take it?

HELYA   My girl friend is going to be sitting here.

VICTOR   Your girl friend isn't going to be sitting here.

HELYA   Young man, that is plain rudeness. You don't think so?

VICTOR   No, I don't. I have a ticket. This row and this seat.

HELYA   Oh, it's probably there. . . . [*Gestures down below.*]

VICTOR   What do you mean, there? Specifically here.

HELYA   But this is a joke, some comic humor. I got the tickets myself.

VICTOR   I got mine myself, too. [*Holds the ticket out to her.*] Take a look.

HELYA [*looks*]   Did you buy it personably?

VICTOR   You mean, personally?

HELYA   Oh, as you like—personally. From a brunette in a reddish brown coat?

VICTOR   Now everything makes sense. A lovely girl.

HELYA   Don't praise her, please. I don't want to hear about her.

VICTOR   I guessed something bad had happened. She was in a terrible hurry.

HELYA   Yes, yes . . . I know where she was hurrying.

VICTOR   And everybody all around was asking for a ticket. Just imagine, what a piece of luck.

HELYA [*casually*]   You often come to the Conservatory?

VICTOR   First time. Why?

HELYA   Oh, no reason . . .

VICTOR   I was walking down the street, saw a crowd a block long.
Meant there was something worthwhile going on, obviously. I
rushed to the box office—rats, shut tight. The business manager
wouldn't give me the time of day. What the hell, I thought;
wasn't I going to get in? It has never happened so far. And then
at that point there was your friend, in the reddish brown coat. . . .
What's on today?

HELYA   If you have no objections—Chopin.

[*Noise, applause.*]

VICTOR   Chopin is Chopin. You have a program?

HELYA   Shh, quiet, please. Now, you have to be quiet. [*The lights
go out. Music. The lights come up again in the entr'acte between
the first and second parts.*] Why aren't you going into the foyer?
One can stretch one's legs there.

VICTOR [*after a moment*]   Don't feel like it somehow. Too much
noise, too many people . . .

HELYA   You don't like noise?

VICTOR   It all depends. Right now, no.

HELYA   You like music?

VICTOR   Turns out I do.

HELYA   It was worth coming to make such a discovery.

VICTOR   Stupid of me not to have come here before. Word of honor.

HELYA   Oh, I believe you without your word of honor.

VICTOR   Where are you from—the Baltic states?

HELYA   No, not from the Baltic states.

VICTOR   But you're not Russian.

HELYA   I'm a rich lady making a trip around the world.

VICTOR   Your friend in the reddish brown coat is also traveling
around the world?

HELYA   My friend . . . We won't talk about my friend. She's a
light-headed thing.

VICTOR   All the same, tell me: where are you from?

HELYA   You don't believe that I'm a rich lady?

VICTOR   I don't know. I've never seen one.

HELYA   I'm from Poland, from sister Poland.

VICTOR   Now that makes sense. I did think you weren't one of us.
That is, I mean, not Soviet. That is, I mean . . .

HELYA   I understand what you mean. [*Bells ring.*] Intermission is over.

VICTOR   What are you doing here?

HELYA   I'm studying .

VICTOR   In what sense?

HELYA   In the Conservatory, if you have nothing against it. And my friend is studying in it, too. But she's yours . . . That is, I mean, Soviet. That is, I mean, we live in the same dormitory.

VICTOR   Thanks, I understand.

HELYA   In the same social company and the same student dormitory. She's a future musician, too. And meantime has sold her ticket.

VICTOR   You probably get a big discount. I didn't even think about it—it was pretty cheap.

HELYA   That's all we needed, for her to . . . how do you say—spec-u-late a little. It was enough that she decided to go hear a young man and not Chopin.

VICTOR   But after all, that's understandable.

HELYA   The gentleman thinks so? I look down on her.

VICTOR   There's not a young man hanging around on every corner.

HELYA   I don't know where he hangs around, but he's a dull young man. He doesn't like music, and that makes him different from you. Poor Asya has a constant conflict. Love and duty. Love and work. It's an absolutely awful position.

VICTOR   Well, I haven't anything against him. Because of him, I'm here.

HELYA   You were lucky.

VICTOR   I'm always lucky. I'm a lucky man.

[*Bells ring.*]

HELYA   That's very interesting. It's the first time I've met a man who doesn't hide it.

VICTOR   Why should I?

HELYA   But you're not afraid?

VICTOR   What should I be afraid of?

HELYA   People will find out you're a lucky man and want to test it out, is it true or isn't it?

VICTOR   What next? I wasn't scared by Hitler.

[*Applause.*]

HELYA   That's all. Now—shhh.

VICTOR [*in a whisper*]   What's your name?
HELYA   Hush. Listen to the music.

The lights go out. Music. The lights come back on. A street
lamp. An alley.

HELYA   Here's our alley. And there at the end is our dormitory.
   Thanks. Don't come any farther. Might run into Asya. If she sees
   somebody walked me home, I'll lose . . . how do you say . . .
   moral superiority.
VICTOR   So; Helya; that's *Helena*. In Russian you're simply Lena.
HELYA   So; you're Victor. In Russian you're simply the winner. I'm
   simply Lena, and you're simply the winner. All the same there's
   no point translating. I like my name.
VICTOR   I do too.
HELYA   Every word loses in translation. The gentleman will dis-
   agree?
VICTOR   The gentleman won't. Are there many of you in your room?
HELYA   Two other girls. Two tea roses. The first, Asya, she's a
   singer, like me. You saw her. She's sweet, but has absolutely no
   will of her own. Her young man wraps her up with his little
   finger. But the other one is completely different. She has a strong
   character, huge height, and plays the harp.
VICTOR   And what's her name?
HELYA   Holy Mary, he has to know everything. Vera.
VICTOR   Just think, I'll go to the opera some time, and Carmen—
   will be you!
HELYA   I won't be singing Carmen; I have a different voice. And
   I won't be singing opera. I'll be . . . how do you say . . . a
   chambering singer.
VICTOR   You mean a chamber singer.
HELYA   It's simply awful. I'm forever getting things wrong.
VICTOR   I wish I were half so good in Polish. How many years
   have you been here?
HELYA   This is my first year.
VICTOR   If you hadn't told me, I would never have believed it.
HELYA   All right, I'll let you in on a secret, although it's not to my
   advantage at all. There's another little circumstance. My father
   knew Russian and taught me. He used to say, "Heltsya, you must
   know that language. One day you'll thank me." Apparently he
   was thinking of today.

VICTOR   Well, that goes without saying. But—it makes no difference. You're all right!

HELYA   I simply have a talent for languages. Like every woman.

VICTOR   Now, not every . . .

HELYA   Yes, yes. What does it mean, having a talent for languages? Having a talent for imitation, I'm right? And all women are monkeys.

VICTOR [*with exaggerated grief*]   Even—you?

HELYA   The gentleman doesn't wish me to be like everyone else. That's sweet. And very lifelike. We respect the rules but love the exceptions. I'm very sorry, I'm an awful monkey. I look around and measure everything against myself. This won't suit me, but that is perfect! A lovely hairdo—something energetic about it, something poetic, something provocative—I adopt it. Or I see a lovely way of walking. Elegant—and very purposeful and dashing— almost a flying. That's an absolutely mortal wound—such a way of walking and it isn't mine! It will be mine! I take it. And then I meet a girl; she has such a thought-filling look—it shows great inner depths; very well, I take that look.

VICTOR   Thoughtful look.

HELYA   Well, no matter, you understood me. In general, I'm Jean- Baptiste Molière. He said, *"Je prends mon bien où je le trouve."*

VICTOR   Although it'll lose something in translation, translate that.

HELYA   I'm choking you a little with my French? Right? It means, "I take what's good for me where I find it." There are stories that Molière took two scenes for himself from Cyrano de Bergerac. He was a genius; he was allowed to do anything.

VICTOR   But you?

HELYA   Me, too—I'm a woman. But why are you always asking questions? You're a dangerous man.

VICTOR   I want to ask something else. . . .

HELYA   Wait a minute—I'm doing the asking. Do you study?

VICTOR [*nodding*]   In the Omar Khayyam Institute.

HELYA   Holy Mother of God, he's making fun of me.

VICTOR   In the wine-making school, that's all I mean. Omar Khay- yam is the patron of wine-makers. A singer, ideologist, and in- spirer. We learn him by heart almost in a set order. Our professor said that some day over the entrance there would be carved his immortal words:

> Wine engenders strength in body and soul alike,
> The key to secret mysteries is found in it alone.

HELYA   I understand—you'll be a wine-taster?

VICTOR   Keep quiet and don't make a fool of yourself. . . . You don't understand a thing. I'll be a technologist. I'll create wines.

HELYA   Yes, yes. If you don't become a drunkard, you'll make your name famous.

VICTOR   Wine-makers don't become drunkards. That's out of the question.

HELYA   As a matter of fact, for some reason I forgot that wines are created.

VICTOR   What next! The attitude of a consumer! Though, by the way, a wine is born, like a person.

HELYA   That's a joke, I hope.

VICTOR   Sometime I'll tell you all about it. The most important thing is to find those qualities which make the bouquet. And then the wine has to be matured. The bouquet is made by maturation.

HELYA   That will have to be remembered. But it's already late—it's time to go in.

VICTOR   Helya . . .

HELYA   Yes, yes . . . I'm interested in what you'll say next.

VICTOR   I want to see you.

HELYA   I know, but you shouldn't have shown it. How must you say it—shouldn't have shown or shouldn't show?

VICTOR   I really want to see you very much.

HELYA   You have to be casual, completely casual: when will we see each other again? You have little experience. That's bad.

VICTOR   When will we see each other again?

HELYA   How do I know? Saturday. At eight.

VICTOR   Where?

HELYA   You'll keep on asking everything? On the corner of Świętokrzyskaja and Nowy Świat. In Warsaw I used to agree to meet there.

VICTOR [glumly, almost expressionlessly]   There.

HELYA [with interest]   The gentleman supposes he'll be the first?

VICTOR [still more glumly]   The gentleman doesn't. So, where?

HELYA   But at the same time you can smile. Where, where? You should have thought of something back in the Conservatory. Holy Mary, absolutely no experience at all.

VICTOR   Well, all right. I'll give the order. On the corner of Herzen and Ogaryov Streets. Right by the bus stop.

HELYA   Oh, that Asya . . . Couldn't sell it to a nice old man!

The lights go out. Then come on again. The street corner.
Victor looks at his watch. Helya comes up.

HELYA   Don't look at your watch. I'm here.

VICTOR   I was terribly afraid you weren't coming.

HELYA   So, all the same you are afraid of something.

VICTOR   Imagine, it turned out that it was important.

HELYA   What was?

VICTOR   That you come.

HELYA   Ah—ah . . . I can just imagine.

VICTOR   I'm telling the truth.

HELYA   And I believe it, I believe it. Of course—the truth. Important—of course. I don't have to be convinced at all. I can easily see Warsaw girls come to meet you on the corner every evening.

VICTOR   Warsaw girls know what they're worth.

HELYA   All girls must know what they're worth. Invincibility comes from dignity.

VICTOR   Where'll we go?

HELYA   Heaven help me. Again he's asking questions. Mother of god, what has he been thinking about for three days? You're supposed to dazzle me, to show yourself in the best light. Aren't you inviting me to a restaurant?

VICTOR   When I get my scholarship I will.

HELYA   So. That's a courtly answer. The answer of a madman. Don't be exasperated. I know—you create wines, but you still don't have anything to pay for them with. Be cheerful; everything is ahead. You see I didn't put on an evening gown, and my shoes, too, are on a different mission. Any other variations?

VICTOR   Not for the time being.

HELYA   You really are a lucky man. You don't have to make a choice.

VICTOR   Who knows, maybe I have my own worries.

HELYA   Your only worry this evening is supposed to be me.

VICTOR   That I understand.

HELYA   And besides, your Khayyam says:

> In this world is it wise to flee from lovely maidens
> And the vine, if in the next we'll find them both?

VICTOR   You read Khayyam. That pleases me.

HELYA   You like him that much?

VICTOR   I like the fact that you prepared for our meeting.

HELYA   [*looking him up and down*]   Well, so . . . Thanks for the fore-warn-ing.

VICTOR   But that I don't understand.

HELYA   You're not so harmless as I thought. Have to be on my guard with you.

VICTOR   That's a mistake. You don't have to at all.

HELYA   I prepared? Very well, all right. I won't let you forget that, neither you nor Khayyam.

VICTOR   There's no point in getting angry; let's be friends.

HELYA   All the same, you have no experience whatever. Even if you've noticed something, you should have kept quiet about it. Then you could have some time taken advantage of your discovery. Still, where are we going?

VICTOR   [*weightily*]   I suggest we go to a movie.

HELYA   I knew that's how it would end. And what will we see?

VICTOR   I have no idea. Makes no difference to me.

HELYA   You mean you won't be watching the screen?

VICTOR   Why? I will. From time to time.

HELYA   You're frank about it.

VICTOR   From inexperience, it must be.

HELYA   My father used to warn me: it all starts with the movies.

VICTOR   We won't tell him.

HELYA   Certainly won't. He's gone.

VICTOR   I'm sorry.

HELYA   What can I do with you; that's all right. When Warsaw was taken, we made our way to the country, but that didn't save him. [*Suddenly.*] What would you have done if I hadn't come?

VICTOR   Gone to the dormitory.

HELYA   That's good. Means you have character. Why have you become so serious? Better let's change the conversation. Now you know I'm an orphan and you mustn't have hurt my feelings. What's the right way of saying that—have hurt or hurt?

VICTOR   Either way.

HELYA   Either way—you mustn't. Mustn't hurt feelings.

VICTOR   I am, too, you know. And no mother, either.

HELYA   Poor little boy . . . And he's convinced he's a lucky man.

VICTOR   No matter, I am. That's a fact. So many didn't make it, but I did. Six months in a hospital and—here I am. On the corner of Herzen and Ogaryov Streets.

HELYA   Vitek, not another word about the war. Not one word.

VICTOR   Agreed: peace.

HELYA   If I had known, you wouldn't have waited a minute on that corner of yours.

VICTOR [*bounteously*]   What next? . . . You were divinely late, like a goddess. . . . I was all set to wait a half hour.

HELYA   That much?

VICTOR Girls like it.

HELYA   But that's stupididness. Simply stupid-ity. Why spoil a man's frame of mind if you're going to come anyway? I read somewhere: punctuality is the courtesy of kings.

VICTOR [*with archness*]   And queens.

HELYA   Every woman is a queen. That must be understanding once and for all.

VICTOR You mean understood once and for all.

HELYA   *Dobrze, dobrze*—all right, all right. You always know better than I do what I want to say.

The lights go out. They come on again. An empty receiving room. The long distance, or trunk-call, office. A voice, magnified by the microphone: "Budapest, booth three. Budapest is on the line, booth three."

VICTOR Who are you calling?°

HELYA   With the gentleman's permission, Warsaw.

VICTOR More specifically?

HELYA   Let that be a secret. A little secret refreshes a relationship.

VICTOR You've started refreshing it rather early.

HELYA   It's never too early. That happens only too late.

VICTOR Well, after all, it's your own business.

HELYA   This time the gentleman is right.

VICTOR [*looking around*]   It's not terribly comfortable here.

HELYA   But it's warm. When it gets terribly cold and we've completely turned into little pieces of ice, we'll come here and pretend we're waiting for a call.

VICTOR You're fed up walking the streets. I understand you.

HELYA   Vitek, don't be depressed. We're impoverished students. I'm a poor little girl, but young, and I have . . . how do you say it . . . fresh color to my face.

°They have begun to address each other in the familiar, second person singular form *ty*.

VICTOR   It's a shame I wasn't born in Moscow. At least I would
have a corner of my own.

HELYA   I'm hoarse. I don't know how I'll talk.

VICTOR   You're not hoarse at all. Your voice is what it always was.

HELYA   You don't know, I was really sick for two days. They wrapped
me up in two blankets. Then I got raspberry tea. And then as-
pirin. And then I burned. Like a sinner on a bonfire of the In-
quisition. And then I couldn't restrain myself and I threw everything off. That was ecstasy. I lay there naked and ate an apple.
Vera played the harp—it was just like Paradise.

VICTOR   I'm sorry I wasn't there.

HELYA   Same old story. The minute you have Paradise, the Devil
shows up. Everything is your fault, anyway. Because of you I'll
lose my voice and ruin my career. A singer can't be light-headed.

VICTOR   You never have been.

HELYA   Either you control your temperament or it controls you.
[VICTOR *bends over and kisses her cheek.*] Bravo, bravo.

VICTOR   I can do it again. [*Trying to hide his embarrassment.*]
What time is it? [HELYA *laughs.*] What's so funny?

HELYA   I've noticed that people are interested in time at the most
inappropriate moment.

VICTOR [*glumly*]   I don't know. Never thought about it.

HELYA   Listen, I'll cheer you up. One time Father loaded the cart
with a huge stack of hay. Some Jews were hidden in the stack.
I was supposed to drive them to the next village. And the patrol
had just let me pass on, we hadn't gone two steps on, when an
old man's head pops up out of the stack, his white beard full of
green hay, and he asks, "What time is it?" Mother of god, I can
still see the patrol right there, and he has to know what time is it.

VICTOR   You've cheered me up a great deal. You could have been
killed. Or—worse . . .

HELYA   What could be worse?

VICTOR   You yourself know.

HELYA [*gently, after a moment*]   You're an odd one, Vitek.

VICTOR   Stop it. What's so odd about me?

HELYA   Why be cross? I love odd people. It's cozier living in the
world with them around. Once upon a time in Warsaw there
lived a man like that, Franz Fischer. Father used to tell me about
him. He was an odd one. Or a wise man. It's practically the same
thing. You know, he was the soul of Warsaw. The city was like
an orphan without him. [VOICE, *magnified by the microphone:* "I
have Warsaw. Booth six. Warsaw is on the line. Booth six."] That's

me. [VOICE: "Warsaw—booth six."] Wait a minute, I'll be quick. [*Runs out.*]

[VICTOR *lights a cigarette, waits.*]

VOICE   I have Prague. Booth two. Prague is on the line—booth two. I have Sofia—booth five. Sofia, Sofia—booth five.

[VICTOR *puts his cigarette out.* HELYA *comes back.*]

HELYA   How clearly you could hear everything. As if only next door.

VICTOR   Who did you talk to?

HELYA   Vitek, don't you see—I want you to be tormented and have to guess.

VICTOR   You told me yourself that your mother had gone to your aunt's in Radom.

HELYA   You know, Radom is a marvelous town. It's called the Shoemakers' Capital. Some day I'll go to Radom, and I'll have such a pair of shoes made that you'll right away invite me to the Grand Hotel.

VICTOR   If she's in Radom, who did you talk to?

HELYA   Oh, tragic Russian soul. It immediately craves drama.

VICTOR   If the lady prefers comedy, she needn't answer.

HELYA   I'm not a lady yet. I'm a girl. Or, rather, a little girl.

VICTOR   Sorry, I was wrong.

HELYA   And I've been wrong, too. I thought, we'll have such a light, pleasant romance.

VICTOR   Not the most fatal mistake.

HELYA   [*meekly*]   *Dobrze*—all right. I take it back. Relax. It was a young man.

VICTOR   What's his name?

HELYA   What's the difference? Let's say, Tadek.

VICTOR   And his last name?

HELYA   Jesus Christ—Dymarczik, Stroniarz, Veroczek. What does his name tell you?

VICTOR   I just wanted to know what your name will be, that's all.

HELYA   For concerts, I'll keep my own. Will you come on my concerts?

VICTOR   Come to.

HELYA   Come on, come to—what a difficult language! [*A short pause.*] Vitek, what if I were talking to a girl friend? That's a possible variation, too.

VICTOR   Why should I believe that?

HELYA   Oh, only because it's more pleasant. What time is it?

VICTOR   Really, at the most inappropriate moment.

HELYA   I told you so. Oh, it's so late. Almost twelve. Or rather, almost midnight. That sounds prettier. More poetic. The dormitory is closed at midnight, and they won't let the girls in.

VICTOR   They will. I promise you.

HELYA   Let's go, Vitek. You walk me up to the door and then you'll say: until next time. That's a lovely expression. Only lovers ought to say good-bye like that, right? Until next time. We say good-bye to each other until the next time we see each other. It isn't fair that everybody says good-bye like that. People in love are constantly being robbed.

VICTOR   It's idiotic to say good-bye right now. Plain incredible idiocy. What if I go up to your room? I'll ask that Vera to strum on the harp a little.

HELYA   No, you really are an odd one. Just my luck—to find an odd man. After the war there were hardly any of them left. I guess they were all shot off.

VICTOR   Word of honor, I'll come visit you. You won't chase me away. Maybe you'll even serve tea? All right? Decided?

HELYA   [laughing]   You look just like the expression . . . how does it go? . . . Either gentleman free or slave on his knees?

VICTOR   [almost gravely]   The gentleman is on his knees.

The lights go out. They come back on. A museum. Statues and paintings.

HELYA   Just a moment ago it was Moscow, and now look. . . . What century are we in? Vitek, it's a miracle. Do you believe in miracles?

VICTOR   Everything in the world comes from electricity.

HELYA   Oh, you're terribly full of jokes, but I forgive you because you brought me here.

VICTOR   What could I do, since there was no place to go.

HELYA   Vitek, don't spoil things.

VICTOR   Of the two of us, I'm the rational principle.

HELYA   That's news to me. Oh, look, what a beautiful maiden. Could you fall in love with her?

VICTOR   Men don't love beautiful maidens. They love pretty girls.

HELYA   You're impossible. She's lovely.

VICTOR   And very much out-of-date. Ice-cold.

HELYA   We'll also be out-of-date.

VICTOR   [light-heartedly]   When will that be?

HELYA   Sooner than you think. Remember what Khayyam says.

VICTOR   And what does he say?

HELYA   "The day has flown away, but you did not see it go."

VICTOR   And then he added: "and therefore, let's drink."

HELYA   Just right. You thought that up wonderfully.

VICTOR   I have a clear head.

HELYA   I'm sorry you've never been in Cracow. I would take you to Wawel.

VICTOR   What's that—Wawel?

HELYA   It's an old castle. All the Polish kings are buried there. And many great men. Slowacki, Mickiewicz . . .

VICTOR   That's sort of amusing, isn't it? Poets have a hard time living with kings, but they're buried together.

HELYA   You see, Vitek, the museum affects you, too. You've become very . . . how do you say it . . . profound.

VICTOR   I always am.

HELYA   Queen Jadwiga is in Wawel, too. She was the patroness of the university; the pupils still write messages to her even now.

VICTOR   What do they write?

HELYA   "Dear Jadwiga, help me pass the exam." "Dear Jadwiga, make studying easier for me."

VICTOR   Did you, too?

HELYA   Oh, when I arrived in Cracow, I ran right over to Jadwiga.

VICTOR   I would have loved to have seen your note.

HELYA   Well, I'll tell you, since you're so inquisitive. "Dear Jadwiga, let the math teacher fall in love with me."

VICTOR   And did Jadwiga help you?

HELYA   I guess she did; I passed the exam.

VICTOR   Listen, I have an idea.

HELYA   You're joking, I hope.

VICTOR   [nodding toward a statue]   Let's hide behind this fellow and kiss.

HELYA   That's what I was saying: today, you're . . . in great form. [They go behind the statue and kiss.] What a lovely idea.

VICTOR   The guard is asleep, I think.

HELYA   I was afraid there would be groups going through. I don't like group excursions at all; it's a failing of mine. You don't have to explain anything really, do you, isn't that right? Let people think for themselves.

VICTOR   [quickly kisses her]   Before the guard wakes up.

HELYA   [leaning against the statue]   If worse comes to worst, our athlete will defend us.

VICTOR   We'll defend ourselves.

HELYA   But he's very strong. Just look at his muscles.

VICTOR   See what it means to be athletic.

HELYA   I know, I know—you have two dumbbells under your bed.

VICTOR   What's wrong with that?

HELYA   I'm a little scared of sports. Sportsmen value strength too highly.

VICTOR   That's no sin.

HELYA   Are you very strong?

VICTOR   I'm not weak, naturally.

HELYA   Do you like being strong?

VICTOR   Very much.

HELYA   What do you like about it?

VICTOR   I really don't know . . . I guess a kind of independence.

HELYA   Or maybe the dependence of other people?

VICTOR   I don't go around looking for trouble, but you have to know how to hit back.

HELYA   Yes. But today a man hits back, and sees that it works, and then tomorrow he's the one to strike first.

VICTOR   All right. I'll turn the other cheek.

HELYA   I'm very stupid, Vitek, I'm sure, and you should just cheerfully laugh at me, but I can't help myself. For me strength almost always goes with violence.

VICTOR   Helya, you're talking about fascism. . . .

HELYA   I often think about fascism nowadays. . . . And listen— sometimes it seemed very . . . effective. It seduced whole countries with its muscles.

VICTOR   Listen . . . the war stopped in forty-five.

HELYA   Yes. True. [A *pause*.] It's silly. I asked you not to talk about the war, but I can't forget it a minute myself. Everybody in Poland is like that. Vitek, do you believe in happiness?

VICTOR   Yes, Helya, I do.

HELYA   But I'm afraid of believing. And afraid of life. I'm very ashamed of that, but I'm afraid of it. They say it was the same for people after the first world war.

VICTOR   I don't know. It was a completely different war. Can't compare them. And you shouldn't be afraid. You simply saw too many occupying troops, their patrols, their guns. It will pass.

HELYA   Vitek, you have the fingers of a pianist.

VICTOR   I can't carry a tune in a basket.

HELYA   I'm sure that's not so.

VICTOR   Listen . . .

HELYA   You have another idea?

VICTOR   Nobody will see us behind that goddess.

HELYA   Remember that the bouquet is made by maturation.

VICTOR   You really are a little monkey. [*They go behind the statue and kiss.*] Damn it, that was great!

HELYA   Don't blaspheme!

VICTOR   [*kisses her*]   God will forgive us.

HELYA   But He obviously doesn't forgive those He should. I wouldn't start a correspondence with Jadwiga now. [*He kisses her again.*] Where will we go tomorrow?

VICTOR   I'll think of something.

HELYA   It's nice knowing that somebody is thinking up something for you. How clever you are.

VICTOR   You don't like people thinking for you.

HELYA   That's just what's so awful: it's nice. I guess it's a feminine trait, but too many men have it. Silly, isn't it?

VICTOR   Dialectics, Helya.

HELYA   Oh, what a big word. It explains absolutely everything. Like your electricity.

VICTOR   Citizen, one must believe either in electricity or in God. There's no third choice.

HELYA   Professor, sir, I've become afraid of gods. Of all of them. Even those that offer mercy. Just as soon as man invents a god, he starts sacrificing to him.

VICTOR   That leaves you only electricity.

HELYA   Electricity has its sacrifices, too.

VICTOR   Helya, there's nothing that doesn't.

HELYA   I know, I know. . . . Science requires them, art requires them, and progress requires sacrifices. Vitek . . .

VICTOR   What, Helya?

HELYA   Now I have an idea.

They go behind the statue. The lights go out. They come on again. A room in the dormitory. Helya in dressing-gown and slippers is putting up her hair in front of a mirror. A knock.

HELYA   *Prosze*—come in. [VICTOR *enters with a box in his hands.*] You're so late.

VICTOR   I'm sorry. [*Pulls off his mittens.*]

HELYA   It'll be New Year's even before we get there.

VICTOR   You're not ready yet.

HELYA   I'll be ready in a minute. I simply want to be the most beautiful. After all, I don't belong to myself. Otherwise I don't care, so long as the gentleman is pleased.

VICTOR   Who do you belong to?

HELYA   I must uphold my country's tradition and show that *Polska eszcze ne sginela*—Poland hasn't perished yet.

VICTOR   She certainly hasn't.

HELYA   Oh, Vitek, how sweet you are. You just showed me moral support. When you have to preserve a tradition, you feel great responsibility. It weighs on you.

VICTOR   You'll be a queen, no fear.

HELYA   What's the box in your hands?

VICTOR   The simplest little New Year's present. [*While she hurriedly unwraps it, he sits down and covers his eyes.*]

HELYA   Holy Mary! What lovely little shoes!

VICTOR   I was afraid you'd go off to the Shoemakers' Capital, off to Radom.

HELYA   Vitek, you're a miracle. *Dziękuję bardzo*—thank you, thank you. I would kiss you but I'm afraid of getting lipstick to you.

VICTOR   On you. [*Yawns.*]

HELYA   Oh, never mind. You're always teaching me. But where did you get the *pieniądze*?

VICTOR   I became rich. [*Yawns.*]

HELYA   Pooh, don't you dare yawn. That's disrespectful to my beauty, to my country, and her flag. I got you a present, too. It's not so chic, of course. I'm not so rich as you. I have other qualities. [*Holds a necktie out to him, tries it for size.*] Oh, how lovely! How lovely!

VICTOR   Thanks. I've never worn ties.

HELYA   That's a falsely democratic attitude. You have to stop that.

VICTOR   All right.

HELYA   The wine is on the window sill. Don't forget to take it. It's our contribution to the table. I'll put on my dress now, slip into my new little shoes, and we'll be off. [*He doesn't respond. She goes behind the wardrobe.*] Sit still and don't move. I'm counting on your nobility. Why aren't you talking, Vitek? Is that agreement or protest? [*She comes out in her dress, carrying the shoes.*] What's happened to you? You asleep? [VICTOR *is, in fact, asleep. She quietly puts the shoes on the table and goes over to him. Cautiously takes his hand.* VICTOR *does not stir—he is asleep.* HELYA, *her footsteps barely audible, moves to one side, puts out the overhead light.*

Now only the night-lamp lights the room. She sits down beside VICTOR, *looks at him carefully. Silence. A far-away clock starts slowly striking. Twelve.* HELYA *sits still. From somewhere, music comes in. Again the clock strikes—once.* HELYA *stays sitting in the same position. The music can just barely be heard.* VICTOR *opens his eyes.*] Happy New Year, Vitek.

VICTOR   What time is it?

HELYA   Same as always—at an inappropriate moment. It's already quarter past one.

VICTOR   Did I fall asleep?

HELYA   Like a baby. And slept like an angel.

VICTOR   Forgive me. I'm a gangster.

HELYA   That's putting it too strongly.

VICTOR   I behaved like a pig.

HELYA   On the contrary, like a patriot. Now the beauty queen will be Natasha.

VICTOR   Maybe we can still go?

HELYA   That makes no sense at all. We'll only provoke smiles and questions.

VICTOR   How stupid of me. . . .

HELYA   Vitek, where were you?

VICTOR   Unloading box-cars.

HELYA   That's how you got rich?

VICTOR   All work is honorable.

HELYA   No matter, we'll drink the wine ourselves. I very much want to drink to you.

VICTOR [*opening the bottle*]   Where are your glasses?

HELYA   Here they are. Is it good wine?

VICTOR   Ordinary.

HELYA   But can you drink ordinary wine? Or is that . . . sacrilege?

VICTOR   *Wszistko jedno, panna*—it's all the same.

HELYA   How is a real wine created, Vitek?

VICTOR   It's a long process. From the grape to the wine is a long process. When the crusher presses the must . . .

HELYA   What's the must? Forgive me, I'm completely ignorant.

VICTOR   The skins, the pulp, the seeds . . . As I was saying, at that point we still don't know what kind of wine we'll get. Everything becomes clear only later. Like with a child.

HELYA   And do wine-makers worry?

VICTOR   They worry terribly.

HELYA   You're talking down to me. You're stressing your superiority.

VICTOR   Sometime I'll take you with us when we go out to do field-work. You'll see how the sugar test is made, how the must is fermented and the wine matured.

HELYA   The bouquet is made by maturation.

VICTOR   I see you've really learned that by heart.

HELYA   I like it.

VICTOR   Quality wine is kept a long time. It is matured in oak casks. The oak cask gives it nobility.

HELYA   Are we drinking a quality wine?

VICTOR   An ordinary one, Helinka.

HELYA   What does that mean?

VICTOR   It's aged less than a year.

HELYA   How disgraceful! Aren't they ashamed?

VICTOR   There's no equality in this.

HELYA   Oh, all right. I drink to you, though this wine is unworthy of you.

VICTOR   And I to you.

HELYA   I drink to things being good for you in forty-seven.

VICTOR   And for you.

HELYA   And to things being fine for you and me in this same forty-seven. Probably, I'm a terrible . . . conservative, but I don't want to discover new things about you. Even if they're things about the coming future.

VICTOR   But I want to develop and improve.

HELYA   Don't. Who knows where you'll go, what you'll become? It's so peaceful for me with you now, so clear.

VICTOR   You shouldn't drink any more. We have nothing to eat with it.

HELYA   That's all right, I'm quite sober, I won't do anything stupid. But there's nothing to eat. You slept through it. And especially— the marvelous cake. Natasha's mother is a great *maestro*. I dreamed of the cake today.

VICTOR   You have a sweet tooth.

HELYA   If you only knew what little treats there are on Nowy Swiat. Nothing like them any place else. I used to spend my last zloty on them. Holy Mary, I can't help it, I just love sweet things. Even without them singers become fat ladies, but on top of it I love them.

VICTOR   Did you love sweet words, too?

HELYA   I did, I did. Why hide it? But now you've opened my eyes. Now I'll do a sugar test on every word. Pleased?

VICTOR   You know what distinguishes real wine? The aftertaste.

HELYA   A wonderful word. Only, explain it to me.

VICTOR The taste which remains after you have drunk. The aftertaste. There are certain full-bodied wines which literally roll
around in your mouth.

HELYA [drinks] This doesn't.

VICTOR Naturally. It lacks body.

HELYA What a shocking science—your wine-making. Do you really
take on girls?

VICTOR Girl after girl.

HELYA But I'm better than that. You must honestly admit—I'm
better. I was born at a geographic crossroads. Everything is mixed
together in me, everything, everything! The Roman Catholic
Church and the paganism of the ancient Slavs. Where will you
find another like me?

VICTOR Another so sober?

HELYA Vitek, I'm soberer than you, and you'll be convinced of
that. But now I want to dance in my new shoes.

VICTOR Will you permit them to be put on?

HELYA Prosze pana—if the gentleman please. [He puts her shoes
on.] Turn on the radio. [VICTOR turns it on. They dance.] In all
the houses they're dancing now. In all the cities people are dancing now. In every country. And wishing each other happiness.
Vitek, for some reason I feel sad.

VICTOR I said you shouldn't drink.

HELYA That's not it, that's not it. How can I explain to you?
You'll make up your mind that I'm an hysterical person. I'm just
thinking about how many people are alive at the same time I
am. And I'll never get to know them. There are boundaries and
borders always and everywhere, borders and limits. . . . Limits
of time, limits of space, limits of countries. Limits to our strength.
Only our hopes have no limits.

VICTOR But I did find you.

HELYA Accidentally.

VICTOR Doesn't matter. Jeh pran, jeh pran . . . In short, I take
what's good where I find it.

HELYA That's terribly witty of you. [A pause.] Vitek.

VICTOR What?

HELYA Haven't you any ideas at all?

VICTOR I have one. [Kisses her.]

HELYA [breaking away] What about the af-ter-ta-ste? That it? Did
I say it right?

VICTOR You're a born wine-maker.

HELYA   If I were, we would become drunkards. [*Stopping.*] This music doesn't go with the melody I feel inside.

VICTOR   Then off it goes. [*Switches the radio off.*]

HELYA   I ought to sing you something instead. You want me to?

VICTOR   Are you in voice?

HELYA   Clear as a bell.

VICTOR   Then do.

[HELYA *goes behind the screen. From there:*]

HELYA   And now we have Helena Modlewska!

[*She comes out. A fur piece lies regally over her shoulders.*]

VICTOR   Where did you pick up that dog?

HELYA   That's no dog; it's Vera's fur collar. [*They embrace.*] Ow, you'll squeeze me to death!

VICTOR   [*brushing little hairs of the fur piece off his lips*]   Take off that damn dog; it's shedding.

HELYA   It really is a little.

VICTOR   [*ironically*]   A little . . .

HELYA   Well, I'll take it off.

[HELYA *sings the gay, old song:* "Straszne cię kocham, straszne cię kocham, straszne kocham cię . . ."]

VICTOR   The audience is ecstatic.

HELYA   The performers are tired. [*Sits down.*] *Straszne cię kocham.*

VICTOR   "*Straszne cię kocham*"—that means, "I love a lot"?

HELYA   I love you a lot. You already understand everything.

VICTOR   I'd like to learn Polish.

HELYA   Well, then I'll teach you.

VICTOR   But first marry me.

HELYA   Vitek, you're being slow.

VICTOR   You don't want to?

HELYA   Vitek, it's as if everything had conspired to mix us up. The first night of the New Year, the wine, nobody in the dormitory— we're all by ourselves in the whole world. But it really isn't that way. Tomorrow has already come, and you and I aren't alone in the world. We absolutely have to look ahead.

VICTOR   You're a sensible girl.

HELYA   I told you I was more sober than you.

VICTOR   Unfortunately.

HELYA   Maybe it's the fault of the way I was brought up. It was drilled into us to think about tomorrow.

VICTOR   No more joking. We do a lot of laughing. We cling to it
like a straw. Like to a loop-hole. Laughter is our rear guard. Our
reserve position. Our way out. What more? I don't want a way
out at all.

HELYA   You're right. It's just that I'm afraid of being serious. I've
told you that before—I'm afraid.

VICTOR   But I'm not. There are some things I know. I know I need
you ever so much. What else should I know? Isn't that enough?
I wake up in the morning in order to see you. To hear your voice,
your eternal "how do you say it," your constant "shouldn't have
shown" instead of "shouldn't show," "understanding once and for
all" instead of "understood once and for all," "come on" instead
of "come to." God forbid, if you started saying everything correctly, I'd think it wasn't you anymore. I just put the shoes on
your feet and realized that in my whole twenty-four years I've
never been so happy. I drag everything to you and burden you
with it, and sometimes you don't even notice that. I know I'll
never be bored with you, never want to get away from you to
relax. What you are gives meaning to everything and makes absolutely everything come alive. [HELYA *starts to interrupt him.*]
Don't, because what I'm telling you is the truth. Maybe I shouldn't
talk like this? Most likely, a person has to be restrained; not the
right thing to let yourself go. I really have very little experience.
And where would I have gotten it, anyway? From school I went
right into the war. What did I see? And what do I remember?
People who have experience I've only read about in books. But
I think there's nothing better than saying it all out, not weighing
this and that, or keeping track of every word. Now there, there
are tears in your eyes. I'm sorry. Still, I'll make you happy. I'll
do everything to make your fear go away. So that you'll never be
afraid of anything. I'll watch over you day and night. And not a
shadow of sadness will ever cross your eyes, not even a shadow.
And I'll hear your even breathing. Then, but not before, see, not
before then, I'll breathe easily myself.

*The lights go out. They come on again. Helya stands by
the window, her back to the door.*

VICTOR [*cheerfully*]   I kiss your two hands.
HELYA   Hello.
VICTOR   It would be nice if you would turn around and come over.

HELYA   There; I've turned around.

VICTOR   The gentleman is waiting. The gentleman is getting nervous.

HELYA   I have a terrible headache.

VICTOR   Take something for it and lie down.

HELYA   I did.

VICTOR   A hot-water bottle on the back of your head—and you'll
be resurrected. For life and all its joys.

HELYA   You've been wine-tasting?

VICTOR   There were things to do. [*Picks up music.*] This your music?
[HELYA *nods.*] And this, too?

HELYA   And that, too.

VICTOR   A whole program. You can give concerts. Damn it all, what
a future lies in store for me! Wine, women, and song!

HELYA   I think I'm again more sober than you.

VICTOR   As always. Though you're already dissatisfied. What will
happen when I become your husband?

HELYA   You still want to be?

VICTOR   And very soon. I've done my obedience to your Polish
majesty. Haven't I been a faithful and humble subject? At first,
you said we had to finish the term. I obeyed. After that, you took
me skiing in the country. You argued that we had to get to know
each other. I know I'll never get used to you, thank god, but that
was what you wanted, and again I went along. We spent ten days
at the lodge, and I humbly stepped aside for you. Oh, I don't
disagree—they were ten wonderful days, but they were spoiled
for me by the uncertainty of my position.

HELYA   You're wrong if you think you're being funny.

VICTOR   Being funny? I'm up in arms. I want to be called a *pan-
mlody*. Shall I translate? In Polish that means a newly-wed.

HELYA   You haven't heard a thing?

VICTOR   No. I've been plunged in self-analysis since I got up.

HELYA   Nobody has told you anything?

VICTOR   What? Some news? World-wide? Or local?

HELYA   Local.

VICTOR   Asya has been sent to Dhagestan?

HELYA   They've made a new law.

VICTOR   About what?

HELYA   It forbids . . . marriage to foreigners. From February fif-
teenth on.

VICTOR   Well . . . so? That can't have anything to do with us.

HELYA   May I ask—why not?

VICTOR   We love each other.

HELYA [*flaring up*] You're a fool. [*A pause.*] Forgive me, forgive me, I don't know what I'm saying.

VICTOR I'm sure, I'll answer for it with my head. . . . It's undoubtedly a temporary measure. . . . Apparently, there are thoughtless, foolish marriages. After all, don't forget, I saw plenty myself, watching those foreign girls. We were stationed in Vienna. . . . There were a lot of foolish things. People played at getting married, and then afterwards—nothing but tears and troubles. . . . [*Embraces her.*] Don't worry. . . . Please . . . Don't. You'll be with me.

HELYA With you . . . with you . . . You can't change a thing!

VICTOR Oh, damn it! There it is, that sobriety of yours. If you had listened to me, we'd be married now.

HELYA If it weren't for my being sober, you would now be in a difficult position.

VICTOR And is my position right now any easier?

HELYA Why are you shouting at me?

VICTOR What can we do? What can we do?

HELYA Vitek, my only one . . . Think of something. . . . Think of something. . . . Anything . . . You're a lucky man. . . . You can do anything. You've always been able to think of things very well. I beg you, think of something.

VICTOR Yes, all right, yes, I will. I will.

The light goes out. It comes on again. A street. Helya.
Victor appears. She rushes to him. We hear Victor's voice,
slightly altered for having been recorded:

VICTOR'S VOICE But I didn't think of anything then. Life is life, and sometimes it's more complicated than you think. Soon I was transferred to Krasnodar. I heard nothing more about Helya. Krasnodar is a fine, gay city. In the evenings everybody strolls down Red Street. And so did I, sometimes, but I didn't make any real friends. Friends came later. In the summer we would go out to Abrau-Diurso on field-work. It's surrounded by mountains and lies there below, as if at the bottom of a cup. The northern slope is planted with various kinds of vineyards. In the summer, when the leaves took on their different colors, it was as if a crown had risen before your eyes.

PART II

*After a short pause, music. It is the same Chopin mazurka
as in the first scene. We hear Victor's voice, slightly altered
for having been recorded:* "Ten years went by, and one day
I found myself in Warsaw. It was mild, early autumn. I
knew that Warsaw had been destroyed, but I saw a live and
thriving Warsaw, despite the many ruins all around. There
are few cities in the world that can compare to the capital
of Poland. Just being there makes you lose your head, like
meeting a girl when you're seventeen."

*The lights come up. The counter in a vestibule in front
of the clerk's compartment. On the counter, a telephone.
Victor dials a number. We hear a male voice:* "Slucham."
Victor's voice: "Prosze pani Helenu." *Male voice:* "Heltsya!"
A pause. Footsteps.

HELYA'S VOICE *Slucham.* [VICTOR *coughs to clear his throat.*] *Slucham.*
VICTOR Helya, it's me. [*Pause.*] Can you hear me? It's me.
HELYA'S VOICE [*constrainedly*] Holy Mary . . .
VICTOR At eight I'll be waiting on the corner of Swietokrzyskaja
and Nowy Swiat. Agreed?

[*A pause.*]

HELYA'S VOICE Yes.

*Victor hangs up the phone. The lights go out and come back
up almost immediately. Street noise. Evening. Victor stands
on the corner. Helya appears.*

HELYA I haven't been late?
VICTOR I'm not late.
HELYA Oh, right. He's correcting me again. I'm-e not-e lat-e.
VICTOR No, you're not late. Punctuality is the courtesy of queens.

[*A handshake.*]

HELYA   You've hardly changed at all.

VICTOR   Neither have you.

HELYA   You were supposed to say that I look better than ever.

VICTOR   I meant to hide that, in order to feel more confident.

HELYA   Oh, so? That's something else again.

VICTOR   All your fears were groundless. You became a singer without getting fat.

HELYA   I'm the only one who knows what it cost. . . . My life . . .
how do you say it . . . is no bed of roses. That I mean literally.

VICTOR   What about the little treats on Nowy Świat?

HELYA   You're wicked. They're never supposed to be talked about
even. Cut out once and for all.

VICTOR   What a shame.

HELYA   Cut out, but today we'll make an exception. In honor of
your arrival.

VICTOR   I'm very glad to afford you pleasure.

HELYA   *Dziękuję bardzo pana*—I thank you, sir. How did you get
here, anyway?

VICTOR   There are several of us here. We came for discussions
with our colleagues. Your wine-making isn't worthy of your country. There are only a few vineyards all told.

HELYA   You're right, vineyards are the only thing we don't have.
We have everything else. [*A pause.*] Have you become a scientist?

VICTOR   I defended my dissertation.

HELYA   Congratulations. I was sure that you would get ahead.

VICTOR   That can be much more readily said about you. All Warsaw
knows you.

HELYA   That's the nature of my work. Have you seen the city?

VICTOR   Barely. But my heart has already gone out to it.

HELYA   Here we say that Warsaw was built in seven centuries and
twelve years. There were ninety buildings left standing.

VICTOR   I know it and can't believe it.

HELYA   Where are you staying?

VICTOR   Hotel Sasski.

HELYA   Ah-ah . . . So. Platz Dzerzinskiego. But you've already
been in Lazenki? In Staroe Miasto?

VICTOR   Haven't been anywhere.

HELYA   When did you get in?

VICTOR   Three hours ago.

HELYA   [*studies him slowly*]   Thanks, that's very sweet of you.

VICTOR   And already had an adventure. Two very plump girls were
standing outside the hotel. They probably eat those sweet treats all

the time. One of the men with us asked me in too loud a voice,
"And are these the famous beautiful Polish maidens?" And one
of them turned around, measured me from head to foot, and said,
"Indeed, these are the famous beautiful Polish maidens."

HELYA   Too much tongue-wagging.

VICTOR   Does everybody here understand Russian?

HELYA   Why were you the one your friend asked? Are you con-
sidered a specialist on Polish problems?

VICTOR   I happened to be standing next to him. [*She laughs*:] I
don't understand.

HELYA   The way you looked at me! . . . You haven't changed a bit.

VICTOR [*businesslike*]   Have to think of where we're going, don't I?

HELYA   Today I will think of it. We'll go to Julek's.

VICTOR   What's that?

HELYA   A little restaurant. The *"Pod gwiazdami."* That means,
under the stars. In the open air. You can even hear the singing
of the heavenly spheres. It's Julek Stadtler singing.

VICTOR   Fine, I haven't heard the angels for a long time.

HELYA   You have a view of all of Warsaw from there. And all of
Warsaw likes going there.

VICTOR   Maybe we won't get in. It's Sunday evening.

HELYA   Don't worry. After all, you're with me.

VICTOR   Indeed I am. I'm not used to it yet.

HELYA   Wait. . . . It really is you?

VICTOR [*quietly*]   It is, Helya, it's me. . . .

*The lights go out. They come back on in the "Pod gwiaz-
dami." A little table behind a column. Victor and Helya.
On the other side of the column, clearly, is the main room
where the customers sit and from which come the sounds of
singing, laughing and joking.*

HELYA   I didn't warn Julek that we were coming.

VICTOR   It's even nicer here. Nobody can see us, and we can see
everybody.

HELYA   You like it here?

VICTOR   That Julek of yours is very nice. How old is he? Forty-
five?

HELYA   About.

VICTOR   I like the fact that everything here is family-like, that he comes and sits down at the tables and talks to everybody as if to old friends.

HELYA   It is like that.

VICTOR   But why is he always smoking? I thought a singer shouldn't.

HELYA   Stadtler is above the rules.

VICTOR   Who's that old man with the moustache who is always writing?

HELYA   A newspaperman. He does all his articles here.

VICTOR   It seems to me that everybody knows everybody here. We were met by Pan Hawlik. We sent our things on but decided to go on foot ourselves, to take a look at Warsaw. Pan Hawlik would greet everyone he met.

HELYA   I don't know Pan Hawlik.

VICTOR   But he knows you. "Pani Modlewska! Oh, Pani Modlewska!"

HELYA   How nice of Pan Hawlik.

VICTOR   He's very nice, very polite, very cheerful.

HELYA   How many good qualities just in Hawlik.

VICTOR   And full of the unexpected. On the way we slipped into a Catholic church to hear the choir-boys, and he immediately knelt down.

HELYA   But after all, cheerful believers are no worse than prayer-minded atheists.

VICTOR   He seemed too intelligent and witty for such piety.

HELYA   Ah, Vitek, my country is such a combination of irony and religiousness that it's hard to know whether the irony is covering up the religiousness or the religiousness, the irony. Poles are like that. There's always a little room for everything.

VICTOR   Poles also have an excellent memory: every step I take I see the plaques—"Here Polish blood was spilled."

HELYA   Yes. We learned a lot, but forgot nothing. Let's drink, Vitek.

VICTOR   To what?

HELYA   To a good memory. [*Stadtler's singing can be heard. For a while they listen to it without speaking.*] You wear ties now.

VICTOR   Yes, you taught me to.

HELYA   Maybe that was precisely my historical role in your life. A very austere necktie. Even too austere. Though that's the style of Soviet men abroad.

VICTOR   I wore your tie for a long time.

HELYA   And I wore your shoes. Unlike Hamlet's mother, I wore them out. [*A pause. Stadtler's singing is heard.*] Vitek, I'm going to ask you a silly question. Very stupid, very . . . how do you say it . . . melodramatic. Are you married?

VICTOR   Yes.

HELYA   She, too . . . makes wine?

VICTOR   No. [*A brief pause.*] She's a good woman.

HELYA   Are you saying that to me or to yourself?

[*They listen to Stadtler to the end. The sound of applause.*]

VICTOR   No point my asking you whether or not you're married. I heard his voice on the phone.

HELYA [*nods*]   A very pleasant baritone. I'd say, like a cello.

VICTOR   A good man?

HELYA   He's a music critic.

VICTOR   That's an exhaustive reply.

HELYA   You'd like to know him better? [*With accentuated fright.*] Holy Mary, Julek is looking at me. I'm done for.

[*Stadtler's voice.* "Proszę pánstwa gdzieś gości wśród nas Helena Modlewska. Poprosimy ją zaśpiewać."]

HELYA   What can I do? I'll have to sing. [*She gets up from the table, for a moment disappears and right away reappears with a small microphone in her hand, visible simultaneously to the auditors in the main room, to* VICTOR, *and to us. She sings the old, familiar song,* "Straszne cię kocham, straszne cię kocham, straszne kocham cię." *Everyone joins in with her.* "Straszne kocham cię" *sing all the tables. Everyone sings except* VICTOR. *He smokes and listens. Thunderous applause.* HELYA *returns.*] That was for you.

VICTOR   Thanks.

HELYA   I shouldn't drink, but never mind. If we're going to have a good time, let's have a good one. I'm taking care of it.

VICTOR   Why should you?

HELYA   Vitek, no foolishness. I'm home. You're my guest. And how would you have any zlotys anyway?

VICTOR   I do.

HELYA   Well, wonderful. Buy something for your wife with them.

VICTOR   That means I've never had a chance to take you out.

HELYA   Vitek, I drink to your having changed so little even though you did defend your dissertation. You're just the way you were, and I'm grateful to you for that.

VICTOR   Why haven't you ever come on tour?

HELYA   I was afraid of seeing you, I suppose. You know, I was always afraid of something.

VICTOR   Whenever I'm in Moscow, I go to the Conservatory. Once I heard Vera and her harp.

HELYA   Vera gives concerts in the Great Hall! She always was a
serious girl. But you've heard nothing about Asya?

VICTOR   No, nothing.

HELYA   That's natural. She loved her young man too much. But now
here's a question for you—which of them is happier? Vera or Asya?

VICTOR   First we have to find out what happiness is.

HELYA   Happiness is what can't be explained. You feel it in your
bones. There's a sad song, goes like this: *"Comme le monde est
petit!"* How small the world is! See, we've met, Vitek, you and I!

VICTOR   We leave the day after tomorrow.

HELYA   For where?

VICTOR   To look at your vineyards.

HELYA   Ah, yes . . . I forgot. I forgot why you've come. Vitek, I
feel like making you laugh, you'll laugh until you collapse: I
still love you.

VICTOR [*lingering*]   That's what it seemed to you just now.

HELYA   Not seemed—it's what I live with. It's very silly, I know,
but it's true. Don't worry; everything is all right. The main thing
is I kept on living then, and that wasn't so easy.

VICTOR   Yes, that was far from easy.

HELYA   Whenever I go to Cracow, I walk up to Wawel. I write
messages for Queen Jadwiga: "Dear Jadwiga, send him back to me."
Good? Confess that I've cheered you up.

VICTOR   It's as bad to put one's faith in queens as in kings.

HELYA   You're right; you don't get much that means anything from
them now. I was reading the diary of your last tsar. How did it
go? . . . "I spent the morning abominably. It turned out I was
locked in the toilet." Mother of god . . . The Revolution was
inevitable.

VICTOR   I meant to say nothing. This is your fault. It's almost ten
years now, but I remember everything.

HELYA   Vitek, a hundred times I've thought it was you coming
toward me. I remember the intonations of your voice, your gestures. A hundred times I've caught myself doing the same thing—
somebody was talking to me, but I wasn't listening, I was talking
to you. I walk out on stage and see you in the audience. I'm ready
to argue, at the forfeit of my head, that it's you there in the fourth
row, sixth seat from the left. I lose my mind from hallucinations,
but I'd rather die than be cured. Now answer me—can one live
like that?

VICTOR   What can I say? What?

HELYA [*after a pause*]   It's time. It's late. We have to go.

*The lights go out. A dim light comes on. A street. A street
lamp. Helya and Victor.*

HELYA   Your hotel is around the corner.
VICTOR   What institute is that?
HELYA   The Hungarian.
VICTOR   Why Hungarian?
HELYA   Mary save us, cultural relations. Why did this suddenly
bother you?
VICTOR   I don't know.

[*A pause.*]

HELYA   Have to say good-bye?
VICTOR   Seems so.

[*A kiss.*]

HELYA   I won't let you go.
VICTOR   Helya . . .
HELYA   I won't. [*Kissing him passionately.*] Give you up again?
For another ten years, twenty, thirty? For my whole life? Have
I no rights at all?
VICTOR   But what can we do about it now? Helya, my darling . . .
HELYA   Merciful Father, he doesn't understand. We're never going
to see each other again.
VICTOR   Listen . . . don't. You have to go.
HELYA   You don't understand the main thing. The only thing that's
important. You know what? In a minute you'll push that door
there, and it will swing in, I can even hear the noise it'll make—
tr-r-r. . . . And then it will come back into place—and that'll be
all. And you'll be gone forever.
VICTOR   Calm down. Control yourself.
HELYA   Yes. Yes. I forgot. The bouquet is made by maturation. Then
there will be a marvelous aftertaste. You're very strong, Vitek.
Very strong.
VICTOR   Damn it, I have to be.
HELYA   Have to, have to . . . Damned, hateful strength. There was
reason for my always fearing it. Listen . . . you leave the day after
tomorrow?
VICTOR   Yes.
HELYA   Come with me now, together.

VICTOR   Where?

HELYA   To Sochaczew. It's not far. You'll come back tomorrow.

VICTOR   Wait a minute; what about your husband?

HELYA   Ah-ah . . . *wszistko jedno*. Let's go.

VICTOR   Impossible.

HELYA   But why?

VICTOR   Don't be angry—understand. After all, I'm not single.

HELYA   Holy Mary, I'm losing my mind. You used to laugh at me for being always afraid. But you yourself, remember, weren't afraid of anything. You're a brave man.

VICTOR   A man isn't always free to do what he likes.

HELYA   You're right, you're right. Well, good-bye, farewell.

VICTOR   No, wait. I've been waiting all these ten years. For what? I don't know. Why? I don't know. I knew I shouldn't have called you. But how could I help it? I'm only human.

HELYA   But not free to do what you like.

VICTOR   Right, right, right! That's the way life turned out. And we have to look life straight in the face. And if I try to keep from screaming out now, that doesn't mean that it's easy for me.

HELYA   Don't, Vitek. I understand. And please, I beg you—not another word. [*Goes.*]

VICTOR   [*after her*]   Helya!

HELYA   [*turning back, putting her finger on her lips*]   Not another word.

The lights go out. The familiar melody resounds, a few notes as translucent as drops of water. Then Victor's voice, slightly altered for having been recorded: "Nearly ten more years went by. I arrived in Moscow in the beginning of May. It's pleasant to come to the city at that time of year. The weather was superb, warm, women were already wearing their summer dresses. In the evening everyone poured out on to the streets, and, though I had a very fine, comfortable hotel room, for some reason I didn't want to go back into the hotel. And so I decided to go to a concert which very much interested me."

The lights come up. A small dressing-room just offstage. A little table, a bench. Victor enters. In his hands, a package. Applause comes from the auditorium. Helya flies in. She is in a white dress with barely visible spangles. She has a frowning, displeased expression.

VICTOR   I don't know how to express my gratitude.

HELYA   [*clasping her hands*]   Holy Mary, what a delightful unexpected visitor!

VICTOR   [*having noticed her expression*]   Is this the wrong time?

HELYA   Oh, I'm so fed up with them!

VICTOR   With whom?

HELYA   My business managers. One second; I'll just take another little bow. [*Goes onstage.* VICTOR *puts his package down, goes over to the mirror, fixes his hair, sits down on the bench.* HELYA *comes back.* VICTOR *rises.*] Sit still, sit still.

VICTOR   You sang beautifully. It gave me great enjoyment. You didn't see me? I was in the front row.

HELYA   In the front row? On the right or left? I'm so cross today I can't see anybody.

VICTOR   What happened?

HELYA   Some day their stupidity is going to kill me. Do you realize that the day after tomorrow I have to be in Leningrad, in Kiev on Monday, and on Wednesday in Baku. And in each city they've arranged for three concerts! You might think that I'm a singing machine.

VICTOR   [*gallantly*]   That would never occur to anyone. But as a matter of fact . . . why not arrange your schedule more sensibly?

HELYA   Oh, don't ask. . . . It's always the same thing.

VICTOR   I'll cheer you up in a minute. [*Opens the package, hands her a bottle.*] From one of your audience . . . and the author.

HELYA   How sweet of you!

VICTOR   [*indicating the label*]   Have you noticed how many medals it has won?

HELYA   [*looking at it*]   I counted them first thing.

VICTOR   You see, we, too, accomplished something.

HELYA   You live in Moscow?

VICTOR   No, I'm on a business trip.

HELYA   You look splendid. Your work is good for you.

VICTOR   The ancient Greeks were no fools. And they used to say: "Golden wine gives health and joy."

HELYA   "The key to secret mysteries is found in it alone." I've taken that course.

VICTOR   [*delighted*]   Listen, you have a magnificent memory!

HELYA   Actually, you're easy to recognize. Strange. I can see the audience well. You're a completely . . . how do you say it . . . well-preserved man. I guess the joy of life really does come from wine. Especially since it not only quenches your thirst but also nourishes.

VICTOR [*laughing*] In that sense, our jobs are alike.

HELYA You're right; I sing not merely for the pleasure of it. So, everything is going fine?

VICTOR Seems so.

HELYA Your wife is well?

VICTOR Fine, thanks. Only she's not my wife anymore.

HELYA Holy Mary. There's always a third person.

VICTOR What can you do? Busy people always live under the sword of Damocles.

HELYA It would be nice if what she did didn't give you any complexes. Because nowdays everybody has complexes. The whole world.

VICTOR We wine-makers have our own way of handling problems. And, besides, they say that everything's for the best, isn't that true? And we had no children.

HELYA Of course, that makes everything easier. You live alone?

VICTOR Yes . . . in general, by myself.

HELYA Maybe now you're a third person somewhere yourself? Forgive me, I don't mean to be indiscreet. But whatever happened, it didn't affect your work. What are you now, a bachelor of science or a master?

VICTOR A doctor of science.

HELYA You're simply a hero.

VICTOR Well, hero or not, I have my own laboratory. And how is our friend, the music critic?

HELYA Disappeared. How do you say it—went up in smoke.

VICTOR And the third person?

HELYA Later . . . not right away. But now he, too . . . has gone up in smoke. Like the first. My husbands can't withstand the atmospheric fluctuations.

VICTOR [*laughing*] Though you make yourself at home with them.

HELYA I travel a lot and get tired. I haven't any energy left for men.

VICTOR [*with concern*] It wouldn't hurt you to take a rest. A person must pull the switch, even if it's only once in a while.

HELYA In the summer I'll run off to Mazury. It's wonderfully quiet there.

VICTOR You'll come back ten years younger. Say, what's become of that good man Stadtler?

HELYA   Stadtler's dead.

VICTOR   He can't be!

HELYA   Why are you so surprised? That happens from time to time.

VICTOR   Oh, the poor man! I'm so sorry for him! Well, of course. A lot has happened.

HELYA   That's just it. To be plain, we can already think about the meaning of life.

VICTOR   True. As we did when we were very young.

HELYA   Thinking about it, though, is very easy. Sometimes it's hard to express it.

VICTOR   Still, everything has its own meaning.

HELYA   [*with an ironic smile*]   Even the fact that once upon a time you and I met in the Conservatory?

VICTOR   Absolutely. You don't think so?

HELYA   [*shrugging her shoulders*]   Some sort of meaning, possibly. After all, I became a good singer. And a good singer isn't just the voice.

VICTOR   You know, today I realized that.

HELYA   There, see, you understood it. That's a lot. And on the whole, both of us have nothing to grumble about. No matter what, we didn't stand still.

VICTOR   Thank god, nobody will say that about us.

HELYA   Never mind god, put your faith in electricity. It makes life easier and easier, and people are becoming wiser and wiser. Things are very hopeful.

VICTOR   No denying it, life goes on.

HELYA   And, remember, in all ways. Young men are even marrying foreigners. [*Suddenly remembers something.*] Oh, Madonna. The intermission will be over in a minute, and I haven't rested at all. You always cause only complications.

VICTOR   I'm sorry, I should have thought of that myself.

HELYA   So, you're in the front row? Well, good luck. I'll be in Moscow another day. Call, if you have time.

VICTOR   Good.

HELYA   The Warsaw Hotel, room two-oh-eight. Should you write it down, or will you remember?

VICTOR   I'll remember, of course. Be well.

HELYA   *Dowidzenia,* Vitek. *Bądź zdrów.*

The lights go out. And almost immediately come up again quickly. A street. Street lamps. A melody. Victor is walking

along. Though his lips are compressed, we hear his voice,
slightly altered for having been recorded:

VICTOR'S VOICE   Everything in Moscow changes so quickly. I haven't
been here for six months, and there are so many new things.
Tomorrow will be a dreadfully hard day. Dreadfully hard. Every
time I come, I never have enough free time for myself. But it's
just as well that I don't. Frankly, it's just right this way.

[*He recedes farther and farther. And the evening melody echoes*
after him.]

CURTAIN

NOTES ON THE AUTHORS

PANOVA, VERA FYODOROVNA

Born in Rostov-on-the-Don in 1905. She served as a newspaper correspondent in the Twenties and Thirties. During the Second World War, she was a correspondent attached to a hospital train. Her published work is a long list, including the plays *Ilya Kosogor* (1939), *The Snowstorm* (1941), *Farewell to White Nights* (1960), many stories, and nine novels, among them *Travelling Companions* (1946), *Kruzhilikha* (1947), *The Clear Shore* (1949), *The Seasons* (1953), and *A Sentimental Novel* (1958). She won a Stalin Prize in 1947, 1948, and 1950. In 1960 she visited the United States. Married to an engineer, she lives in Leningrad.

POGODIN (pseud.; real name: STUKALOV), NIKOLAI FYODOROVICH

Born in Rostov-on-the-Don in 1900; he died in 1962. His long career in the theater was always successful, starting with his first play *Tempo* (1929) and including *My Friend* (1932), *Aristocrats* (1934), and a trilogy on Lenin, *Man with a Gun* (1937), *The Kremlin Chimes* (1941), and *The Third, Pathétique* (1958). He won a Stalin Prize in 1941 and a Lenin Prize in 1959.

ROZOV, VICTOR SERGEYEVICH

Born in Yaroslavl in 1913, Victor Rozov went to school in Kostroma, and worked in a factory where he joined the factory theater group. In 1934, he became a pupil in the school attached to the Theater of the Revolution and then a member of the company until the war. Soon wounded, he played to troops after his discharge. In 1949, he entered the drama section of the Literary Institute in Moscow. His plays include *Her Friends* (1950), *A Page of Life* (1951), *Good Luck!* (1954), and *Alive Forever* (1956). The latter play, which was staged by Efremov for the opening of The Contemporary Theater, was adapted from his 1943 play *The Serebrisky Family* and subsequently made into the film *The Cranes Are Flying. In Search of Happiness* came out in 1957; *Unequal Battle* in 1958; *Before Supper* in 1963; *On the Wedding-Day* in 1964; and *The Reunion* in 1967. Rozov has written several film scenarios, including the 1960 *A,B,C,D,E.* He lives with his family in Moscow and has traveled widely.

SHVARTS, EVGENY LVOVICH

Born in 1904, he died in 1958, having lived most of his life in Leningrad where he worked in S. A. Marshak's Children's Literature Publishing House and edited the magazine *The Hedgehog*. From 1929 on, his children's plays and tales were regularly published, but his serious, satiric comedies were held back until 1960, the year in which his *Plays* was published posthumously and in which *The Naked King* and *The Shadow* were put on to wildly enthusiastic audiences. Lidiya Chukovskaya, in her book *In an Editor's Laboratory*, has left an affectionate memoir of Shvarts. He also worked in films, writing the scenario for *Cinderella* and the internationally successful *Don Quixote* (1957), adapted from Bulgakov's 1938 play.

ZORIN, LEONID GENRIKHOVICH

Born in Baku in 1924, he was early noticed by Maxim Gorky, who highly praised the teen-aged Zorin's work. His first play was put on in Baku in 1941; after the war, in 1949, the Maly Theater introduced his work to Moscow *(Youth)*. Zorin has written eighteen plays, of which a number are currently running in Moscow: *Dion* at the Vakhtangov Theater, *Jolly Good Fellows* at the Soviet Army Theater, *The Deck* at the Stanislavsky Theater, and *The Decembrists,* which recently opened, at the Contemporary Theater. His film "Peace to the Newcomer" won a gold medal at the International Venice Festival in 1961. He is presently working on a novel.

SELECTED BIBLIOGRAPHY

TRANSLATIONS

Anthology of Russian Plays. Vol. 2. (Includes *The Sea Gull,* Chekhov; *The Lower Depths,* Gorky; *The Puppet Show,* Blok; *He Who Gets Slapped,* Andreyev; *The Days of the Turbins,* Bulgakov; *The Bedbug,* Mayakovsky; *The Shadow,* Shvarts). Ed. and tr. by F. D. Reeve. N.Y.: Vintage paperback.

Armored Train 14–69. V. Ivanov. Tr. by Gibson-Cowan and A. Grant. N.Y.: International, 1933.

Best Plays of A. P. Chekhov. (Includes *The Sea Gull, The Cherry Orchard, Uncle Vanya, Three Sisters*). Tr. by Stark Young. N.Y.: Modern Library, paperback.

Chariot of Wrath. L. Leonov. Tr. by N. Guterman. N.Y.: Fischer, 1946.

Distant Point. A. Afinogenov. Tr. by H. Griffith. London: Pushkin Press, 1941.

The Dragon. E. Shvarts. Tr. by E. Hapgood, N.Y.: Theatre Arts paperback.

Four Soviet Plays. (Includes *The Aristocrats,* Pogodin; *An Optimistic Tragedy,* Vishnevsky). Ed. by B. Blake. London: Lawrence and Wishart, 1937.

Four Soviet War Plays. (Includes *The Front,* Korneichuk; *Guerillas of the Ukranian Steppes,* Korneichuk; *Invasion,* Leonov; *The Russians,* Simonov). London: Hutchinson, 1944.

In Search of Happiness. V. Rozov. Tr. by N. Froud. London: Evans, 1961.

Ivanov. A. P. Chekhov. Ed. by J. Gielgud. Tr. by A. Nicolaeff. N.Y.: Theatre Arts paperback.

The Lower Depths and Other Plays. M. Gorky. (Includes *Barbarians, Enemies, Queer People, Vassa Zheleznova, The Zykovs, Yegor Bulychov*). Tr. by A. Bakshy and P. Nathan. New Haven: Yale University Press paperback.

The Man with the Gun. N. Pogodin. In *International Literature,* 7 (1938), 3–40.

Masterpieces of Russian Drama. (Includes *Mystery-Bouffe,* Mayakovsky). Comp. by G. R. Noyes. N.Y.: Appleton, 1933.

The Moscow Character. A. Sofronov. In *Soviet Literature,* 8 (1949), 42–99.

Nine Plays of Chekhov. (Includes *The Cherry Orchard, The Anniversary, The Sea Gull, On the High Road, Three Sisters, On the Harmfulness of Tobacco, Uncle Vanya, The Bear, The Wedding*). N.Y.: Universal Library paperback.

Pavel Grekov. Lench and Voitekhov. In *International Literature,* 10 (1939), 3–40.

Platonov. A. P. Chekhov. Tr. by D. Magarshack. N.Y.: Hill and Wang paperback.

The Promise. A. Arbuzov. Tr. by A. Nicolaeff. London: Oxford University Press paperback.

The Rose and the Cross. A. Blok. Tr. by I. Smith and G. Noyes. In *The Slavonic and East European Review,* XIV (1936), 497–549.

The Russian Question. K. Simonov. In *Soviet Literature,* 2 (1947), 2–26.

Seven Soviet Plays. (Includes *On the Eve,* Afinogenov; *The Orchards of Polovchansk,* Leonov; *Engineer Sergeyev,* Rokk; *Smoke of the Fatherland,* Tur Brothers and Sheinen). Ed. by H. W. L. Dana. New York: Macmillan, 1946.

Six Soviet Plays. (Includes *Fear,* Afinogenov; *Inga,* Glebov; *Squaring the Circle,* Katayev; *Bread,* Kirshon; *Tempo,* Pogodin). Ed. by E. Lyons. Boston: Houghton Mifflin, 1934.

Soviet Scene. Six Plays of Russian Life. (Includes *Far Taiga,* Afinogenov; *The Square of Flowers,* Ilyenkov; *The Chimes of the Kremlin,* Pogodin; *Father Unknown,* Shkvarkin; *Lyubov Yarovaya,* Trenyov). Ed. by A. Bakshy. New Haven: Yale University Press, 1946.

Sunset. I. Babel. Tr. by M. Ginsburg and R. Rosenthal. In *Noonday 3.* N.Y.: Noonday Press, 1960.

Three Soviet Plays. (Includes *The Bedbug,* Mayakovsky; *Marya,* Babel; *The Dragon,* Shvarts). Ed. by M. Glenny. Harmondsworth: Penguin paperback.

HISTORY AND CRITICISM:

An Actor's Handbook. Konstantin Stanislavsky. Tr. by E. Hapgood. N.Y.: Theatre Arts paperback.

An Actor Prepares. Konstantin Stanislavsky. N.Y.: Theatre Arts paperback.

Building a Character. Konstantin Stanislavsky. N.Y.: Theatre Arts paperback.

"Das Märchen lernt von der Zeit: Über das Schaffen von Jewgeni Schwarz." St. Rassadin. In *Kunst und Literatur,* XIV (1966), 608–623.

"Forty Years of the Moscow Art Theatre." Sobolev, Yu. In *International Literature,* 10–11 (1938), 159–170.

Handbook on Soviet Drama. Dana, H. W. L. New York: American Russian Institute, 1938.

Moscow Rehearsals. N. Houghton. N.Y.: Harcourt, Brace, 1936.

My Life in Art. Konstantin Stanislavsky. Tr. by J. Robbins. N.Y.: Meridian paperback.

"New Solutions for the Theater." G. Tovstonogov. In *The Soviet Review,* III (1962), iii, 40–48.

The New Soviet Theatre. Macleod, J. London: Allen and Unwin, 1943.

The New Spirit in the Russian Theatre. Carter, H. London: Brentano, 1929.

"A New View of Don Juan: Samuel Alyoshin's Comedy 'At That Time in Seville.'" V. Revutsky. In *The Slavonic and East European Review,* XLIV (1966), 88–97.

"The Repertoire of the Fifties." F. de Liencourt. In *Literature and Revolution in Soviet Russia, 1917–1962*. N.Y.: Oxford University Press, 1964, pp. 150–169.

Return Engagement. N. Houghton. N.Y.: Holt, Rinehart and Winston, 1962.

Russian Theater from the Empire to the Soviets. M. Slonim. N.Y.: World, 1961.

The Seven Soviet Arts. London, K. London: Faber and Faber, 1937.

Soviet Historical Drama: Its Role in the Development of a National Mythology. S. Roberts. The Hague: Nijhoff, 1965.

The Soviet Theatre. Markov, P. A. London: Gollancz, 1943.

The Stanislavsky Heritage: Its Contribution to the Russian and American Theatre. C. Edwards. N.Y.: New York University Press, 1965.

Stanislavsky on the Art of the Stage. Tr. with an essay by D. Magarshack. N.Y.: Hill and Wang, 1961.

The Theater in Soviet Russia. N. Gorchakov. N.Y.: Columbia University Press, 1957.

"'Théâtralité' contre 'réalisme,'" N. Gourfinkel. In *La table ronde*, 185 (1963), 139–144.

To the Actor. M. A. Chekhov. N.Y.: Harper, 1953.

"V. E. Meyerhold: A Russian Predecessor of Avant-Garde Theater." M. Hoover. In *Comparative Literature*, XVII (1965), 234–250.

"Volodin's Two Plays." V. Revutsky. In *Canadian Slavonic Papers*, VII (1965), 223–234.